샘플로 쉽게 배우는
무역 실무영어 첫걸음

샘플로 쉽게 배우는
무역 실무영어 첫걸음

오시학(경영학 박사) 지음

중앙경제평론사

책머리에

동서고금, 남녀노소를 막론하고 한 번쯤 무역으로 큰돈을 벌고 싶어 하는 사람은 많습니다.

그러나 실행에 옮기기가 쉽지 않은 것이 사실인데, 이는 바로 외국어 때문일 것입니다.

지구상에 있는 수많은 국가에서 다양한 언어를 사용하지만, 무역을 할 때는 주로 영어를 사용하므로 영어만 하면 누구나 무역을 할 수 있습니다.

무역 영어의 특징은 쉬우면서도 난해하다는 양면성이 있습니다.

우선 무역 상담을 할 때에는 물품을 사고팔기 위해 정확한 의사 전달이 중요하기 때문에 가능한 한 쉬운 영어를 사용해야 합니다.

그러나 무역 계약을 체결할 때에는 Incoterms, Letter of Credit 등등 전문 용어를 사용하여야 후일의 분쟁을 예방할 수 있습니다.

즉, 아무리 영어를 유창하게 잘해도 수출입 단계별의 무역 패턴과 무역 전문 용어를 모르면 무역을 할 수 없다는 말입니다.

이 책은 수출입 단계별로 반드시 알아야 할 무역 영어의 샘플을 제시하고 상세히 해설한 책으로, 무역을 하는 사람들에게 필독서 내지는 매뉴얼이라 할 수 있습니다.

중앙경제평론사가 설립되면서부터 30여 년 동안 저자와 각별한 인연을 맺고 무역 분야는 물론 다방면에 걸쳐 양질의 도서를 출판해오신 중앙경제평론사 김용주 사장님과 임직원 여러분들께 깊이 감사드립니다.

저자 오시학

차 례

책머리에   4

1장   초보자도 가능한
       무역 영어

무역 영어는 초보자도 가능한가?   11
무역통신문은 어떻게 작성하나?   14
봉투 기재 방법과 용지 접는 방법   31

2장   거래 개설에 관한
       무역통신문

거래선 알선 의뢰에 관한 무역통신문   37
신용조사에 관한 무역통신문   55

| 거래 제의에 관한 무역통신문 | 70 |
| 거래 수락 및 거절에 관한 무역통신문 | 90 |

3장 매매계약에 관한 무역통신문

총괄계약서 / 일반거래조건협정서	105
상품 및 가격 조회에 관한 무역통신문	113
오퍼에 관한 무역통신문	143
오퍼에 관한 응답 통신문	160
주문에 관한 무역통신문	173
주문 수락에 관한 무역통신문	190

4장 신용장·선적·보험에 관한 무역통신문

신용장에 관한 무역통신문	215
선적에 관한 무역통신문	250
해상 보험에 관한 무역통신문	282

5장 대금 결제·클레임·기타 무역 관련 통신문

대금 결제에 관한 무역통신문	299
클레임 제기에 관한 무역통신문	328
클레임 해결에 관한 무역통신문	342
기타 무역 관련 통신문	354

6장 Incoterms 2020 해설

Incoterms 개념	371
Incoterms 2020 특징	372
Incoterms 2020 무역 조건별 해설	379

부록 자주 쓰는 무역 용어   385

1장

초보자도 가능한 무역 영어

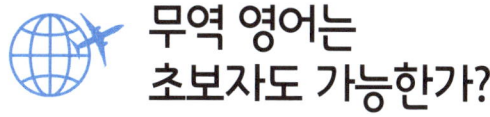
무역 영어는 초보자도 가능한가?

무역 영어란?

영어는 전 세계 어느 국가에서나 통용되므로 만국 공통어라고도 한다. 국제무역을 할 때 서로 다른 언어를 가진 국가 간에 각국의 언어가 사용될 경우, 의사소통 및 해석에 많은 어려움이 생긴다. 따라서 국제무역은 대부분 영어로 이루어진다.

무역 영어(Business English)란 국제 상거래인 무역을 하는 데 사용되는 영어로, 거래제의서신, 물품매도확약서, 매매계약서, 신용장, 선하증권, 보험증권, 상업송장, 환어음 등 무역 거래 전반에 쓰이는 무역통신문(무역서신)과 상대방과의 거래 교섭에 쓰이는 무역 영어 회화를 총칭한다.

무역을 하려면 무역 실무 및 무역 영어에 관한 충분한 지식이 있어야 하는데, 이는 거래 제의에서부터 선적을 완료하고 대금 회수에 이

르기까지 일련의 무역 절차가 일정한 관행에 따라 무역 영어에 의해 이루어지기 때문이다.

영어 초보자도 가능할까?

앞에서 살펴본 바와 같이 무역 영어는 무역통신문과 무역 영어 회화로 구분할 수 있다. 무역통신문은 거래제의서신, 물품매도확약서, 매매계약서, 신용장, 선하증권, 보험증권, 상업송장, 환어음 등 무역 거래에 수반되는 영문 무역 서류를 의미하며, 무역 영어 회화란 거래 상대방과의 거래 교섭에 쓰이는 영어 회화를 의미한다.

따라서 무역통신문은 국제무역에 쓰이는 영문 무역 서류를 작성하고 해석할 수 있는 수준이면 충분하며, 무역 영어 회화는 일반 생활 영어와 동일하다. 그러나 무역통신문을 올바르게 작성하고 해석하려면 수출입 절차와 단계별로 필요한 영문 무역 서류를 알아야 한다. 무역 실무를 모르고 오직 영어에만 능통하다고 무역 영어를 잘하는 것이 아니다. 이를테면 무역통신문에 '꽃피는 봄날' 등 미사여구를 써서 많은 분량의 글을 작성하는 것은 금기 사항이다.

무역통신문은 일정한 양식에 따라 꼭 필요한 내용만 간단명료하게 작성하며, 거래 내용만 명확히 전달되면 충분하다. 따라서 무역통신문은 중학교 영어 수준이면 초보자도 누구나 작성하고 해석할 수 있다. 공부를 위한 영어는 잘 익혀지지 않지만, 무역으로 돈을 벌기 위한 영어는 단번에 귀가 뚫린다는 것을 무역을 해본 사람은 누구나 공감할 것이다.

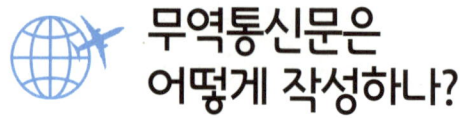
무역통신문은 어떻게 작성하나?

무역통신문의 작성 원칙

무역통신문은 대개 권리와 의무가 수반되기 때문에 정확하고 분명하여야 하며, 간단하면서도 완벽하고 정중하게 작성하여야 한다.

무역통신문의 작성 원칙을 살펴보면 다음과 같다.

① **정확성(Correctness)**
내용과 형식에 있어서 정확하게 (특히 문법 및 문장 구조 면에서)

② **명료성(Clearness)**
의미가 분명하고 쉽게 (오해의 여지가 없게)

③ **간결성(Conciseness)**

용건만 간단히(지나친 생략으로 내용을 손상하지 않는 범위 내에서)

④ **완벽(Completeness)**

상대방이 알아야 할 것은 빠짐없이 완벽하게(특히 상대방이 문의한 내용은 상세하게)

⑤ **예의(Courtesy)**

정중하고 우호적인 태도로(친선 관계를 창출할 수 있도록)

무역통신문의 구성 요소와 배열

무역통신문의 구성 요소는 서두, 작성 일자, 수신인 주소, 서두 인사, 본문, 결문 인사, 서명 등 반드시 포함되어야 하는 필수 구성 요소와 문서 번호, 특정 수신인, 서신의 제목, 서신 책임자 식별 기호, 동봉물 표시, 사본 배부처, 추신 등 필요에 따라 표기되는 부수 구성 요소로 구성되어 있다.

무역통신문의 구성 요소와 배열

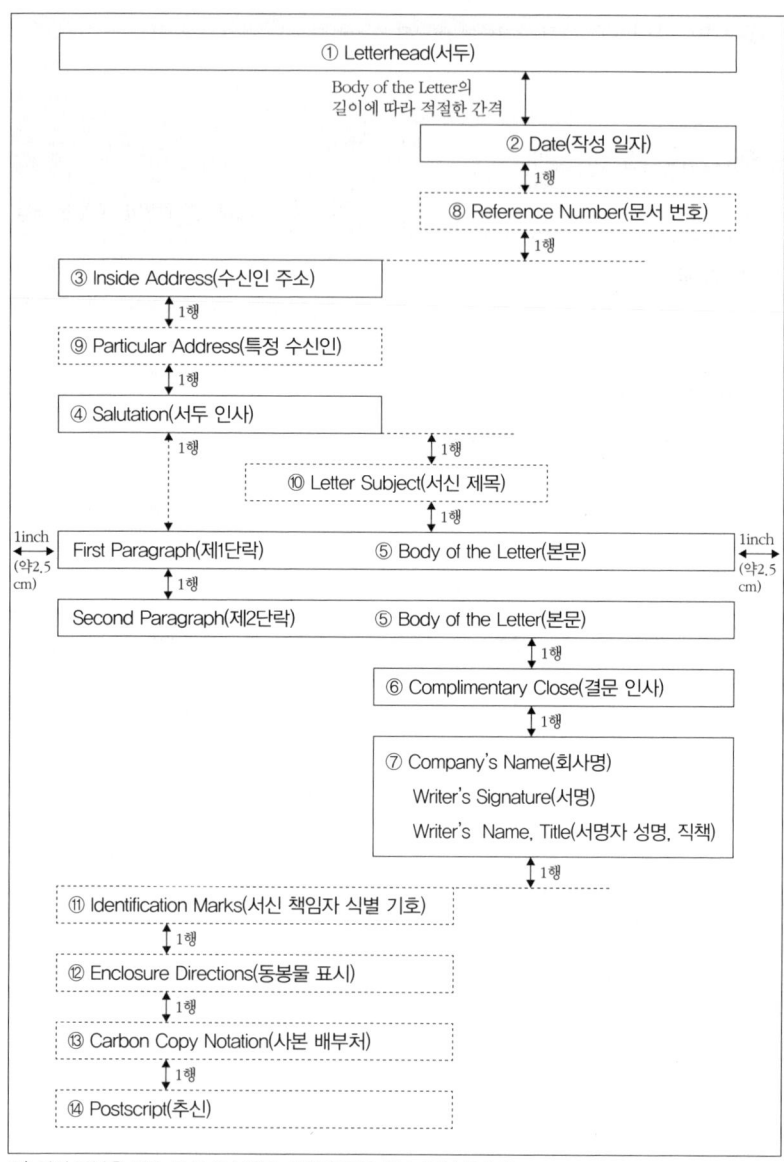

주) 실선 부분은 필수 구성 요소이며, 점선 부분은 부수 구성 요소임.

무역통신문의 필수 구성 요소

① Letterhead(서두)

일반적으로 무역통신문 용지의 윗부분에는 발신자의 상호, 주소, 전신약호, 전화번호, FAX 번호, E-mail, 인터넷 홈페이지 주소 등이 인쇄되어 있는데, 이러한 것을 말한다.

회사 상호의 영문 표기는 개인회사의 경우 Co.(Company) 또는 & Co.(두 사람 이상 여러 사람이 동업한 개인회사)를 쓰고, 주식회사(법인)인 경우 영국계는 주로 Co., Ltd.(Company, Limited) 또는 Pty., Ltd.(Proprietary, Limited)를 사용하며, 미국계는 주로 Inc.(Incorporated/Incorporation) 또는 Corp.(Corporated/Corporation)을 사용한다.

그러나 요즘에는 이에 대한 엄격한 구분 없이 사용하고 있다. 우리나라에서는 주로 Co., Ltd.를 주로 사용해왔으나, 최근에는 Inc. 또는 Corp.도 많이 사용하는 편이다.

그리고 상호 앞에는 문법적으로는 유일무이한 회사이므로 정관사 The가 붙어야 하지만, 요즘엔 상호 앞에 정관사 The를 붙이지 않는 것이 일반적이다. 하지만 'The Asia of Pacific Co., Ltd.'처럼 상호가 of로 수식받는 경우에는 The를 붙인다.

Letterhead의 예

SAMSUNG TRADING CO., LTD.
Manufacturers, Exporters & Importers
"High Quality, High Technology"
#707, 7th Fl. Samsung Bldg., 123 Samsung-dong, Gangnam-gu
Seoul 06170, Korea
TEL+82-2-6228-1472   M.P+82-10-6334-8710   FAX+82-2-6228-8710
E-mail : sihak@itc.co.kr   Website : http://www.itc.co.kr

---

② **Date(작성 일자)**

작성 일자를 표시하는 방법에는 American Style(예컨대 May 10, 2020)과 English Style(예컨대 10th May, 2020)이 있다.

③ **Inside Address(수신인 주소)**

수신인의 회사명과 주소를 기재하는 것으로, 대개 3~4행으로 기재한다. Mr., Mrs., Dr. 등의 호칭은 이름 앞에 오며, Manager, President 등의 직위를 나타내는 말은 이름 뒤에 온다.

Inside Address의 예

XYZ CO., LTD.
345 Wall St., New York
NY 10005, U.S.A.

---

④ **Salutation(서두 인사)**

무역통신문의 본문이 시작되기 전의 인사말로, 우리말의 '근계(謹啓)', 즉 '삼가 아룁니다'에 해당한다. Salutation은 Inside Address에서 1행 정도 아래에 좌측 여백선(Left-hand Marginal Line)부터 시작하며, Inside Address 수신인의 단·복수에 따라 Salutation을 맞춘다. Salutation에는 American Style(예컨대 Gentlemen:)과 English Style(예컨대 Dear Sirs,)이 있으며, 예의 정도에 따라 다음과 같은 Salutation을 사용한다.

예의 정도에 따른 Salutation의 종류

	Man	Woman
Most Formal	Sir,	Madam,
Formal	Dear Sir, My dear Sir,	Dear Madam, My dear Madam,
Less Formal	Dear Mr. Kim, My dear Mr. Kim,	Dear Mrs. Kim, My dear Mrs. Kim,
Friendly	Dear Kim, My dear Kim,	Dear Kim, My dear Kim,

⑤ **Body of the Letter(본문)**

무역통신문의 본문은 그 글의 본 내용으로, 본문의 행간(Between Lines)은 Single Space로 하고 절간(Between Paragraph)은 Double Space로 하는 것이 일반적이다.

무역통신문의 내용이 2페이지 이상일 경우 다음 용지는 Letterhead가 없는 용지를 사용하며, 위에서 2~3행 아래에 수신인의 상호를 기재한 후 페이지 표시 및 날짜를 기재한다. 그리고 약 5행 아래부터 Body of the Letter(본문)의 내용을 계속 기재하면 된다.

본문 두 번째 용지 기재 방법

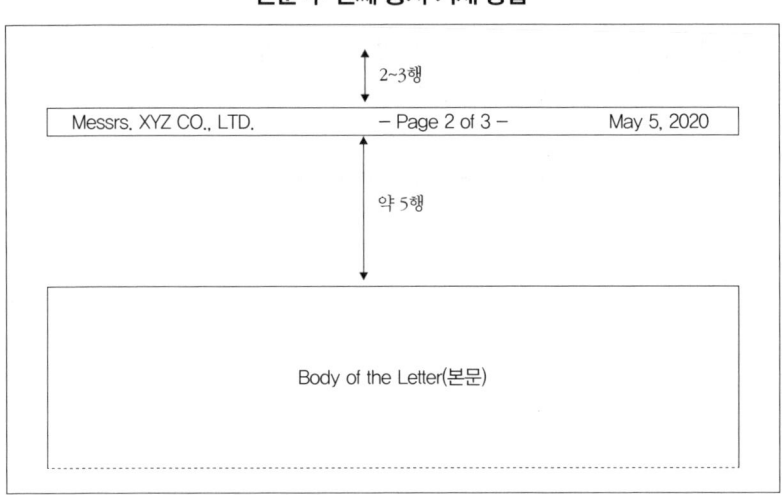

⑥ **Complimentary Close(결문 인사)**

결문 인사는 본문이 끝난 후의 인사말로, 본문 1행 아래 중앙에서 시작한다. 결문 인사의 첫 글자는 대문자로 시작하고, 끝에는 Comma(,)를 찍는다.

예의 정도에 따른 결문 인사의 종류는 다음과 같다.

Complimentary Close의 종류

	Complimentary Close	Remarks
Common Close	Yours truly, Yours very truly, Very truly yours, Yours faithfully, Faithfully yours,	always correct popular in U.S.A. most popular in U.S.A. most common in U.K. sometimes in U.K.
Formal Close	Respectfully, Yours respectfully, Respectfully yours, Very respectfully yours, Regards, Best regards,	
Personal & Friendly Close	Sincerely, Yours sincerely, Sincerely yours, Very sincerely, Most sincerely, Cordially, Cordially yours,	

⑦ **Signature(서명)**

서명은 그 서한의 책임 소재를 분명히 하기 위해 자필로 하여야 한다. 서명 위에는 회사명을 쓰며, 서명 밑에는 'Robert H. Brown, Manager in Export Department'와 같이 서명자의 성명과 직책 및 부서명을 쓴다. 대리 서명의 경우에는 'By Robert H. Brown for Tom H. Baker, President' 등과 같이 표시하고 서명한다. for 대신에 on behalf of 또는 p.p(per procuration) of 등의 표현을 쓰기도 한다. 그리고 서명자

성명과 직책 사이에 Comma(,) 또는 Slash(/)를 넣어 구분하기도 한다.

Signature의 예

• 자필 서명의 경우	SAMSUNG TRADING CO., LTD. *Kil-Dong Hong* Kil-Dong Hong, President
• 대리 서명의 경우	SAMSUNG TRADING CO., LTD. *Chul-Soo Kim* Chul-Soo Kim, Manager for Kil-Dong Hong, President

무역통신문의 부수적인 구성 요소

⑧ Reference Number(문서 번호)

Reference Number는 File Number라고도 하며, 무역통신문의 정리나 조회의 편의상 일련번호를 부여하는 것으로, Inside Address 위 Date 아래에 약어로 Ref. No.로 기재하는 것이 일반적이다.

⑨ Particular Address(특정 수신인)

무역통신문 내용의 성질에 따라 상대편 회사의 특정 부서 또는 특정인에게 보내기를 원할 때 사용하며, 'Attention : David K. Brown, Manager in Import Department' 또는 'Attn. : Robert H. Brown,

Purchasing Manager' 등과 같이 기재한다.

⑩ Letter Subject(서신 제목)

무역통신문 전체의 내용을 한눈에 쉽게 파악할 수 있도록 'Subject : ' 또는 're : ' 등을 명시하고 무역통신문의 제목을 붙이는 것이 전통적이었으나, 요즘은 이와 같은 제목, 즉 'Subject : ' 또는 're : '라는 용어가 사족이므로 Underline을 하거나 대문자에 흑자체로 하여 가운데에 배열하는 것이 일반적이다.

Letter Subject의 예

```
Subject : Business Proposal
re : Business Proposal
Business Proposal
BUSINESS PROPOSAL
```

⑪ Identification Marks(서신 책임자 식별 기호)

Identification Marks는 서신 책임자의 책임 소재를 명확히 하기 위해 서명자(Signer), 서신 작성자(Dictator) 및 타이피스트(Typist) 등의 성명 첫 글자를 서명란의 아래 좌측 여백선에서부터 기재한다. 예컨대 Robert Brown이 서명자이고, William Samuelson이 서신 작성자, Jane Baker가 타이피스트인 경우, 'RB/WS/JB' 또는 'RB:WS:JB' 또는 'RB-WS-JB'로 표기한다.

그러나 요즘은 문서 기안자와 작성자 그리고 타이피스트가 따로 구분되어 있지 않고 한 사람의 담당자가 컴퓨터로 모든 업무를 한꺼번에 처리하므로 서신 책임자 식별 기호를 표시하지 않는 것이 일반적이다.

⑫ Enclosure Directions(동봉물 표시)

무역통신문에 동봉물이 있을 경우에는 Identification Marks 줄 밑에 'Encl.: Price List' 등으로 표기하며, 동봉물이 여러 개일 때는 Encls.로 표기한다.

⑬ Carbon Copy Notation(사본 배부처)

서신 작성자가 서신의 사본이 제3자에게 송부되었다는 것을 알릴 필요가 있을 경우에는 'C.C.(또는 cc) : Mr. Robert Brown in Accounting Dept.' 등과 같이 표기하여 그 내용이 Accounting Dept.의 Mr. Brown 에게도 사본으로 송부되었음을 알린다.

⑭ Postscript(추신)

본문에서 누락된 내용이나 특히 강조할 사항을 추가로 명시할 때 사용한다(예컨대 P.S. : Your fax of May 20 has just reached us. We are examining your limit price.).

무역통신문의 배열 방식

무역통신문의 배열 방식에는 Blocked Style, Indented Style, Mixed Style 등이 있다.

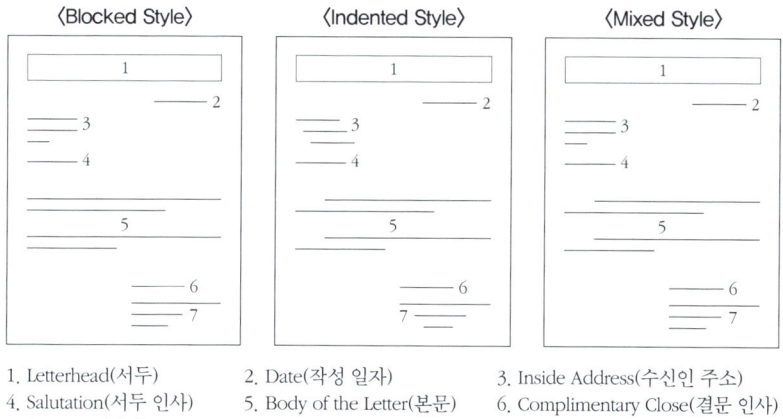

무역통신문의 배열 방식

1. Letterhead(서두)　　2. Date(작성 일자)　　3. Inside Address(수신인 주소)
4. Salutation(서두 인사)　5. Body of the Letter(본문)　6. Complimentary Close(결문 인사)
7. Signature(서명)

Blocked Style

Date, Reference No., Letter Subject, Complimentary Close, Signature 부분을 제외한 무역통신문의 모든 부분을 왼쪽 여백선에 수직으로 배치하며, Salutation, Body of the Letter 및 Complimentary Close에만 구두점을 찍고 여타 구성 요소의 행 뒤에는 구두점을 찍

지 않고 개방하는 Open Punctuation을 사용하는 것이 일반적이다. Blocked Style은 주로 미국계의 진취적인 회사에서 사용한다.

과거 Telex를 많이 사용하던 때에는 요금 절감을 위해 무역통신문의 모든 내용이 왼쪽부터 시작하는 Full Blocked Style이 일반적이었다. 그러나 요즘은 Fax 및 E-mail 등 통신수단의 발달과 요금 인하로 Modern Blocked Style이 일반적이다. 보통 Blocked Style이라 하면 Modern Blocked Style을 말한다.

Indented Style

Inside Address, Signature의 각 행과 Body의 각 Paragraph의 제1행을 윗줄보다 오른쪽으로 약 5~10Space의 간격을 두고 시작하며, 대개 구두점을 찍는 Closed Punctuation을 사용한다.

Indented Style은 주로 영국계의 보수적인 회사에서 사용한다.

Mixed Style

Hybrid Style 또는 Semi-blocked Style이라고도 하며, Body의 각 Paragraph의 제1행을 약 5~10Space의 간격을 두고 시작하는 것 이외에는 Blocked Style과 동일하다.

[샘플 1] Blocked Style(Open punctuation)

NATIONAL INDUSTRIES INC.

3800 East Elm Street

Des Molnes, Iowa 50328, U.S.A.

May 20, 2020

XYZ Co., Ltd.
240 Wells Boulevard
Madison 5, Winsor, Canada

Attention : Henry J. Foster, Importing Dept.

Dear Mr. Foster,

This letter illustrates the blocked style with open punctuation.

Every line begins at the left margin, and no punctuation is used at the end of any line in the heading and the inside address. Typists find this style a great convenience.

Many modern businessmen favor the streamlined appearance of such letters, although others hesitate from the forms to which they have been accustomed.

                                            Yours truly,

                                            NATIONAL INDUSTRIES INC.

                                            Morton Weller

                                            Morton Weller, Manager

                                            Credit Department

[샘플 2] Indented Style(Closed Punctuation)

WEST COST CORP.
458 W. Wells Street
Los Angeles, California, U.S.A.

April 5, 2020

Hankuk Trading Co., Ltd.
    C.P.O. Box 123
        Seoul, Korea

Attention : Mr. Kil-Dong Hong, Director

Dear Mr. Hong,

    This letter illustrates the indented style with closed punctuation.

    Before the typewriter came into common use for business correspondence, this form was widely employed. Many conservative organizations still use the indented form, but it now strikes the reader as old-fashioned.

    Each line of the address is indented five spaces more than the preceding line. The beginning of each paragraph is indented five or ten spaces.

    The complimentary close begins a few spaces to the right of the center of the page. Each line of the signature is indented three spaces from the beginning of the complimentary close. Closed punctuation is used in the address but not in the date and the signature.

                                   Yours truly,

WEST COST CORP.

Larry Frank

Larry Frank, President

[샘플 3] Mixed Style(Open Punctuation)

BELLINGHAM FURNITURE CO.

3947 N. Street, New Washington
Washington D.C. 20012, U.S.A.

November 14, 2020

General Range, Inc.
302 Trimble Street
Lansing, MI 49821, U.S.A.

Attention : Mr. Samuel, Credit Department

Gentlemen :

    The mixed style is the same as the blocked except that the paragraphs are indented five or more spaces.

    This model letter illustrates other features common to many letters.

    The attention line here is at the left margin, two lines below the inside address. In mixed style it could be indented with the paragraphs. It could also have been typed in all capital letters. If you wanted Mr. Samuel's name in the salutation, you would type his first name(or two initals) and his surname above attention. Then you would omit the attention line and use "Dear Mr. Samuel," in the salutation.

An enclosure notation is usually abbrertated "Encl."and the specific item may be indicated "Check".

          Very truly yours,

          BELLINGHAM FURNITURE CO.
          William Hemphill
          William Hemphill, President

Encl. Check

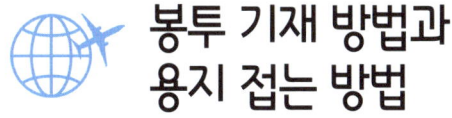
봉투 기재 방법과 용지 접는 방법

봉투에 주소를 기재하는 방법

　봉투의 4분의 1 왼쪽 상단부에는 편지를 보내는 발신인의 주소를 기재하고, 하단부 중앙에는 편지를 받는 수신인의 주소를 기재한다.
　항공편으로 보낼 경우에는 우표 밑에 Via Airmail이나 Air Mail 또는 Par Avion이라고 표시한다. 우편물의 내용물을 표시할 경우에는 Letter(편지), Printed Matter(인쇄물), Parcel(소포), Small Packet(소형 포장물), Sample of Merchandise(상품 견본) 등으로 표시한다.
　등기나 속달의 경우에는 수신인 주소 좌측 하단에 Registered(등기) 또는 Express(속달)라고 표시한다. 그리고 긴급을 요하는 편지는 Urgent 또는 Immediate를 명기한다.
　특정 수신인(Attention)이나 친전(Private/Personal/Confidential)을 표시할 경우에는 수신인 주소의 좌측에 표시한다.

서류의 송달 방법은 우체국(Post Office)이나 UPS(United Parcel Service) 와 같은 국제 택배편/국제 급송 서비스(International Courier Service)를 이용한다.

편지봉투 주소 기재 방법

편지지를 접는 방법

편지봉투가 큰 사이즈인 대봉투의 경우는 편지지를 3등분하여 접는다.

대봉투의 경우 편지지 접는 법

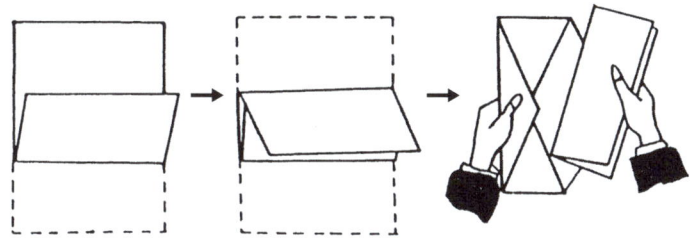

소봉투의 경우 편지지 접는 법

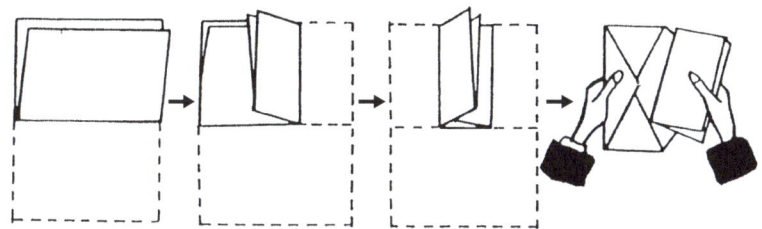

2장

거래 개설에 관한 무역통신문

거래선 알선 의뢰에 관한 무역통신문

거래선 발굴을 위한 해외시장 조사 방법

해외시장 조사(Overseas Market Research)는 수출 절차의 최초 단계로, 특정 상품에 대한 판매 가능성(Selling Feasibility)을 조사하는 것을 말한다.

해외시장 조사는 우선 목표 시장의 전반적인 개황(정치, 경제, 사회, 문화, 풍토, 기후, 언어, 종교 등)을 조사한 다음, 취급 상품에 대한 세부적인 내용(무역 관리 제도, 시장 특성, 수요와 공급, 유통 구조, 경쟁 대상 등)을 조사한다.

해외시장 조사 내용

구분	주요 조사 내용
• 일반 사항	• 정치, 경제, 사회, 문화, 풍습, 기후, 인구, 언어, 종교 등
• 경제 동향	• 경제성장, 국민소득, 물가, 임금, 고용, 국제수지 등
• 산업 동향	• 산업 구조(특히 관련 산업) 등
• 무역 동향	• 대외 무역 구조(특히 품목별, 지역별, 경쟁국 진출 동향)
• 무역 관리 제도	• 수출입 관리 제도 및 절차, 외환 관리 제도, 통화 정책, 관세 정책, 대한 수입 규제 등
• 시장 특성 및 유통 구조	• 소비자 계층, 상관습 및 구매 시기와 유통 구조 등
• 시장 접근 방법	• 수입상, 중개상 등
• 교역 현황	• 우리나라와의 전체 교역량 및 해당 품목의 수입 규모 등
• 기타	• 항만, 통신 시설 등

거래선을 발굴하는 방법

해외시장 조사를 통해 자사 제품이 시장성이 있는 목표 시장이 선정되면 다음과 같은 방법을 통하여 거래선을 발굴해야 한다.

거래선 발굴 방법

구분	주요 거래선 발굴 방법
인터넷 이용	• 인터넷을 이용하여 해외 고객을 검색·발굴하거나 홈페이지를 개설하여 자기 회사 및 취급 상품을 해외 고객에게 알림
자체 홍보물 이용	• 자체적으로 홍보물을 제작하여 주요 잠재 고객에게 배포

구분	주요 거래선 발굴 방법
국내외 발간 해외 광고 매체 이용	• 국내 발간 매체 　– 한국무역협회 : 　　《Korea Export》(연 2회) 　　《Mart Korea》(월간) 등 　– 대한무역투자공사(KOTRA) : 　　《Korea Trade & Business》(월간) 　　《Korea Trade》(연 8회) 등 • 해외 발간 매체 　– 미국 경제 전문지 : 　　《The Wall Street Journal》 등 　– 영국 경제 전문지 : 　　《The Financial Times》 등
해외 공공기관 이용	• 각국의 상공회의소 및 수출입 관련 기관에 거래 알선 의뢰 Circular Letter 발송
사절단 및 전시회 이용	• 무역사절단, 전시회 및 박람회 등에 참가
직접 방문	• 해당 지역 직접 방문(우리나라 무역업계가 시장을 개척한 주된 방법)

거래선 알선 의뢰에 관한 무역통신문 작성 방법

거래선 알선 의뢰에 관한 무역통신문은 주로 각국의 상공회의소나 취급 상품 관련 기관에 발송하는 거래 알선 의뢰 Circular Letter다. 거래 알선 의뢰 Circular Letter에는 취급 상품 등 자기 회사를 소개하고, 거래 희망 거래선을 알선해주기 바란다는 취지를 명시한다. 그리고 자기 회사의 신용조회처로 거래 은행명을 알려주고, 회신해주면 고맙겠다는 말로 끝을 맺는다.

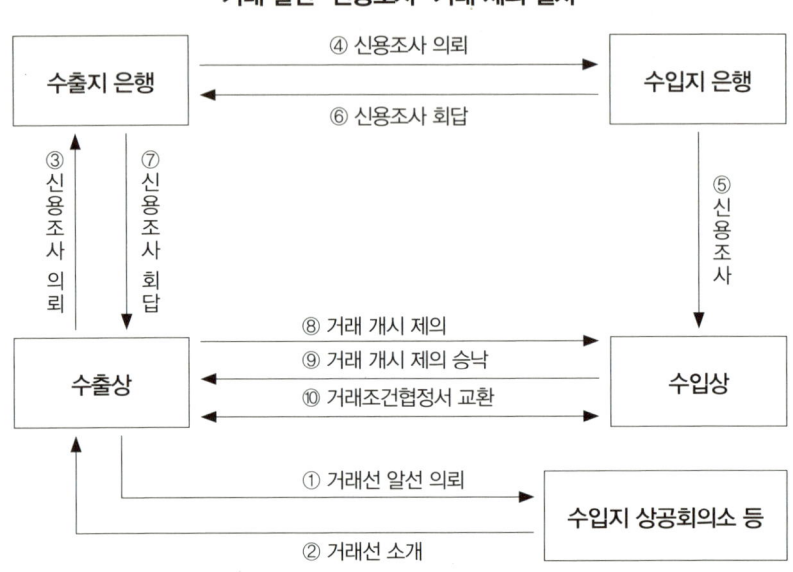

거래선 알선 의뢰에 대한 회신 작성 방법

거래선 알선 의뢰를 받은 기관은 이에 대한 회신으로 거래선을 소개하는 소개장을 발송한다. 거래선 소개장에는 일반적으로 거래선 알선 의뢰 내용을 곧 게재할 것이라는 내용과 관심 있는 거래선을 몇 군데 소개해주면서 추가 정보가 필요하면 요구하라는 내용을 담고 있다.

[샘플 1] 거래 알선 의뢰

SAMSUNG TRADING CO., LTD.

Manufacturers, Exporters & Importers

"High Quality, High Technology"

#707, 7th Fl. Samsung Bldg., 123 Samsung-dong, Gangnam-gu

Seoul 06170, Korea

TEL+82-2-6228-1472   M.P +82-10-6334-8710   FAX+82-2-6228-8710

E-mail : sihak@itc.co.kr   Internet : http://www.itc.co.kr

May 1, 2020

New York Chamber of Commerce[1]
99 Church St., New York
N.Y. 10007, U.S.A.

Attn.[2] : To whom it may concern

Gentlemen :

SEEKING FOR IMPORTERS OF BLUE JEANS

We are long-established[3] exporters of all kinds of blue jeans and have close connections with[4] the leading manufacturers here.

We would appreciate it very much if you could[5] introduce to us some reliable importers who are interested in this line[6] of business.

For any information concerning our financial standing[7] and reputation, please refer to the Samsung Branch of Shinhan Bank(123 Samsung-dong, Gangnam-gu, Seoul 06170, Korea Tel+82-2-6228-1472, Mobile+82-10-6334-8710, Fax+82-2-6228-8710).

Your kind attention would be highly appreciated and we are looking forward to[8] your favourable reply.

Yours very truly,

SAMSUNG TRADING CO., LTD.

Si-Hak Oh

Si-Hak Oh, Manager
Export Department

해설

※ 이 샘플은 청바지 수입상을 물색하고 있는 수출상이 뉴욕상업회의소에 청바지 수입에 관심 있는 믿을 만한 수입상을 소개해달라고 부탁하는 예문이다.

1) Chamber of Commerce : 상업회의소(商業會議所)

   (cf) Chamber of Commerce and Industry : 상공회의소(商工會議所)

2) Attn. : Attention의 약어. 참조(인)

3) long-established : 창업한 지 오래된

4) have close connections with ~ : ~와 밀접한 관계를 가지고 있다

5) We would appreciate it very much if you could ~ : 귀사가 ~을 해주시면 대단히 감사하겠습니다(it는 가목적어이며 if 이하 절이 진목적어임)

6) line : 품목, 상품(= item, commodity, article)

7) financial standing : 재무 상태, 신용 상태(= credit status)

8) look forward to : ~을 기대하다

[샘플 2] 거래 알선 의뢰

June 5, 2020

The Chamber of Commerce
of the State of New York
65 Liberty St., New York
NY 10022, U.S.A.

Gentlemen :

We are long-established exporters of all kinds of porcelain and have wide and close connections with[1] the leading manufacturers here.

We are trying to extend our business[2] to your market[3] and shall be obliged if you will[4] introduce to us some reliable firms[5] in your city who are interested in handling[6] porcelain.[7]

As to our credit standing,[8] Shinhan Bank will supply you with necessary information.[9]

We thank you for your trouble in advance[10] and wait for your favourable reply.

Yours very truly,

HANKUK TRADING CO., LTD.

Kil-Dong Hong
Kil-Dong Hong, Export Manager[11]

해설

※이 샘플은 도자기 수출상이 뉴욕상업회의소에 도자기 수입에 관심 있는 수입상을 소개해달라고 부탁하는 예문이다.

1) have wide and close connections with ~ : ~와 광범하고 밀접한 관계를 가지고 있다
2) extend our business : 당사의 영업 활동(거래선)을 확장하다
3) your market : 귀사의 시장
4) shall be obliged if you will ~ : ~해주시면 감사하겠습니다
5) reliable firms : 신뢰할 만한 상사(회사)
6) be interested in handling ~ : ~을 취급하는 데 관심 있는
7) porcelain : 도자기(= chinaware)
8) As to our credit standing : 당사의 신용 상태에 대해서(는)
9) supply(provide) 사람 with 사물 = supply(provide) 사물 for 사람 : ~에게 ~을 공급(제공)하다
10) thank you for your trouble in advance : 미리 (장차 발생할) 귀사의 노고(수고)에 감사한다. 이러한 표현은 당연히 수고를 해줄 것이라고 단정을 하거나 강압적인 느낌을 주기 때문에 가능한 한 사용을 자제하는 것이 바람직하다.
11) Export Manager : 수출부장

[샘플 3] **거래 알선 의뢰**

20th April, 2020

Singapore Chinese Chamber
of Commerce and Industry
47 Hill Street, Singapore

Dear Sirs,

Since 1980 we have been exporting blue jeans and are now trying to extend our activities[1] to your market.

We shall be obliged, therefore, if you will kindly introduce[2] us to some of the most reliable importers interested in this line and insert the following announcement in your publication[3] :

"Korean Exporters offer blue jeans, having wide connections with first-class manufacturers.[4] Please write or fax to ABC Co., Ltd., 123 Samsung-dong, Gangnam-gu, Seoul, Korea. Tel No.+82-2-6228-1472, Mobile+82-10-6334-8710, Fax No.+82-2-954-8718."

For any information concerning our credit standing and reputation,[5] we are permitted to mention Shinhan Bank, Seoul as a reference.[6]

We are waiting for[7] a favourable reply from you.

Yours faithfully,

ABC CO., LTD.

Si-Hak Oh

Si-Hak Oh, Managing Director[8]

해설

※ 이 샘플은 청바지 수출상이 싱가포르의 화교상업회의소에 청바지 수입상을 소개해 달라고 부탁하는 예문이다.

1) extend our activities : 당사의 영업 활동(거래선)을 확장하다
2) introduce : 소개하다
3) insert the following announcement in your publication : 귀 출판물(간행물)에 다음과 같은 공고를 삽입(게재)하다
   (cf) announcement는 무료 공고, advertisement는 유료 광고
4) having wide connections with first-class manufacturers : 일류 제조업체들과 광범한 거래 관계를 가지고 있다
5) credit standing and reputation : 신용 상태 및 평판
6) reference : 신용조회처(선)
7) be waiting for ~ : ~를 기다리다
8) Managing Director : 상무, 전무

[샘플 4] 거래선 소개

May 20, 2020

ABC Co., Ltd.
123 Samsung-dong, Gangnam-gu
Seoul 06170, Korea

Dear Mr. Oh,

    In reply to[1] your letter of May 10,[2] 2020, we have arranged to insert your announcement in the next issue of our bulletin,[3] a copy of which will be sent to you upon publication.[4]

We also suggest you contact⁵⁾ the following firms who may be intererested in the import of your goods :

XYZ Co., Ltd.
50 Liberty St., New York
N.Y. 10005, U.S.A.

LMN Co., Ltd.
35 East 25th St., New York
N.Y. 10035, U.S.A.

While these firms have been long-established and enjoy a good reputation⁶⁾ as the leading importers of blue jeans, we, of course, assume no responsibility for⁷⁾ them.

They will give you their references from whom you will be able to obtain information about their financial standing and reputation.

We are happy to recommend⁸⁾ these firms and shall be pleased to supply further information.

Very truly yours,

New York Chamber of Commerce

Jane R. Baker
Jane R. Baker, Secretary

해설

※ 이 샘플은 청바지 수출상으로부터 거래선 알선 의뢰를 받은 뉴욕상업회의소가 청바지 수입상 회사 2군데를 소개해주는 예문이다.

1) In reply to : ~에 답하여(= answering)
2) letter of (dated) May 10 : 5월 10일 자 편지
3) in the next issue of our bulletin : 당사의 간행물(출판물) 다음 호(판)에
4) upon publication : 출판하자마자, 출판 즉시
5) suggest you contact ~ : ~와 접촉할 것을 제안하다
6) enjoy a good reputation : 좋은 평판을 향유하다(누리다)
7) assume no responsibility for ~ : ~에 대한 책임을 부담하지 않는다(떠맡지 않는다)
8) recommend : 추천하다, ~을 권하다

[샘플 5] 거래선 소개

15th May, 2020

ABC Co., Ltd.
123 Samsung-dong, Gangnam-gu
Seoul 06170, Korea

Dear Sirs,

    In compliance with your request[1] of 20th April, we have arranged to insert your announcement in the next issue of our bulletin,[2] a copy of which will be sent to you upon publication.

    We also suggest the following firms, though we advise you to write to them direct for their references and make necessary credit inquiries.[3]

    Federated Enterprise (Co.) Ltd.
    Suite 06-16, Orchard Plaza

Orchard Road, Singapore 0922
Attn. : Mr. Wang Chien Sheng, General Manager

Singapore Overseas (Co.) Ltd.
15-N, Realty Centre
Enggor Street, Singapore 9011
Attn. : Mr. Lim Thiam Hong, Managing Director

If there is anything further we can do for you, please do not hesitate to let us know.[4]

Yours faithfully,

SINGAPORE CHINESE CHAMBER
OF COMMERCE AND INDUSTRY
Chua Pen Leng
Chua Pen Leng, Secretary

해설

※ 이 샘플은 거래선 알선 의뢰를 받은 싱가포르 화교상공회의소가 거래선 회사 2군데를 소개해주는 예문이다.

1) In compliance with your request : 귀사의 요청에 따라
2) bulletin : 회보, 출판물
3) credit inquiries : 신용조회
4) do not hesitate to let us know : 주저하지 말고 당사에 알려주십시오

거래선 알선 의뢰 및 소개에 유용한 표현

- We are *old and well-established* exporters of Surgical and Medical Tools and are now *looking for* a reliable firm to act as our agent in your city.

  당사는 설립된 지 오래되고 잘 알려진 수술 의료 기구 수출업체로, 현재 귀 시에 당사의 대리점으로 활동할, 신뢰할 만한 기업(회사)을 찾고 있는 중입니다.

- We *have no connections* in your market and are looking for a reliable concern(firm) who can *do business with* us.

  당사는 귀 시장에 거래선을 가지고 있지 않으므로, 당사와 거래할 수 있는 믿을 만한 기업을 찾고 있습니다.

- We wish to *open an account(enter into business, do business) with* a reliable firm in your city.

  당사는 귀 시에 있는 믿을 만한 기업과 거래를 개시하기를 원합니다.

- *We shall be happy if* you will *inform* us *of* the names and addresses of some reputable toy makers in your city.

귀 시에 있는 믿을 만한 몇몇 장난감 제조업체들의 상호 및 주소를 통보해주시면 감사하겠습니다.

- *We shall be obliged if* you will introduce to us some importers who *are interested in* handl*ing* canned provisions.

  귀 시에 있는 통조림 식품을 취급(거래, 수입)하는 데 관심 있는 몇몇 믿을 만한 수입 업체들을 소개해주시면 감사하겠습니다.

- We would *appreciate* receiv*ing* from you a list of suppliers so that we may contact them direct.

  당사가 직접 그들과 접촉할 수 있도록 공급 업체(공급선)의 목록을 제공해주시면 감사하겠습니다.

- Concerning(Regarding) our *financial(credit) standing(status, position)*, please *refer to* The Bank of Seoul, Ltd., Seoul.

  당사의 재무 상태에 대해서는 서울에 있는 서울은행에 조회하시기 바랍니다.

- While these concerns(firms) are generally considered trustworthy, we *assume no responsibility for* them.

  이 기업들은 일반적으로 믿을 만한 것으로 사료되지만, 당사는 이에 대한 책임은 지지 않습니다.

- *As requested(At your request)*, we are *sending herewith (enclosing, attaching)* a list of our members having offices in Kuala Lumpur.
  귀사의 요청에 따라 당사는 쿠알라룸푸르에 사무소를 가지고 있는 당사 회원사들의 목록을 동봉합니다.

- Havit Bank, Seoul will *provide(supply)* you with the necessary information.
= Havit Bank, Seoul will *provide(supply)* the necessary information *for* you.
  서울에 있는 한빛은행이 귀사에 필요한 정보를 제공할 것입니다.

시간에 관한 유용한 표현

on, in, at

- *in* the morning(afternoon, evening)
  오전(오후, 저녁)에
- *on* Monday morning

월요일 아침에

- *on* the morning of the 10th April

  4월 10일 아침에(특정일)

- *on* the 5th of June(on June 5)

  6월 5일에

- *in* September, 2020

  2020년 9월에

- *at* the beginning(end) of August

  8월 초순(하순)에

- *in* the middle of October

  10월 중순에

by(완료)/till, until(계속)

- The work will be finished *by*(not later than, latest, on or before) the end of this month.

  이달 말까지 그 작업은 완료될 것이다.

- Let's wait *till* he comes.

  그가 올 때까지 기다리자.(부사절 시제 주의)

- She stayed there *until* 7:00.

  그녀는 7시까지 거기서 기다렸다.

before/by, after/from

- The goods must be shipped *before* March 20.

  그 화물은 3월 19일까지 선적되어야 한다.

- The goods must be shipped *by*(not later than, latest, on or before) March 20.

  그 화물은 3월 20일까지 선적되어야 한다.

- The law will come into *after* May 15.

  그 법은 5월 16일부터 효력이 발생할 것이다.

- The law will come into *from*(on or after) May 15.

  그 법은 5월 15일부터 효력이 발생할 것이다.

from ~ to ; through

- *From* June 1 *to* September 5

  6월 1일부터 9월 5일까지(영국식)

- *(From)* June 1 *through* September 5

  6월 1일부터 9월 5일까지(미국식)

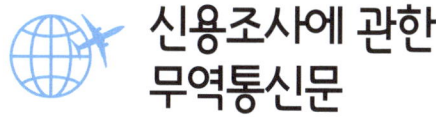# 신용조사에 관한 무역통신문

신용조사 방법

앞에서 살펴본 바와 같이 해외시장을 조사하고 거래선을 발굴하면, 거래 상대방의 신용 상태를 확인하는 신용조사(Credit Inquiry)를 해야 한다.

신용조사의 내용 및 방법과 신용조사 서신 작성 시 포함해야 할 사항은 다음과 같다.

신용조사 내용 및 방법

구분	신용조사 내용 및 방법
신용조사 내용 (3C's)	• 평판(Character) : 계약 이행에 대한 평판, 성실성 등 • 재무 상태(Capital) : 대차대조표(Balance Sheet), 손익계산서(Profit and Loss Statement) 등 지불 능력에 직결되는 재무 상태 • 생산·영업 능력(Capacity) : 생산량, 매출액 등 생산·영업 능력
신용조사 방법	• 은행 조사(Bank Reference) : 거래 은행을 이용한 가장 일반적인 신용조사 방법(유료) • 동업자 조사(Trade Reference) : 거래선을 이용한 신용조사 방법(회신 봉투 및 서식을 동봉하면 상대편의 부담이 경감됨)(무료) • 기타 : 상대국의 상업회의소, 협회, 조합 등이나 대한무역진흥공사, 신용보증기금, 한국수출보험공사 등에 의뢰
신용조사 서신 작성 시 포함 사항	• 조사하고자 하는 상사명 및 주소 • 조사하고자 하는 이유 • 조사 내용에 대해 비밀을 엄수하겠다는 약속 • 감사의 말과 협조의 부탁

신용조사에 대한 회답 작성 방법

신용조사에 대한 회답장에는 신용조사 대상 업체의 창업 이래 사업 경력, 경영 규모, 채무 이행의 확실성 여부, 세인의 평판 등을 알려주되, 제공한 정보에 관해 책임을 지지 않고 또한 극비로 취급해줄 것을 요청한다.

[샘플 6] 신용조사 의뢰

15th May, 2020

Hanvit Bank, Ltd.
10 Myung-dong, Jung-gu
Seoul 04534, Korea

Dear Sir,

We wish to enter into business relations with[1] the following firm :

Pacific Trading Co., Inc.
30 Water Street, New York, N.Y. 10003, U.S.A.

Would you please get information[2] for us on their financial status and reputation? Their bank, we are told, is

North-East Bank of America
85 Broad Street, New York, N.Y. 10004, U.S.A.

We assure you that[3] any information that you may give us will be kept in strict confidence.[4]

Yours very truly,

ABC CO., LTD.

Si-Hak Oh
Si-Hak Oh, Export Manager

해설

※ 이 샘플은 수출상이 거래 은행에 거래를 개시하고자 하는 상대 회사와 상대 회사의 거래 은행을 알려주면서 거래 상대방의 신용조회를 의뢰하는 예문이다.

1) enter into business relations with : 거래 관계를 개설하다
2) information : 정보
   (cf) ask for information : 문의하다, 조회하다
3) we assure you that : 당사는 귀사에게 that 이하 사실에 대하여 약속하다
4) be kept in strict confidence : 극비로 취급되다

[샘플 7] 신용조사 의뢰

15th May, 2020

Citi Bank, Ltd.
40 Liberty St., New York
N.Y. 10005, U.S.A.

Attn. : Tom H. Baker, Manager
        Credit Department

Dear Sirs,

CREDIT ENQUIRY

    Your bank was given as a reference of XYZ Co., Ltd. of Liberty St., New York, who are interested in the import of blue jeans.

    We would appreciate it very much if you could inform us of their financial standing and reputation. Any information provided by you will be treated as strictly confidential,[1] and expense will be paid by us upon receipt of your bill.[2]

Your prompt reply would be highly appreciated.

Your truly,

HANVIT BANK, LTD.

Woo-Young Lee
Woo-Young Lee, Manager[3]
Foreign Exchange Dept.

해설

※ 이 샘플은 수출상으로부터 신용조회 의뢰를 받은 한빛은행이 수입상의 거래 은행인 시티은행에 수입상의 신용 상태를 조회하는 예문이다.

1) be treated as strictly confidential : 엄격히 비밀로 취급되다
2) upon receipt of your bill : 귀사의 대금청구서(계산서)를 받자마자
3) Manager : 부(서)장

[샘플 8] 신용조사 의뢰

April 20, 2020

S. Abbott Company
1060 North Point, San Francisco
CA 94109, U.S.A.

Attn. : Mr. S. Abbott, President

Dear Mr. Abbott :

CREDIT ENQUIRY

The Pan-Pacific Corporation of 160 Pine Street, San Francisco, CA 94111, U.S.A., has recently proposed to open an account with[1] us and given your name as a reference.

We shall appreciate it if you will inform us of your own experience[2] with this firm by filling in the blanks below[3] and returning this letter to us in the enclosed envelope.

Any information you may give us will be held in strict confidence, and when an opportunity comes,[4] we shall be only too[5] glad to reciprocate.[6]

Sincerely yours,

ABC CO., LTD.
Si-Hak Oh
Si-Hak Oh, Director[7]

Enc. Envelope 1

★★★★★★★★★

1. Do they have an account with you now? Yes _____ No _____
2. How long have they had the account with you? _____ years
3. On what terms[8] _____
4. How do they pay? Prompt _____ Medium _____ Slow _____
5. Have you ever had trouble in collecting?[9] _____
6. What line of credit[10] have you extended? _____
7. Other information you think useful to us :

해설

※ 이 샘플은 거래 상대방의 거래선에 거래 상대방의 신용 상태를 조회하는 예문이다.

1) open an account with ~ : ~와 거래 관계를 개시하다(= enter into business relations with, do business with)
2) inform 사람 of 사물 : ~에게 ~을 통지하다
3) fill in the blanks below : 아래 공란에 채우다
4) when an opportunity comes : 기회가 오면
5) only too : 대단히
6) reciprocate : 보답하다
7) Director : 이사(理事), 중역(重役)
8) terms (of payment) : 대금 결제 조건
9) collecting : 대금 회수
10) line of credit : 신용대출의 한도

[샘플 9] 신용조사에 대한 회답

May 30, 2020

Hanvit Bank, Ltd.
10 Myung-dong, Jung-gu
Seoul 104534, Korea

Gentlemen :

REPLY TO CREDIT ENQUIRY

XYZ Co., Ltd.
345 Liberty St., New york, N.Y. 10005, U.S.A.

The above firm has been engaged in importing blue jeans for over twenty years and has sufficient capital for their requirements. As far as we know, all their obligations have been paid promptly.

We believe that because of their steady and sincere way of conducting business,[1] they can enjoy a good reputation among the leading wholesalers in our district.[2]

Please note that this information is furnished without any responsibility on our part[3] and should be treated in strict confidence.

Yours truly,

CITI BANK, LTD.

Charles H. Brown
Charles H. Brown, Manager
Credit Department

해설

※이 샘플은 수출상 거래 은행인 한빛은행으로부터 청바지 수입상의 신용조회를 의뢰받은 시티은행이 한빛은행에 수입상의 신용 상태를 통보해주는 예문이다.

1) steady and sincere way of conducting business : 견실하고 성실한 거래 행위
   (cf) sincerely : 성실하게, 진정으로
2) in our district : 우리(이곳) 지역에
3) without any responsibility on our part : 당사 측에 여하한 책임 없이

[샘플 10] 신용조사에 대한 회답

June 5, 2020

Hanvit Bank, Ltd.
10 Myung-dong, Jung-gu
Seoul 04534, Korea

Dear Sir,

REPLY TO CREDIT ENQUIRY

Pacific Trading Co., Ltd.
30 Water Street, New York, N.Y. 10003, U.S.A.

The above firm started business here in June, 1925, and has sufficient capital for their requirements.[1] All their obligations, as far as we know, have been paid promptly. In our opinion, they are considered good for[2] any normal engagements.

Yours very truly,

THE NORTH-EAST BANK OF AMERICA

George S. Walker
George S. Walker, Manager

해설

※이 샘플은 한빛은행으로부터 신용조회를 의뢰받은 노스이스트은행이 신용조사 대상 기업의 신용 상태를 긍정적으로 통보해주는 예문이다.

1) requirements : 요구 조건
2) good for ~ : ~을 이행할 능력이 있는

[샘플 11] 신용조사에 대한 회답

April 20, 2020

ABC Co., Ltd.
123 Samsung-dong, Gangnam-gu
Seoul 06170, Korea

Gentlemen :

    The firm you inquired about in your letter of April 5 is one of the most reliable importers in this city.

    We have been doing business with them for more than ten years and there has been not a single instance[1] in which they failed to meet their obligations.[2] Their senior partner[3] is an active businessman, about forty years old, with unlimited resources[4] and sound judgement.[5]

    You will run no risk in dealing with[6] them, though of course this is our personal opinion, for which we assume no responsibility.

    We hope that this information will prove useful to you and ask you to treat it with utmost discretion.

Very truly yours,

PHILIPPINES ADVANCE, INC.
Aldo Portolano
Aldo Portolano, President

해설

※ 이 샘플은 수출상으로부터 신용조회를 의뢰받은 수입상 거래선이 수출상에 수입상의 신용 상태를 긍정적으로 통보하는 예문이다.

1) a single instance : 단 한 번의 사례(예)
2) failed to meet their obligations : 채무를 이행하지 못하다
3) senior partner : 동업자 중 상급자
4) unlimited resources : 무한한 잠재력
5) sound judgement : 건전한 판단
6) You will run no risk in dealing with ~ : 귀사는 ~와 거래하는 데에 아무런 위험도 없을 것이다

신용조사 의뢰 및 회답에 유용한 표현

- We *should appreciate it if* you would *supply* us *with* detailed information on the status of this firm.
이 기업의 재무 상태에 대한 상세한 정보를 당사에 제공해주시면 감사하겠습니다.

- Aster Import, Inc. of the following address has proposed to *open an account with* us and given us the under-mentioned bank as reference.
다음(아래) 주소의 아스터 수입상사가 당사와 거래를 개시하자는 제의를 해 왔으며, 그들은 당사에 아래 명시된 은행을 신용조회처로 알려 왔습니다.

- Please let us know frankly and without *responsibility on your part* whether you consider it safe to trust them with a business up to, say, US$200,000.00.
예컨대 미화 20만 달러까지는 그들과 신용거래를 하는 것이 안전한지 여부를 솔직하게, 그리고 귀사 측의 책임 없이 당사에 알려 주십시오.

- During the past five years, they have caused us some trouble *in regard to* their payments. It would be advisable for you to use caution.

  지난 5년 동안 그들은 대금 결제와 관련하여 당사에 얼마간의 어려움을 주었습니다. 그러므로 귀사가 주의를 기울이는 것이 바람직할 것입니다.

- As the firm *in question* has recently suffered heavy losses, *it* would be advisable *for* you *to* take every precaution in dealing with them.

  그 기업은 최근에 심한 손실을 입었으므로, 귀사가 그들과 거래를 하는 데 사전에 철저히 주의하는 것이 바람직할 것입니다.

- Last April we *were obliged to take legal steps* in order to protect ourselves. Since then we have sold them several small orders on *C.W.O.*(Cash With Order, T/T With Order, T/T in Advance, Advance Payment by T/T, Cash in Advance by T/T) terms.

  지난 4월 당사는 당사를 보호하기 위해(대금 결제를 받기 위해) 법적 조치를 취하지 않을 수 없었습니다. 그 이후로는 그들에게 선불 조건으로 소량의 주문품을 팔았습니다.

- Please note that this information is given *without obligation on our part*.

  이 정보는 당사 측에 책임 없이 제공됨을 주지하시기 바랍니다.

- We regret that we are not *in a position* to give you the informations you seek *in regard* to the firms mentioned in your letter of May 10. We are indeed unaware that they had given our name as a reference.

  당사는 유감스럽게도 5월 10일 자 귀사의 편지에서 언급한 그 기업들에 대해 귀사가 원하는 정보를 줄 수 없습니다. 당사는 그들이 왜 당사를 신용조회처로 제시했는지 정말로 알 수 없습니다.

- We are permitted to mention The Bank of Seoul, Ltd. as our reference.

  당사는 서울은행을 당사의 신용조회처로 알려드립니다.

- Please give us at least two references.

  최소한(적어도) 두 개의 신용조회처를 알려주시기 바랍니다.

- *Regarding* our financial standing, *please refer* to The ABC Bank.

당사의 신용 상태에 대해서는 ABC은행에 조회하시기 바랍니다.

- *As to other matters*, we will *supply* you, upon request, *with* any information that you may require.

  여타 사항에 대해서는 귀사가 필요로 하는 정보를 요청받는 즉시 귀사에 제공해드리겠습니다.

- The firm(company) you referred to(in question) has been engaged in the export of electric appliances since 1985, and is enjoying a very good reputation in this city.

  귀사가 언급한(당해) 그 회사는 1985년 이래 전기제품의 수출에 종사해왔으며, 이 시에서 매우 좋은 평판을 누리고 있습니다.

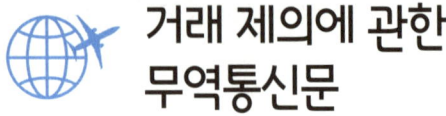
거래 제의에 관한 무역통신문

거래 제의 방법

신용조사를 한 결과 거래 상대방의 신용 상태가 확실하면 다음과 같은 요령에 의해 거래 제의 서신(Circular Letter/Business Proposal Letter)을 Mail이나 Fax 또는 Telex를 통해 발송한다.

거래 제의 서신 작성 요령 및 유의점

작성 요령	유의점
• 상대방을 알게 된 동기	• 간단명료한 문장
• 거래 제의 회사의 취급 상품 및 거래 국가	• 과장된 회사 소개를 삼가고 취급 상품과 거래 국가 등을 간략히 소개 • 품질의 우수성과 경쟁력 있는 가격 강조
• 거래 제의 목적	• 해당 시장을 상대 회사를 통해 처음 개척하고자 한다는 점을 강조
• 신용조회처	• 주로 자기 거래 은행명 및 주소
• 정중한 결론	• 거래 관계가 개설되면 상호 이익을 바탕으로 한다는 점을 언급

대리점에 대한 신청 제의는 어떻게 하나?

대리점에 대한 신청 제의는 본인이 직접 수출입을 하려는 것이 아니고, 수출입 거래선을 소개해주고 수수료를 받는 것을 업으로 하는 무역 대리업자(Offering Agent : 속칭 오퍼상)의 역할을 제의하는 것이다. 대리점에 대한 신청 제의 시 유의할 사항은 일반 대리점(Agency), 독점 대리점(Sole Agency), 그리고 배타적 독점 대리점(Exclusive Agency) 중 어느 것을 원하는지 명확히 해야 한다는 것이다. 그 이외의 사항은 일반 수출입 거래 제의 편지와 동일한 방법으로 작성하면 된다.

[샘플 12] 거래 제의

SAMSUNG TRADING CO., LTD.

Manufacturers, Exporters & Importers

"High Quality, High Technology"

#707, 7th Fl. Samsung Bldg., 123 Samsung-dong, Gangnam-gu

Seoul 06170, Korea

TEL+82-2-6228-1472   M.P+82-10-6334-8710   FAX+82-2-6228-8710

E-mail : sihak@itc.co.kr   Website : http://www.itc.co.kr

June 1, 2020

Mikuk Co., Ltd.
50 Liberty St., New York
N.Y. 10005, U.S.A.

Attn. : Robert H. Brown, Manager
        Purchasing Dept.

Gentlemen :

BUSINESS PROPOSAL

    Your name has been given by[1] the Chamber of Commerce of your city[2] as one of the leading importers of blue jeans in your country.

    We are large manufacturers and exporters in Korea producing all kinds of blue jeans using latest computerized manufacturing facilities.

    We have been exporting our products in Japan, U. K., and France, etc. In order to diversify our existing market,[3] we are interested in supplying our products to you on favorable terms.

Upon receipt of your request for our samples, catalogue and price list, we could submit our samples with competitive prices to you.

As to our credit standing,[4] we refer you to Hanvit Bank, Ltd. or any of the commercial banks[5] in Korea.

We are looking forward to your favourable reply.

Yours very truly,

SAMSUNG TRADING CO., LTD.
Si-Hak Oh
Si-Hak Oh, President

해설

※이 샘플은 청바지 수출상이 뉴욕상업회의소를 통하여 알게 된 청바지 수입상에 거래 제의를 하는 예문이다.

1) Your name has been given by ~ : 귀사의 이름을 ~을 통하여 알게 되었다
2) Chamber of Commerce of your city : 귀 시의 상업회의소, 즉 뉴욕시의 상업회의소
3) In order to diversify our existing market : 기존 시장을 다변화하기 위하여
4) As to our credit standing : 당사의 신용 상태에 대해서는
5) commercial banks : 시중 은행

[샘플 13] 거래 제의

June 15, 2020

Pacific Trading Co., Inc.
30 Water Street, New York
N.Y. 10003, U.S.A.

Gentlemen :

BUSINESS PROPOSAL

Your name and address have been given us by The Chamber of Commerce of your city as large importers of porcelain, and we are writing you with a keen desire of opening an account with you.

We have been doing business for over thirty years as exporters of porcelain and have extensive and close connections with first-class porcelain makers[1] in this country. We have, up to the present,[2] been exporting various kinds of porcelain, especially tea sets, to Britain, Sweden, Germany, Italy, and the Netherlands, and have been enjoying a good reputation because of the excellent quality, quick delivery[3] and competitive prices[4] of our goods.[5]

It is our custom to trade on an irrevocable letter of credit,[6] under which we draw a draft at 30 d/s.[7]

As to our standing, we wish to refer you to[8] The Bank of Seoul, Ltd., Seoul. We will supply you, upon request,[9] with any other information that you may require.

We look forward to your favorable reply by return.[10]

Yours very truly,

HANKUK TRADING CO., LTD.
Kil-Dong Hong
Kil-Dong Hong, Export Manager

해설

※ 이 샘플은 도자기 수출상이 수입상에 도자기 거래를 제의하는 예문이다.

1) first-class porcelain makers : 일류의 도자기 제조업체
2) up to the present : 현재까지
3) quick delivery : 조기 인도, 신속한 인도
4) competitive(reasonable) prices : 경쟁적인(합리적인) 가격
5) goods : 상품(항상 복수형)
6) irrevocable letter of credit : 취소불능신용장
7) draw a draft at 30 d/s(days after sight) : 일람 후 30일 결제 조건의 환어음을 발행하다
8) wish to refer you to ~ : ~에 신용조회를 하기 바란다
9) upon request : 요청을 받자마자
10) by return : 회신 편에

[샘플 14] 거래 제의

16th January, 2020

Austral Farming Supplies Pty. Ltd.[1]
P. O. Box 75, Glebe, N.S.W. 2037
Australia

Dear Sirs,

Having heard from the KITA(Korea International Trade Association), Seoul that you are interested in Farm and Garden Machinery,[2] we are writing to you with a keen desire to do business with you.

As you will see in the enclosed pamphlet, we have been established here for over thirty years as general importers and exporters.[3] In farming equipment, we enjoy a specially advantageous position, because we have an affiliated company[4] which manufactures engines for farming applications, besides having wide and direct connections with first-class builders[5] of agricultural machines.

We know very well the requirements of the Australian farming industry and shall be able to serve you immediately upon hearing from you.

We do business on[6] an Irrevocable Letter of Credit, under which we draw a draft at 60 d/s.

For any information as to our standing, please refer to The Bank of Seoul, and The Hanvit Bank, Seoul.

We look forward to your early and favourable reply.

Yours faithfully,

HANKUK TRADING CO., LTD.
Si-Hak Oh
Si-Hak Oh, President

해설

※ 이 샘플은 농기계 수출상이 농원예용 기계류 수입에 관심 있는 수입상에 거래를 제의하는 예문이다.

1) Pty. Ltd. : Proprietary Limited의 약어. 영국계 주식회사의 일종으로, 주식이 비공개된 장외기업을 일컫는다.
2) farm and garden machinery : 농원예용 기계류
3) general importers and exporters : 특정 상품에 한정하지 않고 모든 종류의 상품을 수출입하는 종합무역상사
4) affiliated company : 관련 회사, 계열회사, 자회사
5) builders : 기계류 제조업체
6) We do business on ~ : 당사는 ~ 조건으로 거래를 한다

[샘플 15] 거래 제의

June 20, 2020

Hankuk Trading Co., Inc.
123 Samsung-dong, Gangnam-gu
Seoul 06170, Korea

Gentlemen :

    We have recently seen your Pottery advertized in the November issue of Modern Pottery,[1] and are very interested in your goods.

    We have always enjoyed an ever-increasing demand[2] for good coffee cups here and we have now many enquiries for high quality Korean-made Coffe Cups of colorful designs, and would be very pleased to have your lowest prices for A-356 and B-485 on FOB Pusan. Also we shall appreciate your sending us two samples each by return airmail.[3] We are ready to place a large order with[4] you if the prices and designs are satisfactory.

    Thank you for your prompt attention to this matter.

                           Sincerely yours,

                            PACIFIC TRADING CO., LTD.
                            Robert H. Brown
                            Robert H. Brown, Purchasing Manager

> **해설**

※ 이 샘플은 수입상이 도자기 간행물 광고란을 보고 수출상에 도자기 거래 제의를 하는 예문이다.

1) in the November issue of Modern Pottery : 《현대도자기》11월호에
2) an ever-increasing demand : 보기 드물게 증가하고 있는 수요
3) by return airmail : 항공 회신 편에
4) place a large order with : ~에게 대량 주문을 하다

[샘플 16] **대리점 신청 제의**

March 12, 2020

Taurus Corporation
105 West Ninth Street, Wilmington
DE 19899, U.S.A.

Gentlemen :

    Your name and address have been given us by Jones & Co. of your city as large exporters of various chemical products. We understand that you have not yet been represented[1] here and we wish to offer our services as your agents for Korea.

    For the past twenty years we have been importing Chemicals[2] and Dyestuffs[3] from your country. Being regular suppliers[4] to the leading mills[5] and printing factories, we shall be able to secure constant orders for your goods.

    If you care to avail yourselves of[6] our services, please inform us of your terms and conditions of agency as well as of the main lines you are handing. Details of our trade and references are stated in the enclosed brochure.[7]

We believe that mutually profitable business will result if you kindly accept this proposal.

Very truly yours,

HANKUK CO., LTD.
Si-Hak Oh
Si-Hak Oh, President

Encl. "Introducing Hankuk Co., Ltd."

해설

※ 이 샘플은 한국회사가 미국에 있는 화공약품 수출상에 한국 내에 화공약품 대리점을 하고 싶다고 대리점 신청 제의를 하는 예문이다.

1) be represented : 대리점을 두다
2) chemicals : 화공약품
3) dyestuffs : 염료
4) regular suppliers : 정기적 납품업자
5) mill : 공장
   (cf) spinning mill : 방직공장
6) avail oneself of ~ : ~을 활용하다, ~을 이용하다
7) brochure : 업무 안내 등의 소책자

[샘플 17] 대리점 신청 제의

15th March, 2020

Pioneer Chemical Co., Ltd.
196, Cannon Street, London
E.C. 4, England

Dear Sirs,

　We have recently learned from our friends[1] in your city, Messrs. Brown & Co., Ltd., that you are seeking a reliable sales agent in Seoul to increase the sale of your products. Following our friends' suggestion, we wish to offer you our services[2] if you have not yet represented here.

　We are old-established dealers in leather goods having numerous and valuable connections,[3] and are confident that we can do a large turnover[4] for you if we are appointed as your agent.

　Should you be disposed to consider[5] our offer, we wish you would let us have your terms and conditions.[6]

　As to our financial status etc., Shinhan Bank, Seoul, Korea will give you any information that you may require.

　We wait for your prompt and favourable reply.

　　　　　　　　　　　　　　Yours faithfully,

　　　　　　　　　　　　　　HANKUK CO., LTD.
　　　　　　　　　　　　　　Han-Dong Kim
　　　　　　　　　　　　　　Han-Dong Kim, President

해설

※이 샘플은 서울에 판매 대리점을 물색하고 있는 영국 회사에 대리점을 하고 싶다고 제안하는 예문이다.

1) friends : 거래선
2) wish to offer you our services : 귀사에 당사의 서비스를 제공하기를 원한다
3) numerous and valuable connections : 다수의 유용한 거래선
4) do a large turnover : 대량 매상고(매출액)를 올리다
5) Should you be disposed to consider ~ : ~을 고려하기를 원하면
6) your terms and conditions : 거래 조건. terms는 통상 지불에 관한 조건, conditions는 지불 이외의 기타 조건을 말한다.

[샘플 18] 독점 대리점 신청 제의에 대한 회신

25th March, 2020

Hankuk Co., Ltd.
123 Samsung-dong, Gangnam-gu
Seoul 01670, Korea

Dear Mr. Lee,

 Thank you for your letter of 18 March and for your comments on our cameras.

 We are still a young company, but expanding rapidly. At present[1] our overseas representation is confined to[2] countries in Western Europe, where our cameras are selling well. However, we are interested in the chance of developing our trade further afield.

When your Mr. Oh is in England, we should certainly like to meet him with a view to[3] discussing your proposal further. If Mr. Oh will get in touch with[4] me to arrange a meeting, I can also arrange for him to look around[5] our factory and see for himself the quality of the materials and workmanship put into[6] our cameras.

Yours truly,

PIONEER CHEMICAL CO., LTD.
Robert H. Brown
Robert H. Brown, Manager

해설

※ 이 샘플은 독점 대리점 신청 제의에 대한 회신으로, 더 검토한 후 결정하겠다는 예문이다.

1) At present : 현재로서는
2) be confined to : ~에 한정(제한)되어 있다
3) with a view to : ~하고자, ~할 목적으로
4) get in touch with : ~와 접촉하다(= contact)
5) look around : 둘러보다
6) put into : 투입되는

[샘플 19] 대리점계약서

AGENCY AGREEMENT

December 1, 2020

This agreement is made between XYZ Co., Ltd.(hereinafter called "Supplier") in New York, U.S.A. and ABC Co., Ltd.(hereinafter called "Agent") in Seoul, Korea, and both parties hereto have agreed as follows :

1. Sales area :"Agent" shall act as a (sole) sales agent for the "Supplier" with the geographic area of Republic of Korea as well as the area mutually agreed upon.
2. Sales products : Blue Jeans
3. Agent shall do its best to promote sales of above products and all sales transactions should be confirmed in advance by "Supplier".
4. Commission rate will be (3)% of the purchase amount, and such commission must be paid within (30) days after shipment.
5. This agreement is effective from (December 1 in 2020), and remain effective for (5) years. This agreement shall be extended by mutual agreement.
6. Supplier shall observe those regulations described in international agreement provisions as regulated in Korean Anti-trust and Fair Trade Acts, against which agent shall not be bound by Supplier.
7. Any disputes or claims which can not be resolved amicably between the parties hereto shall be settled by arbitration in accordance with the Commercial Arbitration Rules of Korean Commercial Arbitration Board in Korea.
8. In the event of the agency contract being terminated by the Supplier, for any reason other than willful misconduct on the part of the agent, the agent shall be entitled to an amount to be paid to him by the Supplier by way of compensation for loss of goodwill suffered by the agent.

Supplier :	Agent :
XYZ Co., Ltd.	ABC Co., Ltd.
456 Wall St., New York	123 Samsung-dong, Gangnam-gu
N.Y., U.S.A.	Seoul, Korea
Robert H. Brown	*Si-Hak Oh*
Robert H. Brown, President	Si-Hak Oh, President

해설

※ 이 샘플은 국제적으로 널리 사용되는 대리점계약서 예문으로, 국내외 수출 및 수입 등 모든 대리점계약에 사용할 수 있는 가장 보편적인 대리점계약서다.

거래 제의에 유용한 표현

- Through Messrs. Furness, Withy & Co., Inc. in Los Angeles we *have heard(learned, known)* your name and address.
  당사는 로스앤젤레스에 있는 퍼니스 위디 회사로부터 귀사의 상호와 주소를 알았습니다.

- Having heard from Messrs. Green & Company in your city that you *are desirous* of importing Motorcycles from Korea, we are writing to(approaching) you *with a view* to entering into business relations with you.

당사는 귀 시에 있는 그린상사로부터 귀사가 한국에서 오토바이를 수입하기를 바란다는 것을 듣고 귀사와 거래 관계를 개시하고자 귀사에 편지를 보냅니다.

- We have learned that you *are dealing* chiefly *in* toys and sundry goods.
  당사는 귀사가 주로 장난감과 잡화를 취급한다는 것을 알고 있습니다.

- We *are indebted for* your name and address to The State of Illinois Department of Commerce, Chicago, who informed us that you are *looking* for reliable agents to represent you in Korea.
  당사는 시카고에 있는 일리노이주 상무성으로부터 귀사의 상호 및 주소를 알게 되었으며, 일리노이주 상무성은 귀사가 한국에서 귀사를 대리할, 믿을 만한 대리점을 물색하고 있다는 것을 당사에 알려주었습니다.

- Having sufficient capital and intimate knowledge of the trade, we are confident of *being able to* give you full satisfaction.
  당사는 충분한 자본과 무역에 관한 정통한 지식을 가지고 있으므로 귀사를 충분히 만족시킬 수 있다고 확신합니다.

- We trust that you will *be interested in* this proposal and hope that a mutually profitable relationship will soon be established.
  당사는 귀사가 이 거래 제의에 관심을 가질 것으로 믿으며, 상호 유익한 거래 관계가 곧 개설될 것으로 기대합니다.

- It is our desire to *deal in* all kinds of cameras.
  당사는 모든 종류의 카메라를 취급하기를 원합니다.

- We *are given to understand(are informed)* that you are seeking a friend who can act as your agent here.
  당사는 귀사가 이곳에 귀사의 대리점으로 활동할 수 있는 동반자를 물색하고 있다는 사실을 알게 되었습니다.

- Your goods are enjoying a wonderful reputation and commanding a very good sale in this market. If you *are disposed to* establish an agency, please be sure to *appoint us as* one.
  귀사의 제품은 이곳 시장에서 대단한 호평을 받고 있으며 판매 실적도 매우 좋습니다. 만약 귀사가 대리점을 개설할 의향이 있으면 당사를 대리점으로 지명해주시기 바랍니다.

- We advise you to *avail yourselves of* this opportunity.
  당사는 귀사가 이 기회를 이용하시기를 권합니다.

- We *are looking forward to(look forward to, are waiting for, wait for)* serving you again in the near future.
  당사는 가까운 장래에 다시 귀사에 서비스를 제공할 수 있기를 기대합니다.

- We were impressed by the selection of sweaters displayed on your *stand(booth)* at the Autumn Exhibition.
  가을 전시회에서 귀사의 매장에 전시된 스웨터 모음에 깊은 인상을 받았습니다.

- Would you please let us know if *you are represented* here?
  이곳에 귀사의 대리점을 두었는지 알려주시겠습니까?

- If you have anything else to inquire about, *please do not hesitate to write to us*.

만약 귀사가 알고 싶은 그 밖의 다른 것이 있으면, 주저하지 마시고 당사에 편지하시기 바랍니다.

- We have been supplying the same material for the past six years.

  당사는 지난 6년간 같은 제품을 공급해오고 있습니다.

거래 수락 및 거절에 관한 무역통신문

거래 수락 방법

거래 제의를 받은 거래 상대방은 제반 사항을 검토하고 거래를 제의한 회사의 신용조사를 한 후 거래 수락 여부를 결정하게 된다.

거래 수락 시 수락 서신에 포함시켜야 할 내용은 다음과 같다.

① 거래 제의에 대한 감사 표시

② 지속적 거래 및 거래량 증가를 위해 경쟁력 있는 가격, 품질 등에 대한 요구

③ 상호적인 거래 관계 기원

④ 감사의 말로 끝맺음

[샘플 20] 거래 수락

June 10, 2020

ABC Co., Ltd.
123 Samsung-dong, Gangnam-gu
Seoul 01670, Korea

Dear Mr. Oh,

    We thank you very much for your letter of June 1, 2020 in which you expressed your willingness to open an account with[1] us.

We are glad to learn that you are especially interested in exporting blue jeans and in these articles we may say that we are specialists.

    We would appreciate receiving[2] your best CIF New York price on blue jeans as well as several samples by air parcel post.[3]

    If your prices are competitive and merchandise is suitable for our trade, we will be able to place large orders.

    We look forward to hearing from you soon.

                          Cordially yours,

                            XYZ CO., LTD.
                            Robert H. Brown
                            Robert H. Brown, President

해설

※이 샘플은 청바지 거래 제의에 대한 거래 수락 회신으로, 샘플 및 가격 제시를 요구하는 예문이다.

1) open an account with ~ : ~와 거래를 개시하다
2) would appreciate ~ ing : ~해주시면 감사하겠습니다
3) by air parcel post : 항공 소포 우편으로

[샘플 21] 거래 수락

June 30, 2020

ABC Co., Ltd.
123 Samsung-dong, Kangnam-ku
Seoul 135-090, Korea

Gentlemen :

Thank you very much for your letter of June 15, 2020, proposing to do business with us in porcelain.

We are prepared to accept your proposal so long as your goods prove suitable[1] for our market in price and quality. Will you be good enough to[2] send us a copy[3] of your latest catalog, a price list and some samples of your goods?

As to the settlement of account,[4] we are agreeable to your terms.

We hope this will be the beginning of mutually profitable business between us.

Yours very truly,

PACIFIC TRADING CO., INC.

Stanley N. Evans
Stanley N. Evans, Sales Manager

해설

※ 이 샘플은 도자기 거래 제의에 대한 회신으로, 샘플 및 카탈로그, 가격표를 요구하는 예문이다.

1) prove suitable : ~하기에 적당하다고 입증되다
2) Will you be good enough to : Would you be kind enough to와 동일한 표현으로 Would you가 더 간곡한 표현이다.
3) a copy : 1부
4) settlement of account : 대금 결제

[샘플 22] 거래 수락

May 14, 2020

Atlantic Trading Co., Inc.
Suite 1023, One World Trade Center
New York, NY 10048
U.S.A.

Gentlemen :

 Your proposal of April 30 has interested us very much. Our credit files[1] have also been completed with favorable reports from your references, and we are pleased to serve customers of your standing.[2]

 Before starting actual business, however, we wish to come to complete agreement with you as to the general terms and conditions. The enclosed Memorandum is submitted for your comments and is open to your suggestions for improvement. If you have no objection to[3] any of its clauses, please sign it and return the duplicate[4] to us, keeping the original with you.

 The samples you requested have been sent by parcel post and Price List No. 1 is enclosed. Since this is our first quotation[5] to you, please let us have your frank opinion so that we may judge your requirements correctly.

 We are sure that this marks the beginning of our long pleasant relationship, and wait for your inquiries[6] and orders.

          Very truly yours,

          HANKUK TRADING CO., LTD.

Chul-Soo Lee
Chul-Soo Lee, Manager
Export Department

Encls. Memorandum of General Terms and Conditions of Business 1
　　　Price List

해설

※이 샘플은 거래 개시 전에 일반 거래 조건에 대한 합의를 위해 협정서(합의서) 및 가격표를 동봉하면서 검토 및 주문을 요청하는 예문이다.

1) Our credit files : 당사가 의뢰한 신용조회선으로부터 받은 신용조사 보고(결과) 서류
2) customers of your standing : 귀사의 신용 있는 고객
3) have no objection to : 이견이 없다, 이견을 가지지 않다
4) duplicate : 두 번째 원본(= second original)
   (cf) in duplicate : 원본 2부(= in 2 fold)
   　　　in triplicate : 원본 3부(= in 3 fold)
   　　　in quadruplicate : 원본 4부(= in 4 fold)
   　　　in quintuplicate : 원본 5부(= in 5 fold)
   　　　in sextuplicate : 원본 6부(= in 6 fold)
   　　　in septuplicate : 원본 7부(= in 7 fold)
   　　　in octuplicate : 원본 8부(= in 8 fold)
5) quotation : 견적(서). quotation은 확정구속력이 없고, offer는 확정구속력이 있다.
6) inquiry : 조회(= enquiry)

[샘플 23] 거래 제의에 대한 거절

2nd April, 2020

British Sunlight Co., Ltd.
583 High Holborn, London, W.C. 1
England

Dear Sirs,

    We thank you for your letter of 5th March, 2020, offering to open an account with us.

    To our regret, we are not in a position to accept your kind proposal at present, as we have some regular sources of supply[1] in your country, and, moreover, the market[2] here is somewhat dull.[3]

    However, we shall keep your name in our file,[4] and when times take a favourable turn,[5] we will write to you again for your help.

Yours faithfully,

HANKUK TRADING CO., LTD.

Chul-Soo Lee
Chul-Soo Lee, Manager
Export Department

해설

※ 이 샘플은 상대방의 거래 제의에 대해, 현재 상대방 국가에 정기적인 공급선이 있으므로 거래 의사가 없다는 예문이다.

1) regular sources of supply : 정기적인 공급선
2) the market : 시황

3) dull : 침체된(= slow, sluggish)
4) keep your name in our file : 당사의 주소록 명부에 기록하다
5) when times take a favourable turn : 사정이 호전될 때

[샘플 24] 구매 대리점 제의에 대한 거절

20th May, 2020

Agence Generale
Nusantara Bldg., 21st Floor
59 Jalang M. H. Thamrin
Jakarta, Indonesia

Dear Sirs,

Thank you very much for your letter of 10th May offering us your services as agents for the purchase of[1] various Indonesian products.

Yours are exactly the lines we have been importing, but we have at present some regular sources of supply[2] in Makassar. Moreover, the market here is so dull[3] that there is little demand for the goods you handle.

We shall, however, keep your name and address in our files so that we may call for your help when we expand our activities at a favourable turn of the market.[4] In the meantime, please inform us occasionally of the prices of Essential Oils, Spices, Copra and Tapioca.[5]

We thank you for your kind proposal and believe that it will not be long before we can accept it.

Yours faithfully,

HANKUK TRADING CO., LTD.

Chul-Soo Lee
Chul-Soo Lee, Manager
Export Department

해설

※ 이 샘플은 인도네시아 제품의 구매 대리점 제의에 대한 정중한 거절의 예문이다.
1) agents for the purchase of : 구매 대리점(= buying agent, buying office)
2) sources of supply : 공급선
3) the market is dull : 시황 부진
4) at a favourable turn of the market : 시황이 호전될 때
5) Essential Oils, Spices, Copra and Tapioca : 식물성 오일, 향신료, 코프라(야자유의 원료), 타피오카(식용 녹말)

거래 수락 및 거절에 유용한 표현

- The general terms and conditions you drafted are satisfactory to us except Article 4 concerning the Letter of Credit.
  귀사가 초안 작성한 일반 거래 조건은 신용장에 관한 제4조를 제외하고는 만족스럽습니다.

- While many European firms allow us D/A terms, we consider it somewhat humiliating that we have to arrange with our bank to open an L/C for each of our orders.

  많은 유럽 기업들도 당사에 D/A 조건을 허용해주는 반면, 당사가 당사의 매 주문에 대해 신용장을 개설해야 한다는 것은 상당히 굴욕적이라 생각됩니다.

- Please excuse us for the delay in our response to your proposal. We have been making customary inquiries, a process we must *go through* for every new customer.

  귀사의 거래 제의에 대한 당사의 답변이 늦은 것을 용서해주시기 바랍니다. 당사는 모든 새로운 고객에 대해서는 조사를 해야 하는 고객 조회 절차를 취해왔습니다.

- We believe that the market will recover before long, when we shall be pleased to write you again.

  당사는 시장이 멀지 않아 회복될 것으로 믿으며, 그때 다시 귀사에 편지를 드리겠습니다.

- We are now concentrating our efforts on the opening-up of our market in another line. We regret, therefore, that we *do*

not see our way clear to(can not) accept your proposal.
당사는 다른 품목으로 당사 시장을 개시하기 위해 모든 노력을 집중하고 있습니다. 따라서 유감스럽지만 당사는 귀사의 거래 제의를 받아들일 수 없습니다.

- We are glad to hear that our proposal is acceptable to you.
당사의 거래 제의가 귀사에 받아들여졌다는 소식을 듣고 매우 기뻤습니다.

- The Johnson Oil Company hereby appoints the above named company as its exclusive sales agent for the entire country of Korea to sell Johnson Oil Company's products herein named.
존슨 오일 회사는 상기 명시된 회사를 존슨 오일 회사의 제품을 판매할 한국 전 지역에 대한 배타적 독점 대리점으로 지정합니다.

- Sorry to say, we *are not in a position to(can not)* accept your proposal this time.
유감스럽게도 당사는 이번에는 귀사의 (거래) 제의를 받아들일 수 없습니다.

- *(We) Thank you very much for* your great(keen, strong) interest in the compact cars we produce.

= *We greatly appreciate* your special interest in our small(-sized) cars.

= *We are very much obliged* to you for your deep interest in our small(-sized) cars.

당사가 생산하는 소형 자동차에 대한 귀사의 특별한 관심에 감사 드립니다.

- Even though we would like to *do business with* you, we are afraid that we cannot compete here at the price you have quoted.

당사는 귀사와 거래를 하고 싶지만, 유감스럽게도 귀사가 제시한 가격으로는 당사가 이곳에서 경쟁할 수 없습니다.

3장

매매계약에 관한 무역통신문

총괄계약서/일반거래조건협정서

총괄계약서/일반거래조건협정서

총괄계약서(Master Contract)/일반거래조건협정서(Agreement on General Terms and Conditions of Business, Memorandum)란 어느 한쪽의 거래 제의에 대해 상대방이 거래를 수락할 경우, 당사자 간에 향후 모든 거래에 일반적으로 공통 적용되는 내용을 포괄적으로 합의한 계약서다. 총괄계약서/일반거래조건협정서가 체결된 후 매 계약건마다 물품매도확약서(Offer Sheet)나 물품구매주문서(Parchase Order Sheet)가 발행되며, 여기에 당사자 간의 합의가 이루어지면 최종적으로 매매계약이 성립된다. 따라서 총괄계약서/일반거래조건협정서와 물품매도확약서/물품구매주문서가 하나의 계약서를 구성한다.

[샘플 1] 총괄계약서/일반거래조건협정서

Agreement
on General Terms and Conditions of Business

Between ABC Co., Ltd., the Buyer and XYZ Co., Ltd., the Seller

(1) Business : Business is to be transacted between the Sellers and the Buyers as Principals to Principals[1] for the sale of the Seller's Porcelain in New York.

(2) Samples and Quality : The Seller is to supply the Buyer with samples free of charge,[2] and the quality of the goods to be shipped should be fully equal to the sample on which an order is given.

(3) Quantity : The minimum quantity for an order is to be the standard contents of one package stated on Price List. Assortment of various articles is to be accepted so long as[3] the total quantity exceeds the minimum just mentioned.

(4) Prices : Prices are to be quoted in U. S. Dollars on the basis of CIF New York port, Incoterms 2020 unless otherwise specified.

(5) Firm Offer : Firm offers are to remain effective for seventy-two hours after the time of dispatch, Sunday and national Holidays being excepted.

(6) Orders : Except in cases where firm offers are accepted all orders are to be subject to the Seller's final confirmation.

(7) Packing : Proper export wooden case packing is to be carried out, each case bearing the mark ABC in diamond with destination port mark, running case numbers, and the country of origin.

(8) Shipment : Shipment is to be made within the time stipulated in each contract, except in circumstances beyond the Seller's control. The on-board date of Bills of Lading[4] shall be taken as the conclusive proof of the date of shipment.

(9) Insurance : All shipments are to be covered on W. A. for the

invoice amount plus ten per cent, and the insurance policy is to be made out in U. S. Dollars and claims payable in New York.

(10) Payment : Draft is to be drawn at 30 days after sight under Irrevocable Letter of Credit which should be opened in favor of the Seller immediately upon conclusion of a contract, for the value of an order, with full set of shipping documents.

(11) Claim : Any claim exceeding 10 per cent of invoice amount is to be cabled within 14 days after the date of final discharge of goods at destination. Any claim beyond the amicable adjustment between the Seller and the Buyer is to be settled by arbitration in Korea according to the arbitrations rules of the Korean Commercial Arbitration Board.

This Agreement shall be valid on and after July 5, 2020 and remain valid for two(2) years.

For ABC CO., Ltd.
Robert H. Brown
Robert H. Brown, President

For XYZ CO., LTD.
Kil-Dong Hong
Kil-Dong Hong, President

해설

※ 이 샘플은 도자기 수출입 거래에 대한 총괄계약서 예문이다.

1) Principals to Principals : 당사자 대 당사자
2) free of charge : 무료로
3) so long as : ~하는 한
4) The on-board date of Bills of Lading : 선하증권상의 본선 적재일

[샘플 2] 총괄계약서/일반거래조건협정서

Agreement
on General Terms and Conditions of Business

This Agreement entered into between Seoul Trading, Inc., Seoul, Korea, hereinafter called Sellers, and Smith & Co., Ltd., London, England, hereinafter called Buyers, witnesses as follows :

1. Business : Both parties shall act as Principals, and not as Agents.

2. Goods : Goods in business, their unit to be quoted, and their mode of packing shall be as stated in the offer sheet or purchase order sheet.

3. Prices : Unless otherwise specified in fax messages or letters, all prices submitted by either party shall be quoted in Sterling Pound on a CIF London port, Incoterms 2020.

4. Firm Offers : All offers are to be considered "firm" subject to reply being received within four(4) days from and including the day dispatched. Sundays and official Bank Holidays are excepted.

5. Orders : Any business closed by fax shall be final, and orders thus concluded shall not be cancelled unless by mutual consent.

6. Payment : Drafts shall be drawn under Irrevocable Letters of Credit at ninety(90) days after sight, with documents attached, for the full invoice value.

7. Shipment : Shipment is to be made within the time stated in each contract, except in circumstances beyond Seller's control. The date of on-board shall be taken as conclusive proof of the date of shipment.

8. Marine Insurance : All shipments shall be covered by ICC(A) including War & SRCC Risks for the 110% of invoice value, if no other conditions are particulary agreed upon. All policies shall be made out[1] in Sterling Pound and claims payable in London.

9. Quality : Seller shall guarantee all shipments to conform to[2] sample, types or descriptions, with regard to quality and condition of the contracted goods.

10. Force Majeure[3] : Sellers shall not be responsible for any delay in shipment due directly or indirectly to force majeure, such as fires, floods, earthquakes, tempests, strikes, lockouts, mobilization, war, prohibition of export, and any other contingencies which may prevent shipment within the period stipulated. In the event of any of the aforesaid causes arising, documents proving its occurrence or existence shall be submitted to Buyers without delay.

11. Delayed Shipment : In all cases of force majeure provided in the Article No. 10, the period of shipment stipulated shall be extended for period of twenty one(21) days. In case shipment within the period thus extended should still be prevented by a continuance of the causes mentioned in the article or the consequences of any of them, Buyers shall have the option of either to allow the shipment of late goods or to cancel the order by giving Sellers a notice of cancellation by telex.

12. Claim : Claims, if any, shall be submitted within fourteen(14) days after arrival of the goods at destination. Certificates by authorized surveyors must be sent by mail without delay. All claims that cannot be adjusted amicably between Sellers and Buyers shall be settled by arbitration in Korea under the Commercial arbitration rules of The Korean Commercial Arbitration Board.

In witness whereof Seoul Trading Co., Inc. have hereto set their hands[4] in duplicate on the Fifth day of April, 2000, at Seoul, and Smith & Co., Ltd. have hereto set their hands on the Fifteenth of April, 2000, at London, and any of the clauses in this Agreement shall not be changed or modified unless by mutual consent.

Seller :
SEOUL TRADING, INC.
Si-Hak Oh
Si-Hak Oh, President

Buyer :
SMITH & CO., LTD.
Robert H. Brown
Robert H. Brown, President

해설

※ 이 샘플은 거래 상품이 다양하게 많은 경우에 사용되는 총괄계약서/일반거래조건협정서 예문이다.
1) be made out : 발행되다(= be issued)
2) conform : ~와 일치하다
3) Force Majeure : 불가항력
4) set their hands : 서명하다(= signed)

총괄계약서/일반거래조건협정서 작성 시 유용한 표현

- The Seller shall not be responsible for the delay in shipment *due directly or indirectly to force majeure*, such as fires, floods, earthquakes, tempests, strikes, war, and any other contingency, which prevent shipment within the period stipulated.
매도인은 약정된 기간 이내에 선적이 불가능하게 하는 화재, 지진, 폭풍우, 전쟁, 파업 및 기타 비상사태와 같은 불가항력에 의해 직접적 또는 간접적으로 선적이 지연된 것에 대해 책임을 지지 않습니다.

- *As a rule* we follow American law to determine legal disputes over contracts.
일반적으로 당사는 계약에 대한 법적 분쟁을 해결하는 데 미국 법률에 따릅니다.

- All disputes arising out of or in connection *with* the present contract shall be finally settled under the Rules of Arbitration of the international Chamber of Commerce by one or more arbitrators appointed in accordance with the said rules.
본 계약과 직접적 또는 간접적으로 관련하여 발생하는 모든 분쟁은 국제상업회의소의 중재 규칙에 의해, 동 규칙에 따라 임명된 1인 이상의 중재인에 의해 최종적으로 해결된다.(국제상업회의소 표준중재조항)

- All disputes *in relation to* this contract shall be finally settled by arbitration in the country of the respondent. In case the respondent is a Korean enterprise, the arbitration shall be held at the Korean Commercial Arbitration Board. In case the respondent is a American enterprise, the arbitration shall be held at the American Commercial Arbitration Association.

본 계약과 관련된 모든 분쟁은 피신청인 국가에서 중재에 의해 최종적으로 해결된다. 피신청인이 한국 회사인 경우, 중재는 대한상사중재원에서 이루어진다. 피신청인이 미국 회사인 경우, 중재는 미국상사중재원에서 이루어진다.(피신청인주의 중재조항의 예)

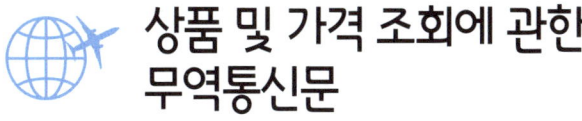

상품 및 가격 조회에 관한 무역통신문

상품 및 가격 조회 방법

거래 제의에 대한 수락이 이루어지면 그다음은 상품(Item, Commodity, Article) 및 가격(Price) 등에 대한 구체적인 거래 조회가 이루어진다.

일반적으로 거래 조건에 대한 조회 내용은 상품(Item, Commodity, Article), 품질 및 명세(Quality, Descriptions, Specifications), 수량(Quantity), 가격(Price), 선적(Shipment), 보험(Insurance), 대금 결제(Payment) 등이다.

상품 소개/가격 조회와 Offer/Acceptance 절차

Incoterms 2020의 11가지 무역 조건

Rules for any mode or modes of transport 어떠한 단일 또는 복수의 운송 방식에 사용 가능한 규칙	Rules for sea and inland waterway transport 해상운송과 내수로 운송에 사용 가능한 규칙
1. EXW : Ex Works	8. FAS : Free Alongside Ship
2. FCA : Free Carrier	9. FOB : Free On Board
3. CPT : Carriage Paid To	10. CFR : Cost and Freight
4. CIP : Carriage and Insurance Paid to	11. CIF : Cost, Insurance and Freight
5. DAP : Delivered At Place	
6. DPU : Delivered at Place Unloaded	
7. DDP : Delivered Duty Paid	

주) Incoterms는 International Rules for the Interpretation of Trade Terms의 약어로, 무역 조건의 해석에 관한 국제 규칙(약칭 International Commercial Terms)을 말함.

[샘플 3] 샘플 및 가격표 송부

July 19, 2020

Pacific Trading Co., Inc.
30 Water Street, New York
N.Y. 10003, U.S.A.

Gentlemen :

We thank you very much for your letter of June 30 and for the Agreement on General Terms and Conditions of Business which reached us yesterday.

We are pleased to send you herewith[1] our Price List giving our lowest possible prices.[2] The samples of our products have been sent you today separately.[3]

If you examine our prices, you will see that it is to your advantage[4] to place your orders with[5] us.

We are really glad that business relations have now been opened between you and us, and hope to do business with you for a long time.

Yours very truly,

HANKUK TRADING CO., LTD.

Chul-Soo Lee
Chul-Soo Lee, Export Manager

Inc. 1 Price List

해설

※이 샘플은 가격표를 동봉하면서 주문을 요청하는 예문이다.

1) send you herewith : 동봉한 바와 같이 ~을 귀사에 보내다
2) giving our lowest possible prices : 당사가 제시할 수 있는 가장 낮은 가격을 기재한
3) separately : 별편으로, 별도로
4) your advantage : 귀사에 유리한
5) place your orders with ~ : ~에게 발주하다, 주문하다

[샘플 4] 상품 및 가격 조회

May 30, 2020

Hankuk Co., Ltd.
19th floor, Eti Bldg.
13 Myung-dong, Jung-gu
Seoul 04534, Korea

Attn. : To whom it may concern

Gentlemen :

    Having found in the "Wire Journal[1]" that you are the export agent of "Hankuk" wire drawing machines,[2] we wish to know whether you can offer the equipment[3] which produces steel wires for making pasture fencing.[4]

    We are leading merchants of wires and fences in Uruguay and are now planning to set up our own plant[5] here in Montevideo to meet ever-increasing local demands.[6] The machine we are most interested in is a type capable of drawing a 5.5mm rod down to 3.2mm and 2.8mm wires.[7]

We shall be obliged, therefore, if you will porpose a machine with details, stating the price, delivery and other terms.

Very truly yours,

PACIFIC TRADING CO., INC.
Robert H. Brown
Robert H. Brown, Engineering Manager

해설

※ 이 샘플은 우루과이 수입상이 한국기업에 울타리용 철조망 생산 기계에 대한 가격, 납기, 명세 등을 조회하는 예문이다.

1) Wire Journal : 출판물 이름
2) wire drawing machines : 신선기(伸線機)
3) equipment : 기계, 설비(집합명사로서 통상 불가산명사로 취급)
4) fencing : 울타리, 울타리 재료
   (cf) an iron fencing : 철책
5) plant : 공장
6) local demands : 현지의 수요
7) drawing a 5.5mm rod down to 3.2mm and 2.8mm wires : 5.5mm 봉을 3.2mm 및 2.8mm로 뽑아내는

[샘플 5] 상품 및 가격 조회

2nd June, 2020

Hankuk Co., Ltd.
19th floor, Eti Bldg.
13 Myung-dong, Chung-ku
Seoul 100-020, Korea

Dear Sirs,

    For some time we could not do any business because of our sluggish market,[1] but we are pleased to inform you that our Government has eased the duties on[2] some textile goods.

    It is most likely that our customers will lay in[3] fairly large stocks of polyester fabrics,[4] and we are anxious to[5] have your latest prices together with samples for the following :

    Polyester Satin, Polyester De-chine, Polyester Jacquard Palace, 44″×20/50 yds., plain dyed[6] or screen-printed[7] in five colourways.[8]

    We expect to obtain orders for at least 30,000 yards of each item and the time of shipment required would be August/September.[9] Please quote prices on CIF & C[10](3%) Jeddah as usual.

    We trust that this will received your prompt attention and interesting business will be realized after a long interval.

                                Yours faithfully,

                                PACIFIC TRADING CO., INC.

Robert H. Brown
Robert H. Brown, Import Manager

해설

※ 이 샘플은 폴리에스테르 직물의 가격 조회에 대한 예문이다.

1) sluggish market : 시황 부진
2) eased the duties on : ~에 대한 수입 관세를 경감하다
3) lay in : 사들이다
4) polyester fabrics : 폴리에스테르 직물(합성섬유의 일종)
5) be anxious to : 열망하다, 갈망하다
6) plain dyed : 무지염(無地染)
7) screen-printed : 모양염(模樣染)
8) colourways : 배색(配色)
9) August/September : 8월 1일에서 9월 31일 사이 선적(연월 선적)
10) CIF & C : Cost, Insurance, Freight and Commission의 약어. 운임, 보험료, 수수료 포함 가격 조건

[샘플 6] 상품 및 가격 조회

5th June, 2020

Hankuk Trading Co., Ltd.
123 Samsung-dong, Kangnam-ku
Seoul 135-090, Korea

Dear Sirs,

We are very glad to know from your letter of 20th May that you have kindly accepted our proposal. To inform you of our general requirements, we are enclosing

A Schedule of Requirements[1]

for various commodities asked for by many customers of ours throughout the world. If you can secure these articles or at least some of them, we assure you of our best cooperation in realizing business.[2]

We recommend the list to your careful study and ask you whenever you refer to it not to miss pointing to[3] the item number.[4] In case you have any merchandise on hand which is not found in the list, please do not hesitate to quote on it the lowest prices CIF European port and FOB Korean port in either the German mark[5] or your currency.[6]

All your quotations should be as completely detailed as possible in order to[7] avoid unnecessary further inquiries.

We hope that we can develop profitable business, and wait for good news from you.

> Yours faithfully,
>
> PACIFIC TRADING CO., INC.
>
> *Robert H. Brown*
>
> Robert H. Brown, General Manager
>
> Enc. Schedule of Requirements
> P. S. Just now we received the following inquiry :
> 6,000 meters Welded Carbon Steel Pipes, 900mm×13mm[8]

해설

※이 샘플은 수입상이 다양하게 요구하는 상품의 목록을 첨부하며 가격을 조회하는 예문이다.

1) A Schedule of Requirements : 필요품 일람표
2) realizing business : 거래를 실현하다, 매매계약을 체결하다(= materialize business)
3) miss pointing to : 지적하는 것을 잊어버리다(망각하다)
4) item number : 품목번호
5) German mark : 독일 마르크 통화(= Deutschmark ; DM)
6) your currency : 귀국 통화
7) in order to ~ : ~하기 위해
8) 900mm×13mm(= 900mm OD×13mm WT) :
    외경(OD ; Outside Diameter) 900mm, 두께(WT ; Wall Thickness) 13mm

[샘플 7] 카탈로그 및 가격표 송부

June 5, 2020

D. Mantero & Cia, S. A.
Casilla Cerreo No. 27
Montevideo, Uruguay

Gentlemen :

    Thank you very much for your letter of May 30. As requested, we are enclosing our general catalog in which all the models of "Samsung" machines are illustrated[1] and explained.

    Your attention is invited to pages 8 to 10 featuring[2] Model CD-550×5, which, we believe, will best suit your purpose.

    The price would be approximately two hundred and thirty thousand dollars for one machine in the U.S. currency on FOB Busan port for shipment in six to eight months depending on how many machines you require.

    If you are interested in the above range of price and delivery,[3] we are ready to enter into further discussions with you on technical details and payment terms.

Very truly yours,

SAMSUNG MACHINE SALES, LTD.

Kil-Dong Hong
Kil-Dong Hong, Director
Sales Department

Encl. Catalog 1

해설

※ 이 샘플은 카탈로그를 동봉하며 가격을 제시하는 예문이다.

1) illustrated : 도해된, 도시된
2) featuring : 특징을 나타낸
3) price and delivery : 가격 및 인도

[샘플 8] 샘플 및 가격표 송부

17th June, 2020

Saudi Textile Co., Ltd.
P. O. Box 3467
Jeddah
Saudi Arabia

Dear Sirs,

Your letter of 2nd June delighted us very much with very good news. We have immediately dispatched the samples you requested, five for each item, and are pleased to quote on them as the enclosed Price List.

While your market was quiet,[1] ours has been very active[2] with a rush of orders[3] from Australia. Under the circumstances, we have quoted the very best prices with deliveries[4] as near as August or September.

We thank you very much for your inquiry and expect to receive your order as soon as possible.

Yours faithfully,

HANKUK CO., LTD.

Jin-Ho Kim

Jin-Ho Kim, Manager
Textile Department

Enc. Price List

해설

※ 이 샘플은 가격표를 동봉하면서 주문을 요청하는 예문이다.

1) quiet : (시장 상태가) 한산한, 부진한
2) active : 거래가 활발한
3) a rush of orders : 주문 쇄도
4) deliveries : 인도
    (cf) near deliveries : 근일 인도

[샘플 9] 가격표 동봉 및 주문 요청

April 15, 2020

Messrs. H. Wilson & Co., Inc.
50 West Street, New York
N.Y. 10004, U.S.A.

Gentlemen :

We thank you for your inquiry of April 5 and are pleased to enclose a price list for our goods.

You will find that our prices are much lower than those our competitors will offer.[1] This is because we have close connections with the first-class makers here. We can assure you that, in spite of the low prices, our goods are excellent in quality.

We are looking forward to your early order.

Yours truly,

HANKUK TRADING CO., LTD.

Chul-Soo Lee

Chul-Soo Lee, Sales Manager

Inc. 1 Price List

해설

※ 이 샘플은 가격표를 동봉하며 주문을 기대하는 예문이다.

1) those our competitors will offer : 당사의 경쟁사들이 제시하는 가격(= dprices that our competitors will offer)

[샘플 10] 가격 인하 요구

July 15, 2020

Hankuk Trading Co., Ltd.
123 Samsung-dong, Gangnam-gu
Seoul 06170, Korea

Gentlemen :

    We have received with thanks your letter of July 10 and samples of Porcelain which you were good enough[1] to send us.

    Although your Tea Set B has impressed us favorably,[2] we regret that your price is not competitive, as it is much higher than those of your competitors.[3]

    We trust that you will make every effort[4] to revise your price.[5]

                                Yours very truly,

                                  PACIFIC CO., LTD.

                                Robert H. Brown
                                Robert H. Brown, President

해설

※ 이 샘플은 가격 인하를 요구하는 예문이다.

  1) good enough : 친절한(= kind enough)
  2) impressed us favorably : 당사에 호감을 주다
  3) than those of your competitors : 귀사의 경쟁 회사의 가격보다
  4) make every effort : 모든 노력을 다하다
  5) revise your price : 귀사의 가격을 고치다(인하하다)

[샘플 11] 가격표(Price List)

SAMSUNG TRADING CO., LTD.

Manufacturers, Exporters & Importers

"High Quality, High Technology"

#707, 7th Fl. Samsung Bldg., 123 Samsung-dong, Gangnam-gu,

Seoul 06170, Korea

TEL+82-2-6228-1472 M.P+82-10-6334-8710 FAX+82-2-6228-8710

E-mail : sihak@itc.co.kr Website : http://www.itc.co.kr

July 10, 2020

Pacific Trading Co., Inc.
30 Water Street, New York
N.Y. 10003, U.S.A.

Dear Sirs,

PRICE LIST

Thank you very much for your fax of July 7, 2020. We are pleased to send you our price list as below.

Item	Description	Unit Price(FOB Pusan)	Minimum Quantity
Porcelain	Tea Set A Tea Set B Tea Set C	@US$9.80 per doz @US$10.30 per doz @US$11.50 per doz	100 dozen each

Note +The above all prices are subject to[1)] market fluctuations[2)] and our final confirmation.
　　+All prices are based on[3)] T/T in advance or L/C at sight.
　　+We are prepared to allow you a 5% discount off the price list if the total quantity of order amounts to 500 doz.

We are looking forward to your valued order.

                              Yours truly,

                              SAMSUNG TRADING CO., LTD.

Kil-Dong Hong
Kil-Dong Hong, Export Manager

해설

※ 이 샘플은 도자기에 대한 가격표 예문이다.
1) be subject to : ~에 따르다, ~의 조건이다
2) market fluctuations : 시장 가격 변동
3) base on : ~에 의거하다, ~에 근거하다

[샘플 12] 가격표

SAMSUNG TRADING CO., LTD.
Manufacturers, Exporters & Importers
"High Quality, High Technology"
#707, 7th Fl. Samsung Bldg., 123 Samsung-dong, Gangnam-gu,
Seoul 06170, Korea
TEL+82-2-6228-1472 M.P+82-10-6334-8710 FAX+82-2-6228-8710
E-mail : sihak@itc.co.kr Website : http://www.itc.co.kr

                                          7th June, 2020

Saudi Textile Co., Ltd.
P. O. Box 3467, Jeddah

Saudi Arabia

PRICE LIST

Prices are subject to market fluctuations.[1]

Item No.	Sample No	Descriptions	Unit Price (per yd.)	Shipment
TS-1005	101	Polyester Satin, dyed and white, 44"×20/50 yds., 50D×75D, 215×68, 1000 yds. min. per colour[2]	US$1.80	in July
TS-1008	102	Polyester De-chine, screen-printed in equal 5 colourways, 44"×21/26 yds., 60D×75D, 192×116, 3000 yds. minimum per design[3]	US$ 2.20	in July
TS-5000	103	Polyester Jacquard Palace, dyed and white, 44"×20/28 yds., 50D×50D, 245×98, 1000 yds. minimum per colour	US$ 2.50	in August

Note +Prices are on CIF & C(3%) Jeddah in U.S. dollars.
  +Maximum quantity available : 30,000yds for each item if orders reach us before 15th July
  +Packing : 20 pieces in a seaworthy[4] carton box.

E. & O. E.[5]

SAMSUNG TRADING CO., LTD.

Jun-Ho Park
Jun-Ho Park, Manager
Textile Department

> **해설**

※ 이 샘플은 폴리에스테르 원단에 대한 가격표 예문이다.
1) Prices are subject to market fluctuations : 가격은 시장 가격 변동에 따라 바뀔 수 있다
2) 1000 yds. min. per colour : 색상당 최소 주문량(수주량) 1,000야드
3) 3000 yds. minimum per design : 디자인당 최소 주문량(수주량) 3,000야드
4) seaworthy : (해상운송 및 선박의) 내항성 있는, 항해에 적합한
5) E. & O. E. : Errors and Omissions are Excepted의 약어. 오류(오기) 및 누락은 제외한다. 즉, 가격표상의 오류 및 탈루 내용에 대하여 책임을 지지 않는다는 표현이다.

상품 및 가격 조회에 유용한 표현

- Please quote us *rockbottom prices on* CIF London in Sterling Pound for 1,000kgs each style.
  각 스타일당 1,000kg에 대하여 영국 스터링 파운드화로 런던까지의 운임 보험료를 포함한 가격 조건으로 최저 가격을 당사에 제시해주십시오.

- Please quote only on what you have in stock for immediate shipment and send us *proforma invoices* together with samples.

즉시 선적할 수 있는 재고 수준을 당사에 알려주고, 샘플과 함께 견적송장을 당사에 보내주십시오.

- *We effect insurance on* our goods. So you may quote on CRF New York or FOB your port in U.S. dollars.
  당사 제품에 대해 당사가 보험을 부보합니다. 그러므로 귀사는 미국 통화로 CRF 뉴욕 또는 FOB 귀국 항구 조건에 대한 가격을 제시하면 됩니다.

- *We are enclosing* specifications of small Diesel engines for agricultural implements and ask you to submit your estimate with full particulars including the possible time of shipment.
  당사는 농기구용 소형 디젤 엔진의 명세서를 동봉하며, 선적 가능 시기를 포함하여 세부 내역을 담은 귀사의 견적(서)을 송부해줄 것을 요청합니다.

- For an order of this size we expect *a quantity discount off* your price list.
  이 규모의 주문에 대해서는 당사는 귀사의 가격표에서 수량 할인을 기대합니다.

- The article for which you inquired on May 10 *is temporarily out of stock*, but we will let you know by fax tomorrow when it will *be ready for* shipment.

  5월 10일 귀사가 조회한 제품이 일시적으로 재고가 없습니다. 그러나 언제 선적할 준비가 될지(언제 선적이 가능할 것인지)를 내일 팩스로 알려드리겠습니다.

- Please note the prices are without engagement and *subject to change without notice*.

  그 가격은 구속력이 없으며, (사전) 통지 없이 변경 가능한 조건임을 주지하시기 바랍니다.

- We are sorry that we *are unable to* quote the prices on the goods you required, since they *are out of make* now.

  귀사가 요구한 제품에 대한 가격을 제시할 수 없어 유감입니다. 그 제품은 더 이상 생산되지 않기 때문입니다.

- The catalog we enclose gives you but(only) an outline of the vast range of our products. A *trial order* will *convince* you *of* the excellence of our goods.

  당사가 동봉한 카탈로그는 광범한 당사 제품의 개괄적인 사항만 나타냅니다. 시험 주문을 하면 당사 제품의 우수함을 귀사에서 납득할 것입니다.

- For the initial order, please *arrange with* your bank to open an Irrevocable Letter of Credit at 60 days after sight.
  최초 주문을 이행하기 위해 귀사의 거래 은행에 일람 후 60일에 대금이 결제되는 취소불능신용장을 개설하도록 조치해주시기 바랍니다.

- We will *do all in our power* to merit your confidence and give you full satisfaction.
  당사는 귀사의 신뢰를 받고 귀사를 완전히 만족시키기 위해 전력을 다하겠습니다.

- We are sure that these goods will meet your requirements, and we *look forward to* your first order.
  당사는 이들 제품이 귀사의 요구 조건을 충족시킬 것으로 확신하며, 귀사의 첫 주문을 기대합니다.

- We *shall be glad* to receive by return of post your lowest prices, CIF Yokohama or FOB shipping port for your products,

together with samples.
당사는 회신 편으로 샘플과 함께 CIF 요코하마 또는 FOB 선적항 조건으로 귀사의 최저가를 받았으면 좋겠습니다.

- *As (you) requested*, we are pleased to quote you the prices on Cotton Thread at 72cents per lb., CFR Singapore.
  귀사가 요청한 바와 같이, 당사는 귀사에 면사에 대하여 CFR 싱가포르 조건으로 파운드당 72센트로 가격을 제시합니다.

- We *are prepared to* allow you *a 5% discount off* the list prices.
  당사는 귀사에 목록 가격에서 5%를 할인할 준비가 되어 있습니다.

- We regret that business cannot be completed at the present prices, and therefore keener(lower) prices are necessary.
  당사는 유감스럽게도 현재 가격으로는 거래가 성사될 수 없습니다. 그러므로 더 싼 가격이 필요합니다.

- We wish you to understand that each of the prices given is for one case, which is the *minimum quantity of an order* that we can book(accept).
  각 가격은 한 상자에 대한 가격이며, 한 상자는 당사가 수락할 수 있는 최소 주문량임을 이해해주시기 바랍니다.

- *In accordance with(at)* your request in your fax of April 10, we send you herewith our catalog.
  4월 10일 자 귀사의 팩스에서 귀사가 요청한 바와 같이 당사의 카탈로그를 동봉합니다.

- The price of our Cotton Handkerchiefs, which you inquired about in your fax of May 5, is US$ 5.00 per dozen, FOB Pusan.
  5월 5일 자 귀사의 팩스에서 조회한 당사의 면 손수건 가격은 FOB 부산 조건으로 1다스당 미화 5달러입니다.

- Please send us by airmail 3 *copies of* catalog of your goods, together with a price list.
  가격표와 함께 귀사 제품의 카탈로그 3부를 항공우편으로 보내주십시오.

- Since our prices are reduced to the minimum, there is no room for further discount.
  당사의 가격이 최저까지 내려가 더 이상 할인을 할 여지가 없습니다.

- Article No. 12 *looks like(resembles)* No. 14 in pattern.

  품목번호 12번은 패턴(유형)이 14번과 비슷합니다.

- We usually deal on a 20% quantity discount *for an order of 1,000 units or more*.

  당사는 통상 1,000단위 이상의 주문에 대해서는 20% 수량 할인을 하여 거래합니다.

- The enclosed quotations are valid until the end of July.

  동봉된 가격제시서는 7월 말까지 유효합니다.

- If there are any items that interest you, please let us know. We will send you samples *on hearing* from you.

  귀사의 관심을 끄는 품목이 있으면 알려주십시오. 요청한 즉시 귀사에 샘플을 보내드리겠습니다.

- Please note that this estimate is for *a minimum order of 200 cases*.

  이 견적서는 최소 주문량 200상자에 대한 것이라는 사실을 주지하시기 바랍니다.

- We enclose a list showing the items we require, and would be glad to receive your quotations as soon as possible.
  귀사가 요구(필요)하는 품목을 나타내는 목록을 동봉하오니 가능한 한 빨리 귀사의 가격제시서를 받을 수 있으면 기쁘겠습니다.

- The article is enjoying a very good reputation *among* the Korean consumers.
  그 품목은 한국 소비자들 사이에 대단히 좋은 평판을 누리고 있습니다.

- We presume that the items shown on *pages 18 to 20* will find the largest sale in your market.
  당사는 18쪽에서 20쪽 사이에 표시된 품목이 귀 시장에서 가장 큰 판매고를 올릴 것으로 생각됩니다.

- This machine is easy to *operate*.
= It is easy to *operate* this machine.
  이 기계는 작동하기가 쉽습니다.

- This is an excellent opportunity *for* you *to* buy a stock of high quality products at prices we cannot repeat.

이번이 당사가 다시는 반복할 수 없는 가격으로, 귀사가 고품질의 재고품을 살 수 있는 절호의 기회입니다.

- As soon as our present stock has *run out*, we shall have to revise our prices.
  당사의 현재 재고가 바닥나는 즉시 당사는 당사의 가격을 수정(인상)하여야 할 것입니다.

- We will send you separately our catalogs requested in your fax of September 12.
  당사는 9월 12일 자 귀사의 팩스에서 요구한 당사의 카탈로그를 별도로 귀사에 보내드리겠습니다.

- We *are doing our best* to keep our prices as low as possible without sacrificing quality.
  당사는 품질을 저하시키지 않고 가능한 한 낮은 가격을 유지하기 위해 최선을 다하고 있습니다.

- We believe there is a promising market in our area for your products so long as they are moderately priced.
  귀사 제품의 가격이 적절히 책정되는 한, 이 지역에 귀사 제품이 유망한 시장이 있다고 믿습니다.

- The enclosed catalog will help you make the best choice for your purpose.
  동봉된 카탈로그는 귀사가 귀사의 목적에 맞는 최상의 선택을 하는 데 도움을 줄 것입니다.

- The terms of payment are given in the Price List. We fear you have overlooked them.
  대금 결제 조건은 가격표에 표시돼 있습니다. 당사는 귀사가 그것을 놓칠까 봐 염려됩니다.

- We enclose *a copy* of our latest catalog. Please choose from it some items that will satisfy you.
  당사는 당사의 최근 카탈로그 1부를 동봉합니다. 그 카탈로그에서 귀사에 만족을 주는 품목들을 선택하시기 바랍니다.

- Ours is a highly competitive market and we have been *compelled to* cut your prices to the minimum.
  당사의 시장은 대단히 경쟁이 치열한 시장이므로 당사는 귀사의 가격을 최소 수준까지 깎지 않을 수 없었습니다.

- We will send you *a copy of* the manual as soon as it is made.
  당사는 매뉴얼이 만들어지자마자 바로 그 매뉴얼 1부를 귀사에 보내드리겠습니다.

- You are right in choosing this particular line as it is very popular in many markets.
  이 특정 품목은 많은 시장에서 대단히 인기가 있으므로 귀사가 그 품목을 선택하는 것은 옳은 것입니다.

- The Korean won currency has risen by more than 20 percent against the U.S. dollar since September 2020, making Korean goods more expensive abroad.
  한국 원화가 2020년 9월 이래 미국 달러화에 대해 20% 이상이나 평가절상됨으로써 한국 제품이 해외에서 더 비싸졌습니다.

- We hope you will send us a more detailed explanation of the machine so that we can easily understand its mechanism.
  그 기계의 메커니즘을 쉽게 이해할 수 있도록 그 기계에 대한 좀 더 상세한 설명서를 보내주시기 바랍니다.

가격 및 금액에 관한 표현

가격 인상 · 인하

- raise(increase) prices
  가격을 인상하다
- lower(reduce, cut(down)) prices
  가격을 인하하다
- mark up(down) all the goods in the shop
  상점에 있는 모든 제품의 가격을 인상(인하)하다

가격 상승 · 하락

- prices rise(go up, advance)
  가격이 상승하다
- prices fall(go down, decline, drop)
  가격이 하락하다

비싼 가격 · 저렴한 가격

- high(exorbitant, prohibitive) prices

높은(비싼) 가격

- low(reasonable, competitive, moderate, popular, reduced, keen) prices

저렴한 가격

가격·금액에 관한 전치사

- He paid an high price *for* the watch.

  그는 그 시계에 대하여 높은 가격을 지불했다.

- They sell merchandise *at* reduced prices now.

  그들은 이제 인하된 가격으로 제품을 판다.

- She bought the cloth *at* 6 dollars a yard.

  그녀는 야드당 6달러에 그 옷을 팔았다.

- We sold those books *at* US$2.00 each.

  당사는 그 책들을 권당 2달러에 팔았다.

오퍼에 관한 무역통신문

수출 계약 의사 표시인 오퍼 방법

청약(Offer)이란 청약자(Offeror)가 피청약자(Offeree)에게 일정한 조건으로 계약을 체결하고 싶다는 의사 표시를 말하며, 우리나라에서는 Offer Sheet를 대외무역법상 '물품매도확약서'라 칭한다.

이론상으로 계약 체결을 희망하는 의사만 분명하면 Offer라는 용어를 사용할 필요가 없지만, 실무상으로는 단순한 가격 제시(Price Quotation)와 헷갈리는 것을 피하기 위해 'We offer ~'와 같이 Offer라는 단어를 사용하는 것이 바람직하다.

[샘플 13] 오퍼

6th February, 2020

Messrs. Osaka Trading Co., Ltd.
3-6 Bingomachi 2-chome
Chuo-ku, Osaka
541 Japan

Dear Sirs,

We thank you very much for your inquiry of 15th January against which we make the following firm offer subject to your reply being received here by the 10th[1] March, 2020.

Article	: Cotton Yarns,[2] 20S and 30S
Quantity	: 33,000 lbs.[3] (4 FCL's[4]) each
Quality	: Carded Yarn,[5] Made-up on Cones, for towelling,[6] weaving[7] or knitting[8]
Prices	: 82¢ per lb. for 20S and 112¢ per lb. for 30S, C & F Japanese port in the U. S. currency
Shipment	: in March, 2020
Packing	: 100 lbs. in one carton and 80-83 cartons[9] in one 40′ shipping container[10]

Owing to the rush of orders from your country, the market here is very strong and our stocks are almost exhausted. Under the circumstances, the prices we have offered are the rockbottom and the delivery is the nearest possible.

We advise you, therefore, to accept this offer without loss of time.

Yours faithfully,

HANKUK TRADING CO., LTD.

Jin-Ho Kim

Jin-Ho Kim, President

해설

※ 이 샘플은 타월·직물·편물용 원추형 보플면사에 대한 오퍼 예문이다.

1) subject to your reply being received here by the 10th : 10일까지 귀사의 회신이 도착하는 조건으로
2) cotton yarns : 면사(綿絲)
3) lb(s). = pound(s) ≒ 0.4536kg
4) FCL : Full Container Load의 약어. 컨테이너 1개를 가득 채울 만큼의 만재 화물(滿載貨物). LCL(Less than Container Load)은 컨테이너 1개를 못 채우는 소량 화물(小量貨物)
5) carded yarn : 보플실
6) towelling : 타월류
7) weaving : 직물류
8) knitting : 편물류
9) cartons : 종이류
10) shipping container : 선적 컨테이너
    (cf) TEU = Twenty feet Equivalent Unit = 8′ ×8′ ×20′
        FEU = Forty feet Equivalent Unit = 8′ ×8′ ×40′

[샘플 14] 오퍼

April 3, 2020

Sovereign International Limited
Suite 505, 43 York Street
Toronto, Ontario M5J 1R7
Canada

Gentlemen :

After the Easter sales,[1] alert buyers[2] are setting their eyes on winter sales. Believing that you are also preparing for the next season, we offer firm as follows :

2,000 dozen Nylon Ski Gloves[3] for Ladies,
one size fits all,[4]
at US$ 55 per dozen FOB Incheon port
for shipment June/July,
subject to your acceptance received here by April 10.

With the turn of the month, prices of all nylon goods have made a sudden advance.[5] But we have kept the rise to the minimum specially for you. So it would be to your interest to accept this offer without hesitation.[6]

Very truly yours,

ORIENTAL TRADING CO., LTD

Jang-Soo Lee
Jang-Soo Lee, Managing Director

해설

※이 샘플은 여성용 나일론 스키 장갑에 대한 오퍼 예문이다.

1) the Easter sales : 부활절 세일
2) alert buyers : 주도면밀한 바이어
3) nylon ski gloves : 나일론 스키 장갑
4) one size fits all : 모든 사람에게 맞는 한 사이즈(= free size)
5) made a sudden advance : 돌연 가격을 상승시키다
6) without hesitation : 주저하지 말고, 곧, 즉각

[샘플 15] 오퍼

8th August, 2020

Delco Machinery Sales Pty. Ltd.
267-271 Cleveland Street
Redfern, N.S.W.
Australia

Dear Sirs,

re : Rod Breakdown Machine

Thank you very much for your inquiry by fax of 6th August requesting us to quote one new or used "SAMSUNG" rod machine on CIF Sydney basis. You say that the machine will be supplied to a local cable plant for their urgent expansion programme and the machine has to run on their AC 415V 50 HZ power supply.[1]

We have immediately contacted Samsung Machine Company and make you the following offer for one used machine subject to being unsold.

      Article : One 11-Die Heavy-duty Rod Breaker
            "SAMSUNG" Model AH-11, complete with Electrics,
            Used but Reconditioned with a 1-year guarantee
Specifications : Inlet size 8.0mm copper rod
              Outlet size 1.6-2.3mm copper wire
              Running speed[2] 1,500m.p.m.
              Drive 220KW DC motor and Control
Price : US$38,000.00 CIF Sydney
Terms[3] : 1/3 by bank transfer on contract[4]
          1/3 by draft at sight on shipmen[5]
          1/3 by draft at sight on erection[6]
Shipment : Within two months after initial payment
Approx. weight & measurement : 30,000 kgs & 67CBM

"SAMSUNG" rod machines are in great demand among cable producers at home and abroad, and the manufacturer has a 12 month backlog of orders[7] for new machines.

The machine offered above was built and supplied to a cable works here as late as last year, but for some reason they no longer need the equipment.

Since this offer is a bargain as well as an answer to your urgent request, we firmly believe that you will accept this sooner than any other interested party.

                    Yours faithfully,

                    HANKUK TRADING CO., LTD.
                    Jang-Soo Lee
                    Jang-Soo Lee, Director

해설

※ 이 샘플은 삼성 모델의 중고 선재인출기를 재고 잔유 조건으로 오퍼하는 예문이다.

1) power supply : 공급 전원
2) running speed : 운전 속도
3) terms : 지불 조건(= payment terms, terms of payment)
4) by bank transfer on contract : 계약 시 은행 송금으로
5) by draft at sight on shipment : 선적 시 일람불환어음으로
6) by draft at sight on erection : 최후 설치 완료 시 일람불환어음으로
7) a 12 month backlog of orders : 12개월 분량의 주문 잔고

[샘플 16] 오퍼

July 20, 2020

Pacific Trading Co., Inc.
30 Water Street, New York
N.Y. 10003, U.S.A.

Gentlemen :

In accordance with your letter of July 15, we are pleased to offer you as follows, subject to your reply reaching us by July 26.

Item & Description : Porcelain Tea Set B
Quantity : Four Hundred(400) Dozen
Unit Price : at US$10.00 per dozen C.I.F. New York
Shipment : During August
Payment Terms : Under an irrevocable L/C[1] with draft at 30 days after sight

This is the best offer we can make at present and we trust that you will accept this offer without loss of time.[2]

Yours very truly,

HANKUK TRADING CO., LTD.

Min-Ho Kim

Min-Ho Kim, Export Manager

해설

※ 이 샘플은 도자기 커피잔을 오퍼하는 예문이다.

1) L/C : Letter of Credit의 약어. 신용장
2) without loss of time : 즉각

[샘플 17] 물품매도확약서(Offer Sheet)

SAMSUNG TRADING CO., LTD.
Manufacturers, Exporters & Importers
"High Quality, High Technology"
#707, 7th Fl. Samsung Bldg., 123 Samsung-dong, Gangnam-gu
Seoul 06170, Korea
TEL+82-2-6228-1472   M.P+82-10-6334-87180   FAX+82-2-6228-8710
E-mail : sihak@itc.co.kr   Website : http://www.itc.co.kr

June 30, 2020

XYZ CO., LTD.
50 Liberty St., New York
N.Y. 1005, U.S.A.

Gentlemen :

OFFER SHEET NO. 123

We are pleased to offer you the following goods on the terms and conditions as stated below.

Item	Commodity & Description	Quantity	Unit Price (CIF New York)	Amount
Blue Jeans	Men's Blue Jean : Style No. 500	25,000pcs.	@US$20.00per pc.	US$500,000.00
	Women's Blue Jean : Style No.600	25,000pcs.	@US$20.00per pc.	US$500,000.00
Total	-	50,000pcs.	-	US$1,000,000.00

Origin : Republic of Korea
Shipment : From Pusan port, Korea for transportation to New York port, U.S.A. not later than October 31, 2020, partial shipment allowed and transhipment not allowed
Insurance : Seller to cover 〔the CIF price plus 10% against ICC(A) including War and Strikes Risks with claims payable in New York in the same currency as the draft〕
Payment : Under an irrevocable documentary L/C at sight to be opened in favour of Samsung Trading Co., Ltd., Seoul, Korea
Documents Requried :
    1) Signed Commercial invoice in 3 copies
    2) Full set of[1] clean on board ocean Bills of Lading, made out to order of shipper, blank endorsed,[2] marked "Freigh prepaid" and Notify "XYZ Co., Ltd."

   3) Insurance Policy or Certificate endorsed in blank for full invoice value plus 10%, against ICC(All Risks) including War and Strikes Risks with claims payable in New York[3] in the same currency as the draft.[4]
   4) Packing list in 3 copies
   5) Certificate of orgin in duplicate
Inspection : Seller's inspection to be final before shipment
Packing : Export standard packing
Shipping Marks :

       <XYZ>

       NEW YORK
       BOX NO 1/UP
       MADE IN KOREA

Validity : By September 30, 2020

Your valued acceptance would be highly appreciated.

         Yours very truly,

Date of acceptance :
(Confirmed and) accepted by : SAMSUNG TRADING CO., LTD.
           Si-Hak Oh
           Si-Hak Oh, President

해설

※ 이 샘플은 수출상이 수입상에 청바지를 오퍼하는 예문이다.
 1) Full set of : 전통(全通)의
 2) blank endorsed : 백지 배서된(= endorsed in blank)
 3) with claims payable in New York : 클레임 발생 시 뉴욕에서 보험금이 지급되고
 4) in the same currency as the draft : 환어음에 표시된 것과 동일한 통화로

오퍼에 유용한 표현

- We have(take) *the pleasure to offer(pleasure in offering)* you (firm) the following goods :

  One container-load of Polyester Palace,

  Item No. TS-5100, Anti-Static Finish

  at US$1.30 per yd., CIF Hong Kong

  Shipment in October, 2020

  Subject to your reply reaching us by Monday noon

  당사는 다음 제품을 아래와 같이 오퍼합니다.

  폴리에스테르 한 컨테이너 물량

  품목번호 TS-5100, 정전기 방지 (마감) 처리

  CIF 홍콩 조건으로 야드당 미화 1.30달러

  2020년 10월에 선적

  귀사의 회신이 월요일 오후까지 당사에 도달할 조건

- We have so many inquiries for this lot that we offer it *subject to being unsold*.

  당사는 이 품목에 대해 대단히 많이 조회를 받으므로 재고 잔유 조건으로 오퍼합니다.

- Large orders are rushing in from Indonesia and near futures *are* fast *running* out. We believe, therefore, that the above offer is excellent in both price and delivery.

  인도네시아로부터 대량 주문이 쇄도하고 있어 근일물(최근 선적 조건의 물품)은 빠르게 소진되고 있습니다. 그러므로 당사는 상기 오퍼가 가격과 인도 면에서 모두 우수하다고 믿습니다.

- The market is strong with a sign of stiffening further. We advise you, therefore, to accept this offer without hesitation.

  시장이 더 강세 신호를 보이며 강합니다. 그러므로 당사는 귀사가 주저 없이 이 오퍼를 수락하시길 권합니다.

- If, on receipt of this offer, you fax us your acceptance, we shall be able to ship the goods on the "Arirang" which *leaves* Pusan *for* New York on August 15.

  이 오퍼를 받자마자 당사에 귀사의 수락을 팩스로 보내주시면, 당사는 8월 15일 부산을 출발하여 뉴욕으로 가는 아리랑호 편에 그 제품을 선적할 수 있을 것입니다.

- We offer you firm the following items *subject to* your immediate reply by tele-transmission.

당사는 전신으로 귀사의 즉각적인 회신을 받는 조건으로 다음 제품을 귀사에 확정 오퍼를 합니다.

- We can accept your offer *on condition that* the delivery be made promptly.
  당사는 인도가 즉시 이루어지는 조건으로 귀사의 오퍼를 수락할 수 있습니다.

- We venture to say that there is no firm that could make you a more favorable offer.
  당사는 귀사에 (이보다) 더 유리한 오퍼를 할 수 있는 기업은 없다고 감히 말하고 싶습니다.

- *In view of* the rising trend of the materials, we would advise you not to miss this opportunity.
  원재료의 상승 추세를 비추어 볼 때 당사는 귀사에 이 기회를 놓치지 않기를 권하고 싶습니다.

- We believe that *a trial order* will convince you that the goods we are offering are excellent value for money.
  귀사의 시험 주문은 당사가 오퍼하고 있는 제품이 돈 벌기에 탁월

한 가치가 있다는 것을 납득시킬 것이라 믿습니다.

- This is an exceptional opportunity for you to buy a stock of high-quality products at these prices. So we hope you will *take full advantage of it*.
이번이 귀사가 이 가격으로 양질의 재고품을 살 수 있는 예외적인 (절호의) 기회입니다. 그러므로 귀사가 이 기회를 백분 활용할 것으로 기대합니다.

- *In accordance with(At)* your request, we have airmailed our samples.
귀사의 요청에 따라 당사의 샘플을 항공우편으로 우송하였습니다.

- The prices quoted *are subject* to market fluctuation(s).
제시된 가격은 시장 변동에 따라 변동될 수 있습니다.

- If your price is *reasonable(competetive)*, we will send you our order.
만약 귀사의 가격이 저렴하면, 당사는 귀사에 주문을 보내겠습니다.

- Please fax us a firm offer, as this line *is in good demand* in our market.
  당사에 확정 오퍼를 팩스로 보내주십시오. 이 품목이 당사 시장에 충분한 수요가 있기 때문입니다.

- We accept your *firm offer* for 100 cases (of) Thermos Bottle No. 101 for September shipment.
  당사는 9월 선적 조건으로 보온병 101호 100상자에 대한 귀사의 확정 오퍼를 수락합니다.

- We believe it is to your advantage to accept this offer *without loss of time*.
  당사는 귀사가 지체 없이 이 오퍼를 수락하는 것이 이익이라 믿습니다.

- Since those goods are to *be put on sale toward* the end of July, it is absolutely necessary that they reach us *by* June 30.
  그 제품들은 7월 말경까지는(늦어도 7월 31일까지) 판매에 들어가야 하므로 6월 30일까지는 반드시 그 제품들이 당사에 도착해야 합니다.

- This price will remain *open(valid)* until our receipt of your

reply by December 20.
이 가격은 당사가 12월 20일까지 귀사의 회신을 받을 때까지 유효합니다.

- The prices quoted *are subject to* change as the market for raw materials here is very unstable at present.
제시된 가격은 이곳 원재료 시장이 현재 대단히 불안정하므로 변동될 수 있는 조건입니다.

- You will see that *sizable discounts* are offered for larger orders.
귀사는 대량 주문에 대해서는 상당한 규모의 할인이 된다는 것을 알게 될 것입니다.

- Because of their low prices and the small profit margin, we do not offer any *trade discounts* on these items.
저렴한 가격과 소폭의 이윤 때문에, 당사는 이 품목에 대해 더 이상의 거래(개시) 할인을 하지 않습니다.

- You will agree that the price we have offered is *competitive* enough in your market.

귀사는 당사가 오퍼한 가격이 귀 시장에서 충분히 경쟁적이라는 것을 동의할 것입니다.

- This merger will *enable* us to offer you a much wider range of optical goods.
  이 합병이 당사로 하여금 귀사에 더 광범한 안경 제품을 오퍼할 수 있도록 할 것입니다.

- The prices quoted *are subject* to a usual discount of 2 percent.
  제시된 가격은 2%의 통상 할인 조건입니다.

오퍼에 관한 응답 통신문

수입 계약 의사 표시인 Acceptance 방법

승낙(Acceptance)이란 피청약자가 청약자의 청약(Offer)을 수락하여 계약을 성립시키고자 하는 의사를 말한다. Firm Offer의 경우 피청약자가 Acceptance하면 곧 매매계약이 성립된다. 그리고 Acceptance는 Offer의 모든 조건을 무조건 수락하는 것이며, 조건부 승낙은 Counter Offer가 된다.

Offer 및 Acceptance의 흐름도

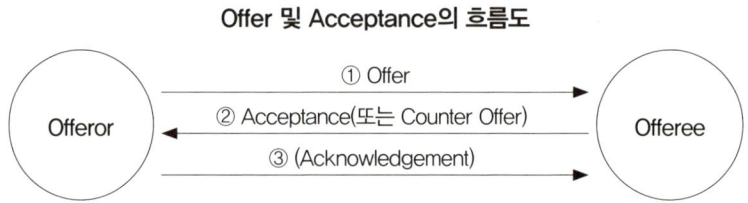

[샘플 18] 오퍼 수락

8th February, 2020

Haji Essa & Sons
Altaf Hussain Road
Karachi-1, Pakistan

Dear Sirs,

We are glad to accept your offer of the 6th February for Cotton Yarns, 20S and 30S, 33,000lbs. each, at 82 and 112 cents per lb. respectively[1] C & F Pusan port in the U.S. currency for March shipment.

To confirm this business, we are sending herewith our Purchase Note No. 100. Please note that the cargo is to be unloaded[2] at Pusan.

For reimbursement,[3] we have arranged with our bankers for an L/C to be opened by tele-transmission.[4]

We accept this offer because the delivery is so attractive. We ask you, therefore, to do everything possible to ensure punctual shipment.[5]

Yours faithfully,

HANKUK TRADING CO., LTD.

In-Ho Kim
In-Ho Kim, Manager
Textile Department

Encl. Purchase Note

해설

※ 이 샘플은 수출상이 제시한 면사 오퍼에 대해 수입상이 수락하는 예문이다.

1) respectively : 각각, 즉 20S에 대해 82센트, 30S에 대해 112센트
2) be unloaded : 하역하다
3) reimbursement : 결제, 변제(= payment)
4) by tele-transmission : 전신으로
5) punctual shipment : 적기선적
   (cf) punctual : 시간(기한)을 엄수하는, 어김없는

[샘플 19] 구매계약서

SAMSUNG TRADING CO., LTD.
Manufacturers, Exporters & Importers
"High Quality, High Technology"
#707, 7th Fl. Samsung Bldg., 123 Samsung-dong, Gangnam-gu
Seoul 06170, Korea
TEL+82-2-6228-1472   M.P+82-10-6334-8710   FAX+82-2-6228-8710
E-mail : sihak@itc.co.kr   Website : http://www.itc.co.kr

8th February, 2020

Haji Essa & Sons
Altaf Hussain Road
Karachi-1, Pakistan

Dear Sirs,

PURCHASE NOTE No.100

This is to confirm having bought from you the following goods at the price and on terms and conditions set forth below :

Article	: Cotton Yarn, Carded, 20S and 30S, Made up on Cones, for towelling, weaving or knitting
Quantity	: 66,000(sixty-six thousand) lbs., : equally divided for each count[1]
Price	: at 82¢ per lb. for 20S and 112¢ per lb. for 30S C & F Kobe
Amount	: $64,020(sixty-four thousand and twenty dollars) in the United States currency
Shipment	: during March, 2020
Packing	: 100 lbs. to be packed in a carton box and 80-83 boxes to be stuffed into one 40-ft shipping container. Totally eight full containers
Shipping Mark[2]	: △ OTC / KOBE with number 1 & up

Please sign it and return the duplicate.

SELLER :
HAJI ESSA & SONS
Ayub Khan
Ayub Khan, President

BUYER :
SAMSUNG TRADING CO., LTD.
In-Ho Kim
In-Ho Kim, President

해설

※ 이 샘플은 수입상이 작성한 구매계약서 예문이다.

1) equally divided for each count : 각 번호별로 균등하게 배분되다
2) Shipping Mark : 화인(貨印), 하인(荷印)

   with number 1 & up

문자로 풀어쓰면 OTC in triangle over Kobe with numbers one and up.

[샘플 20] 조건부 승낙(Counter Offer)

April 10, 2020

Oriental Trading Co., Ltd.
P. O. Box 230, Seoul
Korea

Gentlemen :

　　Your offer of April 3 on 2,000 dozen(24,000 pairs) Ski Gloves for Ladies at US$55 FOB Kobe port is certainly attractive in price, but we need the goods here by the end of July.

　　Therefore, your offer will be acceptable if you can ship the whole lot in June.

　　As we leave all the other particulars to your discretion,[1] we believe that it will not be too difficult for you to ship the goods in the usual manner during June.

Please confirm this by fax.

Very truly yours,

SOVEREIGN LIMITED

S. P. Jones

S. P. Jones, Manager

해설

※ 이 샘플은 여성용 스키 장갑 오퍼에 대한 6월 선적 조건으로 counter Offer하는 예문이다.

1) leave ~ to your discretion : ~을 귀사의 재량에 맡기다

[샘플 21] 조건부 승낙

July 25, 2020

Hankuk Trading Co., Ltd.
123 Samsung-dong, Gangnam-gu
Seoul 06170, Korea

Gentlemen :

    We have received with thanks[1] your firm offer for four hundred(400) dozen Porcelain Tea Set B, for which we would like to make you our counter offer.

    Your offer of July 20 is acceptable if the price is US$9.50 per dozen and the total amount US$3,800. Please reply by fax.

You must remember that competition in this line is very keen and that your competitors are offering lower prices than yours.

We are looking forward to your confirmation.

Yours very truly,

PACIFIC TRADING CO., INC.
Robert H. Brown
Robert H. Brown, Manager

해설

※ 이 샘플은 도자기 커피 세트 오퍼에 대하여 가격 인하를 요구하는 Counter Offer 예문이다.

1) We have received with thanks ~ : 당사는 ~를 감사히 받았다

[샘플 22] 오퍼 거절

12th August, 2020

Hankuk Trading Co., Ltd.
123 Samsung-dong, Kangnam-ku
Seoul 135-090, Korea

Dear Sirs,

We thank you for the trouble you took in making us an offer for a "SAMSUNG" rod machine, at which we were a little disappointed.

Your price is almost on the same level as those for the new machines with similar specifications[1] which have been offered by some European manufacturers. The customers at whose request we made the inquiry turned to an Italian source.[2]

Since they are big producers of cables here, their opinion may be useful to you. They say that Korean sell good machines with excellent after-sales service, so they could put up with[3] slightly higher prices for new makes, but expected a much lower price tag for second-hand units.

But please do not be discouraged.[4] We will work harder to secure orders for you if you assist us with reasonable prices and deliveries, whether machines are new or used.

Yours faithfully,

PACIFIC TRADING CO., INC.
Robert H. Brown
Robert H. Brown, Manager

해설

※ 이 샘플은 중고 기계 오퍼 가격이 거의 새 기계 수준이어서 실망했다는 오퍼 거절의 예문이다.

1) with similar specifications : 유사한 사양(명세)을 가진
2) Italian source : 이탈리아 공급선
3) put up with ~ : ~을 감내하다, ~을 참다
4) do not be discouraged : 낙심하지 마라

[샘플 23] 조건부 승낙의 수락

July 27, 2020

Pacific Trading Co., Inc.
30 Water Street, New York
N.Y. 10003, U.S.A.

Gentlemen :

　We thank you for your counter offer of July 25 for Porcelain Tea Set B and are pleased to confirm your counter offer of July 25 has been accepted.

　Please note, however, that we have specially accepted your request solely because we wish to make this the forerunner[1] of many future orders from you.

　We hope you will send us your formal order by return, which we will execute with our best attention.[2]

　　　　　　　　　　　　　Yours very truly,

　　　　　　　　　　　　　PACIFIC TRADING CO., INC.
　　　　　　　　　　　　　Robert H. Brown
　　　　　　　　　　　　　Robert H. Brown, Manager

해설

※ 이 샘플은 첫 거래를 성사시키기 위해 Counter Offer를 수락하는 예문이다.

1) forerunner : 선구자
2) best attention : 최선의 주의(배려)

오퍼에 대한 응답과 관련된 유용한 표현

- We are glad to accept your firm offer of July 18 on 1,000cases (of) Tin Plates No. 50 at US$990 per 1,000kgs. on CIF Pusan.
  당사는 CIF 부산 조건으로 1,000킬로그램당 미화 990달러로 주석판 50번 1,000상자에 대한 7월 18일 자 귀사의 확정 오퍼를 수락하여 기쁩니다.

- We thank you very much for your offer of July 30 on Borax but *regret* our inability *to* accept it as we are overstocked at present.
  당사는 붕사에 대한 7월 30일 자 귀사의 오퍼에 대하여 감사드립니다. 그러나 유감스럽게도 당사는 현재 재고가 지나치게 많아 귀사의 오퍼를 수락할 수 없습니다.

- We have to make a counter offer to yours of July 15 on *Polyester/Cotton Blended Poplin* S/# T-4004. One of our important customers is ready to buy 10,000 yards for September shipment if you can reduce the price to US$1.10 per yard on CIF Busan port.
  당사는 폴리에스테르와 면이 혼합된 포플린(옷감) S/# T-4004에 대한 7월 15일 자 귀사의 오퍼에 대해 조건부 승낙을 해야 합니다. 당사의 중요한 고객 중 한 고객이, 귀사가 가격을 CIF 부산항 조건으로 야드당 미화 1.10달러로 깎아줄 수 있다면, 9월 선적 조건으로 10,000야드를 구매할 준비가 되어 있습니다.

• Let us congratulate ourselves on the realization of this initial business, to which we hope you will *pay your very best attention*.
본 최초 거래 실현에 축하하며, 당사는 귀사가 최선의 배려를 할 것으로 기대합니다.

• The price you offered is about 30% higher than the level *workable* to us. So we refrained from making a counter offer.
귀사가 오퍼한 가격은 당사가 실행할 수 있는 수준보다 약 30% 높습니다. 그래서 당사는 조건부 승낙을 하는 것을 자제했습니다.

• We are pleased to accept your offer of August 3, and wish you to send us your *Sale* Note immediately.
당사는 8월 3일 자 귀사의 오퍼를 기꺼이 수락하며, 즉시 귀사가 작성한 매도계약서를 보내주시길 바랍니다.

- All our customers say that your prices are about 20% higher than those offered by *European sources of supply*.

  당사의 모든 고객들은 귀사의 가격이 유럽 공급선이 오퍼한 가격보다 약 20% 높다고 말합니다.

- Your prices are quoted on CFR Yokohama port basis, but we wish you to let us know your CIF Yokohama prices.

  귀사의 가격은 CFR 요코하마 항구로 제시되어 있습니다만, 당사는 귀사가 CIF 요코하마 가격으로 당사에 알려주기를 바랍니다.

- Your request for a price reduction for this article is not necessarily unreasonable, but, *as matters stand(as the matter stands)*, we wish you to accept the terms of payment originally agreed upon.

  이 품목에 대한 귀사의 가격 인하 요청이 반드시 부당한 것은 아니지만, 현 상태로는 귀사가 당초 합의된 대금 결제 조건을 먼저 수락하시기를 바랍니다.

- We would like to consider the problem of maintenance before deciding which model to install in our plant.

  당사는 어떤 모델을 당사의 공장에 설치할 것인가를 결정하기 전에 유지(보수) 문제를 (먼저) 고려하고 싶습니다.

- Your *selling offer* was disappointing, as we had expected lower prices.
  당사는 더 싼 가격을 기대했는데, 귀사의 매도 오퍼는 실망스러웠습니다.

- We have to point out that your products are priced too high for this market.
  당사는 귀사 제품의 가격이 이곳 시장에는 너무 높게 책정되었다는 것을 지적해야만 합니다.

- These goods are *too* high in price *for* us to purchase.
  = These goods are *so* high in price *that* we *cannot* purchase them.
  이들 제품은 가격이 너무 높아 구매할 수 없습니다.

주문에 관한 무역통신문

매매계약 체결 방법

매매계약(Sales Contract)은 어느 한쪽의 Offer에 대해 상대방이 Acceptance를 하게 되면 성립한다. 일반적으로 Seller가 제시하는 Offer를 Buyer가 Acceptance함으로써 매매계약이 성립하지만, 공급 물량이 달리는 인기 상품의 경우는 Buyer가 먼저 Purchase Order(P/O)를 하여 Seller가 Acknowledgement함으로써 매매계약이 성립하는 경우도 있다.

[샘플 24] 시험 주문

February 6, 2020

Hankuk Corporation
123 Samsung-dong, Kangnam-ku
Seoul 135-090, Korea

Attn. : Si-Hak Oh, Managing Director

Dear Mr. Oh,

Subject : Hunting Gloves

We thank you very much for your samples made in your Korean factory, and are glad to place a small order by way of trial[1] for Style No. 1234.

The particulars are given in the attached Purchase Order No. 150. Though small in quantity, this is an important order to decide our furture policy and we expect you to book[2] this order at our price.

As we are in a hurry for[3] the goods, please let us know your acknowledgement by facsimile, upon receipt of which we will open an Irrevocable Letter of Credit through The Chase Manhattan Bank, New York.

Yours faithfully,

THE GLOVE IMPORTS, INC.

Robert H. Brown
Robert H. Brown, President

Encl. Purchase Order

> **해설**

※ 이 샘플은 사냥용 장갑을 시험 주문하는 예문이다.
  1) by way of trial : 시험적으로
     (cf) trial order : 시험 주문
  2) book : 기장하다, 인수하다(= accept)
     (cf) book an order : 주문을 수락하다
  3) be in a hurry for : 급히 필요로 하다

[샘플 25] 시험 주문

April 10, 2020

Hankuk Corporation
123 Samsung-dong, Gangnam-gu
Seoul 06170, Korea

Attn. : Si-Hak Oh, Managing Director

Dear Mr. Oh,

Grass Mats

Thank you for your letter of 20th March together with a catalogue. On looking it through,[1] we found some items would be suitable for our business[2] and are pleased to place a small order with you[3] as a trial.

The particulars[4] are given in the enclosed Order Sheets No. 12-A-3456 in duplicate,[5] one of which is to be sent back to us after signed.

As these goods are urgently[6] requested, we ask you to fax your acknowledgement. On receipt of it, we will arrange with our bank to open a Confirmed Letter of Credit.[7]

Yours faithfully,

THE MATS IMPORTS, INC.
Robert H. Brown
Robert H. Brown, President

해설

※ 이 샘플은 인조 잔디 매트를 시험적으로 수입 주문하는 예문이다.

1) On looking it through : 상세히 살펴보고
2) suitable for our business : 당사의 거래에 적합한
3) place a small order with you : 귀사에 소량의 주문을 하다
4) particulars : 상세한 사항
5) in duplicate : 정부(正副) 2통
6) urgently : 긴급히, 다급하여
   (cf) on urgent business : 급한 일로
7) Confirmed Letter of Credit : 확인신용장

[샘플 26] 구매 주문(Purchase Order)

THE GLOVE IMPORTS, INC.

4815 Twin Knolls Road

Columbia, MD 21045

Tel 301-964-3036, Fax 301-964-3026

10th May, 2020

Hankuk Corporation
123 Samsung-dong, Gangnam-gu
Seoul 06170, Korea

Dear Sirs,

Purchase Order[1] No. 150

We have the pleasure of placing the following order with you :

Commodity & Descriptions	Size Assortment[2] (Style)	Quantity	Unit Price (FOB Pusan)	Amount
Hunting Gloves with Pigskin Leather Patch	Men's Small (Style 101)	20 doz.	US$ 46.56 per doz. each style	US$931.20
	Men's Medium (Style 102)	60 doz.		US$2,793.60
	Men's Large (Style 103)	100 doz.		US$4,656.00
	Men's X-large (Style 104)	60 doz.		US$2,793.60
Total	—	240 doz. (2,880 pairs)	—	US$11,174.40

Shipment	: During March, 2020, from Pusan port, Korea to New York port, U.S.A. and partial shipment not allowed
	The shipping lines and the ship's name[3] to be reported to you later
Packing[4]	: Each pair in a polyethylend bag, six pairs to be further poly-bagged, and 72 pairs in a shipping carton
Shipping Marks	: The shipping cartons to be marked as follows :

One side	Adjacent side
P.O. NO.	STYLE NO.
G.I.I.	QUANTITY
New York	P.O. NO
MADE IN	
(COUNTRY OF ORIGIN)	
C/NOS. 1-UP	

Insurance	: To be covered by us
Payment Terms	: Draft at sight under L/C
Inspection	: By S.G.S. whose certificate is part of the shipping documents
Shipping Samples	: One doz. of each size to be air-freighted before shipment

Your kind acknowledgement would be highly appreciated.

Date of acknowledgement :
Acknowledged by :　　　　　　　THE GLOVE IMPORTS, INC.

Robert H. Brown
Robert H. Brown, President

해설

※ 이 샘플은 사냥용 장갑 구매주문서 예문이다.

1) purchase order : 구매주문서. 간단히 order 또는 p/o 또는 p.o.라고도 한다.
2) assortment : 종류, 유형
3) the shipping lines and the ship's name : 선사명 및 선박명
4) packing : 포장

[샘플 27] 주문(발주)

July 25, 2020

Hankuk Trading Co., Ltd.
123 Samsung-dong, Gangnam-gu
Seoul 06170, Korea

Gentlemen :

    We are pleased to acknowledge your fax of July 27, accepting our counter offer for Porcelain Tea Set B, and now enclose our Order No. 100. We trust that you will find the particulars[1] of our order correct in all respects.[2]

    Please note that we are going to instruct our bankers[3] to open an irrevocable L/C for the amount of this order.

    We hope you will do everything possible[4] to quicken the shipment.

                             Yours very truly,

PACIFIC TRADING CO., INC.

Stanley N. Evans

Stanley N. Evans, Sales Manager

Inc. 1 Order Sheet

> **해설**

※ 이 샘플은 도자기 커피 세트에 대한 주문서를 동봉하며 주문하는 예문이다.

1) particulars : 명세서
2) in all respects : 모든 점에서
3) our bankers : 당사 거래 은행
4) do everything possible : 가능한 모든 조치를 다하다, 전력을 다하다

[샘플 28] 구매 주문

MRB Electronic Services Limited

Romsey, Hampshire S05 8XQ, England

Telephone : (0341) 42428, Fax : (0341) 42976, Telex : 841736 MRB G

10th June, 2020

Hankuk Co., Ltd.
123 Samsung-dong, Kangnam-ku
Seou 135-090, Korea

Attn. : Mr. Dong-Su Kim, Export Manager

 We are pleased to place an order with you for Electric Screwdrivers[1] as follows :

Model Number	Quantity	CIF Southampton	Shipment
(1) M/#[2] D-532	100 pcs.[3]	J¥36,000 per pc.	in August
(2) M/# D-533	100 pcs.	J¥38,000 per pc.	in August
(3) M/# D-534	100 pcs.	J¥40,000 per pc.	in August

This order is based on the samples and prices you sent us on 5th May. Shipping instructions[4] and a credit will be transmitted[5] upon receipt of your acknowledgement.

We are looking forward to your kind acknowledgement.

Yours very truly,

MRB ELECTRONIC SERVICES, LTD.
Robert D. Mollis
Robert D. Mollis, Purchase Department

해설

※ 이 샘플은 전동식 스크루드라이버에 대한 구매 주문 예문이다.

1) electric screwdrivers : 전동식 스크루드라이버
2) M/# : Model Number
3) pcs. : piece(s) = pc(s)
4) shipping instructions : 선적 지시
5) transmit : 전송하다

[샘플 29] 구매주문서(Purchase Order Sheet)

10th July, 2020

Hankuk Trading Co., Ltd.
123 Samsung-dong, Gangnam-gu
Seoul 06170, Korea

Dear Sirs,

ORDER No. 100

This is to confirm our having placed the following order with you for our account and risk[1] :

 Item & Descriptions : Porcelain Tea Set B
 Quantity : Four Hundred(400) dozen
 Price : US$ 9.50 per dozen. CIF New York port
 Shipment : During August, 2020
 Payment Terms : Irrevocable Documentary Letter of Credit at 90 days after sight
 Insurance : To be covered on W. A[2]. for 110% of the invoice amount
 Packing : 1 dozen each to be packed in a carton box and 100 dozen in a wooden case
 Shipping Marks :

⟨PT⟩
NEW YORK
C/# 1/UP[3]
MADE IN KOREA

Your kind acknowledgement would be highly appreciated.

Yours very truly,

Date of acknowledgement :
Acknowledged by :　　　　　　PACIFIC TRADING CO., INC.

　　　　　　　　　　　　　　　Stanley N. Evans
　　　　　　　　　　　　　　　Stanley N. Evans, Sales Manager

해설

※ 이 샘플은 도자기 커피 세트에 대한 구매주문서 예문이다.
1) for our account and risk : 당사의 계산 및 당사의 위험 부담으로
2) W. A. : With Average의 약어. 분손담보
3) C/# 1/UP : Case(Carton box) number one and up 상자 일련번호를 1부터 위로 기재(예컨대 상자가 10개인 경우 1/10……10/10 또는 10-1……10-10으로 기재)

[샘플 30] 구매계약서(Purchase Note)

July 15, 2020

Hankuk Trading Co., Ltd.
123 Samsung-dong, Gangnam-gu
Seoul 06170, Korea

Gentlemen :

PURCHASE NOTE
NO. 1002

　　We have the pleasure to confirm our purchase of the following merchandise[1] from you on the terms and conditions specified below and on the back hereof :

Article	: Silk Blouse, S/No. 1302 Embroiderd in flower design
Quantity	: 300(three hundred) dozens
Price	: At US$30.50 per dozen CIF New York
Shipment	: By October 20
Insurance	: ICC(B) for full invoice amount plus 10%[2]
Payment	: Irrevocable L/C at sight
Packing	: One dozen in a carton and one hundred(100) dozens in a wooden case
Marks	: ◇C.R.N.◇ with numbers 1 and 3 New York
Remarks	: Design and assortment[3] same as your sample No. 1302

Yours sincerely,

PACIFIC TRADING CO., INC.

Stanley N. Evans

Stanley N. Evans, Sales Manager

해설

※ 이 샘플은 실크 블라우스에 대한 구매계약서 예문이다.

1) merchandise : 상품, 제품

   (cf) general merchandise : 잡화

2) for full invoice amount plus 10% : 송장 금액 전액에 10%를 더하여

3) design and assortment : 재료와 배색

주문에 유용한 표현

- ***We have received with thanks**(thank you for)* your letter of September 12 together with samples of Arc Welding Rods, and are now pleased to place the following order with you as a trial.

  당사는 아크 용접봉 샘플과 더불어 9월 12일 자 귀사의 편지를 감사히 잘 받았습니다.

- We are glad to confirm the E-mail message recently exchanged between us *resulting* in our order as per Order Sheet No. 50 enclosed.

  당사는 동봉된 구매주문서 50번과 같이 당사의 주문을 체결시킨 양 사 간에 최근 교환한 전자우편 메시지를 확인하게 되어 기쁩니다.

- As our stock *is running short*, we must have the goods by the end of September at the latest. Should you fail to complete shipment during July, we would have to cancel this order.

  당사의 재고가 빠르게 줄어들고 있으므로 늦어도 9월 말까지는 그 제품을 받아야만 합니다. 만약 귀사가 7월 중에 선적을 완료하지 않으면 이 주문을 취소해야만 합니다.

- Please *effect* insurance on ICC(WA) including War Risks and prepay the premium.
  전쟁 위험을 포함하여 협회적하약관(분손담보 조건)으로 보험을 들어 주시고(부보해주시고) 보험료를 미리 지불해주십시오.

- Please note that *neither* partial shipments *nor* trans-shipments are allowed.
  분할 선적도, 환적도, 허용되지 않음을 주지하시기 바랍니다.

- As these goods are urgently needed, we ask you to ship them *during the first half of July*.
  이들 제품은 급하게 필요하기 때문에, 당사는 귀사에 제품을 7월 상반월(1~15일) 중에 선적할 것을 요청합니다.

- For this order, we *have arranged with* Bank of America, New York, *to open* a confirmed L/C.
  이 주문에 대하여 당사는 뉴욕에 있는 아메리카은행에 확인신용장을 개설하도록 수배(조치)하였습니다.

- We trust that you will fulfil this order *in strict* compliance *with* the instructions we have given in our Order Sheet.
  당사가 구매주문서에 명시한 지시 사항과 엄격히 일치하게 귀사가 이 주문을 이행할 것으로 믿습니다.

- We are pleased to *send* you *herewith* our Order Sheet for one hundred(100) dozen Canned Salmon.
  당사는 연어 통조림 100다스에 대한 당사의 주문서를 귀사에 동봉합니다.

- We hope you will *place an order with* us for at least 500 dozen of the item.
  당사는 귀사가 그 상품에 대하여 최소한 500다스를 주문할 것으로 기대합니다.

- We *have enclosed* our order sheet for the following goods.
  당사는 다음 제품에 대한 당사의 주문서를 동봉합니다.

- If you can *make(effect) shipment* of the item by the end of January, we *are prepared to* order 100 dozen of it.
  만약 귀사가 1월 말까지 상품을 선적할 수 있으면, 당사는 100다스의 상품을 주문할 준비가 되어 있습니다.

- We should *point out* that delivery before Christmas is essential and hope that you can give us that guarantee.
당사는 크리스마스 이전 인도가 필수적이라는 것을 지적하며 귀사가 그것을 당사에 보증할 수 있기를 기대합니다.

주문에 관한 여러 가지 표현

'주문하다'의 표현

- We place an order (with you) for the following goods.
- We order (you) the following goods.
- We order the goods from you.
- We send(give) you an order for the following goods.

'주문을 수락 · 거절 · 취소 · 이행하다'의 표현

- acknowledge(book) an order 수락하다
- decline an order 거절하다

- cancel an order 취소하다
- execute(fill, fulfil, carry out) an order 이행하다

'주문품'의 표현

- order
- the goods ordered
- the goods we (have) ordered
- the goods on our order
- the ordered goods
- our ordered goods

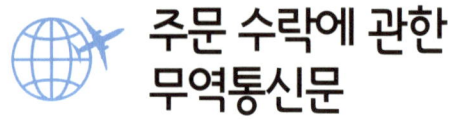

주문 수락에 관한 무역통신문

주문 수락 방법

주문에 대한 수락은 무조건부 수락이어야 하며, 조건을 붙이면 Counter Offer가 된다. 그리고 주문 수락을 하면 매매계약이 성립한다.

매매계약은 후일의 분쟁을 예방하기 위해 매매계약서(Seller가 작성할 경우 Sales Contract 또는 Sales Note라 하며, Buyer가 작성할 경우 Purchase Contract 또는 Purchase Note라 함)를 2부 작성하여 계약 당사자가 서명하고 1부씩 나누어 가지는 것이 원칙이다.

그러나 당사자 간에 지속적으로 거래할 경우, 첫 거래에 앞서 추후 모든 거래에 공통적으로 적용될 조건을 합의한 총괄계약서/일반거래조건협정서를 작성하여 서명한 후 1부씩 보관하고, 이후 반복되는 거래에서는 Offer Sheet나 Purchase Order Sheet에 양자가 서명하고

1부씩 나누어 가짐으로써 Sales Contract에 갈음하는 경우가 많다.

총괄계약을 체결하지 않고 매 거래건마다 매매계약을 체결할 경우, 매매계약서의 기재 내용은 거래할 때마다 개별적으로 결정해야 하는 개별거래조건(표면조항 또는 타이핑조항)과 일반적으로 모든 거래에 공통적으로 적용되는 일반거래조건(이면조항 또는 인쇄조항)이 있다.

[샘플 31] 주문 수락

February 10, 2020

Mr. Peter Brown, President
The Glove Imports, Inc.
Columbia, Maryland
Fax No. 301-964-3026

Dear Peter :

Hunting Gloves

Thank you for your facsimile letter of February 6 and we are pleased to acknowledge your P. O. No. 150 for 240 doz. Hunting Gloves Style No. 8624 as per Sales Note No. 21.

The instructions have immediately been given to our factory in China, at which the goods will be ready for shipment in the middle of March. Of course we ourselves will inspect the quality before the delivery.

Since the cargo is shipped from China direct to the United States, we ask you to insert the remarks "A THIRD-PARTY SHIPPER ON B/L[1] ACCEPTABLE" in your L/C.

We thank you very much for this order and we assure you of our best attention to its execution.[2]

Yours very truly,

HANKUK TRADING CO., INC.

Mi-Young Kim

Mi-Young Kim, Managing Director

Incl. Sales Note

해설

※ 이 샘플은 사냥용 장갑 주문에 대한 수락 예문이다.

1) A THIRD-PARTY SHIPPER ON B/L : B/L(선하증권)의 Shipper(송하인)란에 수출상이 아닌 제3자로 되어 있는 B/L, 즉 제3자 선적인 선하증권
2) execution : 실행, 집행
   (cf) carry(put) execution into : ~을 실행(실시)하다

[샘플 32] 수출상이 작성한 매매계약서

SAMSUNG TRADING CO., LTD.

Manufacturers, Exporters & Importers
"High Quality, High Technology"
#707, 7th Fl. Samsung Bldg., 123 Samsung-dong, Gangnam-gu
Seoul 135-090, Korea
TEL+82-2-6228-1471 M.P+82-10-6334-8710 FAX+82-2-6228-8710
E-mail : sihak@itc.co.kr URL : http://www.itc.co.kr

February 10, 2020

Glove Imports, Inc.
4825 Twin Knolls Road
Columbia, MD 21045
U.S.A.

Dear Sirs,

SALES NOTE NO. 123

We are pleased to confirm our sale to you of the following goods on the terms and conditions set forth below :

Descriptions : Hunting Gloves, Nylon Shell, Camouflage-Printed, with Pigskin Leather Patch, Style No. 8624, as per our Spec. No. 4118 attached

Quantity : 240 doz.(2,880 pairs) of the following size assortment :
20 doz. Men's Small 60 doz. Men's Medium
100 doz. Men's Large 60 doz. Men's X-large

Unit Price : @US$46.56(forty-six dollars fifty-six cents) per dozen FOB Busan

Amount	:	US$11,174.40(eleven thousand one hundred and seventy-four dollars forty cents) in the United States currency
Shipment	:	during March, 2020, from Chungdo port, China to St. Louis, U.S.A., the shipping lines and the ship's name to be reported to us later
Packing	:	Each pair in a polyethylene bag, six pairs(1/2 doz.) to be further poly-bagged, and 72 pairs (6doz.) in a shipping carton

Marking :

One Side	Adjacent Side
P.O. NO.	P.O. NO.
⟨G.I.I.⟩	STYLE NO.
	SIZE
ST. LOUIS	QUANTITY
VIA SEATTLE	NET WEIGHT
C/NO. 1 & UP	GROSS WEIGHT
MADE IN CHINA	MEASUREMENT

Insurance	:	To be covered by you
Payment	:	By letter of credit at sight to be opened in our favor

Please sign it and return the duplicate.

BUYER :
GLOVE IMPORTS, INC.
Robert H. Brown
Robert H. Brown, President

SELLER :
SAMSUNG TRADING CO., LTD.
Mi-Young Kim
Mi-Young Kim, President

[샘플 33] 수출상이 작성한 매매계약서(앞면)

ABC CO., LTD.

123 Samsung-dong, Gangnam-gu

Seoul 06170, Korea

TEL+82-2-6228-1472   M.P+82-10-6334-8710   FAX+82-2-6228-8710

E-mail : sihak@itc.co.kr   URL : http://www.itc.co.kr

June 25, 2020

XYZ CO., LTD.
50 Liberty St., New York
N.Y. 1005, U.S.A.

Gentlemen :

SALES CONTRACT NO. 123

We as Seller confirm having sold you as Buyer the following goods on the terms and conditions as stated below and on the back hereof.

Item	Commodity & Description	Quantity	Unit Price (CIF New York)	Amount
Blue Jeans	Men's Blue Jean : Style No. 500	25,000pcs.	@US$20.00per pc.	US$500,000.00
	Women's Blue Jean : Style No. 600	25,000pcs.	@US$20.00per pc.	US$500,000.00
Total	—	50,000pcs.	—	US$1,000,000.00

Origin   : Republic of Korea
Shipping Date   : Not later than July 21, 2020

Shipping Port	: Pusan Port, Korea
Destination Port	: New York Port, U. S. A.
Partial shipment	: Not allowed
Transshipment	: Allowed
Insurance	: Seller to cover the CIF price plus 10% against ICC(A) including War and Strikes Risks with claims payable in New York in the same currency as the draft
Payment	: Under an irrevocable documentary L/C at sight to be opened in favour of ABC Co., Ltd., Seoul, Korea

Documents Requried :

    1) Signed Commercial invoice in duplicate

    2) Full set of clean on board ocean Bills of Lading, to order of shipper, blank endorsed, marked "Freight prepaid" and Notify "XYZ Co., Ltd."

    3) Insurance Policy or Certificate endorsed in blank for full invoice value plus 10%, against ICC(A) including War and Strikes Risks with claims payable in New York in the same currency as the draft.

    4) Packing list in triplicate

    5) Certificate of origin in duplicate

Inspection	: Seller's inspection to be final
Packing	: Export standard packing
Shipping Marks	:

<XYZ>

NEW YORK

BOX NO 1/UP

MADE IN KOREA

Please sign it and return the duplicate.

BUYER :	SELLER :
XYZ CO., LTD.	ABC CO., LTD.
David Jones	*Si-Hak Oh*
David Jones, President	Si-Hak Oh, President

[샘플 34] 매매계약서(뒷면)

(Agreement on) General Terms and Conditions (of Business)

1. Principal to Principal Basis : This contract recognizes the fact that it is on a principal to principal basis between Seller and Buyer.
2. Shipment : The on-board date of shipment shall be taken as the conclusive date of shipment. Partial shipment and/or transshipment shall be permitted, unless otherwise stated on the face hereof. Seller shall not be responsible for nonshipment or late shipment in whole or in part by reason of Force Majeure, such as fires, floods, earthquakes, tempests, strikes, lockouts, and other industrial disputes, mobilization, war, threat of war, riots, civil commotions, hostilities, blockade, requisition of vessel, and any other contingencies beyond Seller's control.
3. Inspection : Inspection performed under the export regulation of Korea is final in respect of quality and/or conditions of the contracted goods, unless otherwise stated on the face hereof.
4. Trade Terms : The trade terms used in this Contract shall be governed and interpreted by the provisions of Incoterms(2000 edition) unless otherwise specifically stated.

5. Infringement : Buyer shall hold Seller harmless from liability for any infringement with regard to patent, trade mark, design and/or copyright originated or chosen by Buyer.
6. Claim : Any claim by Buyer must be made in writing within fourteen(14) days after receipt of the goods at destination stated on the face hereof, and no claim will be recognized if they are used.
7. Arbitration : All disputes, controversies or differences which may arise between Seller and Buyer, out of or in relation to or in connection with this Contracts, or for the breach thereof, shall be finally settled by arbitration in Seoul, Korea in accordance with the Commercial Arbitration Rules of the Korean Commercial Arbitration Board and under the Laws of Korea. The award rendered by the arbitrator(s) shall be final and binding upon both parties concerned.

[샘플 35] 주문 수락(수주)

August 5, 2020

Pacific Trading Co., Inc.
30 Water Street, New York
N.Y. 10003, U.S.A.

Gentlemen :

　　Many thanks for your letter of July 29 and your Order No. 100 for four hundred (400) dozen Porcelain Tea Set B.

　　You will find enclosed[1] our Contract Note No. 501. As you requested, shipment of this order will be made at the earliest date possible,²⁾ probably by the m/s³⁾ "Arirang", leaving Busan about August 20.

We assure you that we will do our best to execute this order so that we may⁴⁾ have repeat orders⁵⁾ from you.

Yours very truly,

HANKUK TRADING CO., LTD.
Soo-Chul Kim
Soo-Chul Kim, Export Manager

Inc. 1 Contract Note

해설

※ 이 샘플은 주문을 수락하며 계약서를 동봉하는 예문이다.

1) will find enclosed : 동봉물을 발견할 것이다, 동봉물을 수취할 것이다
2) at the earliest date possible : 가능한 한 가장 가까운 날짜에
3) m/s : moter ship의 약어. 내연기관 선박
   (cf) s/s : steamship의 약어. 증기기관 선박, 기선
4) so that we may : 당사가 ~할 수 있도록(may = can)
5) repeat orders : 재주문

[샘플 36] 수출상이 작성한 매매계약서(Contract Note)

SAMSUNG TRADING CO., LTD.

Manufactures, Exporter & Importers

"High Quality, High Technology"

#707, 7th Fl. Samsung Bldg., 123 Samsung-dong, Kangnam-ku

Seoul 06170, Korea

TEL+82-2-6228-1471   M.P+82-10-6334-8710   FAX+82-2-6228-8710

E-mail : sihak@itc.co.kr   URL : http://www.itc.co.kr

August 6, 2020

Pacific Trading Co., Inc.
30 Water Street, New York
N.Y. 10003, U.S.A.

Gentlemen:

CONTRACT NOTE[1] NO. 501

This contract note covers our sale to you of the undermentioned[2] goods on the terms and conditions set forth[3] below :

Commodity & Description	: Porcelain Tea set B
Quantity	: Four Hundred(400) dozen
Unit Price	: US$9.50 per dozen, CIF New York
Amount	: US$3,800.00(Say U.S. dollars thirty eight hundred only)
Shipment	: From Busan port, Korea to New York port, U.S.A. not later than August 31, 2020, Parshipment not allowed and transshipment allowed

Payment	: Under an irrevocable L/C with bill(s) of exchange at 30 days after sight to be opened in our favor[4]
Insurance	: ICC(WA) for 110% of invoice value
Packing	: 1 dozen each packed in a carton box and 100 dozen in a wooden case
Shipping Marks	:

<XYZ>

New York
C/# 1/UP
MADE IN KOREA

Please sign and return the duplicate.

BUYER :
PACIFIC TRADING CO., INC.
Robert H. Brown
Robert H. Brown, President

SELLER :
SAMSUNG TRADING CO., LTD.
Soo-Chul Kim
Soo-Chul Kim, Export Manager

해설

※ 이 샘플은 수출상이 작성한 도자기 커피 세트 매매계약서 예문이다.

1) Contract Note : 수출상이 작성한 매매계약서(= Sales Note, Sales Contract)
2) undermentioned : 하기(下記)의, 아래에 언급한
3) set forth : 진술된, 명시된(= stated, described, specified)
4) in our favor : 당사를 수익자로 하여(= in favor of us)

[샘플 37] 대체품 제시

13th June, 2020

Mr. Robert D. Mollis
MRB Electronic Services Limited
Romsey, Hampshire S05 8XQ
U. K.

Dear Mr. Mollis,

We thank you very much for your order by facsimile of 10th June for Electric Screwdrivers Model Nos. D-532, D-533 and D-534, 100 pieces each, and we are glad to book it except the second item which is out of stock at present.

The required time of shipment is so near that we suggest two solutions.[1]

One is that we recommend D-633 as a very good substitute[2] for D-533. Though of a different model, D-633 is the same in bit torque[3] as D-533, and can be applied to the same screw sizes. We offer it at the same price. If you are good enough to accept this, please fax your immediate acceptance and we will ship all the three items in August.

The other is that we may ship D-532 and D-534 in August and D-533 separately in September, if you would rather wait for D-533.

We are sorry for the inconvenience you have been put to,[4] but you may be aware that it is due to the growing popularity of electric tools which are gradually superseding pneumatic[5] ones in the tool market.

We await your instructions by e-mail or facsimile and assure you that if you accept either of the two suggestions, we shall execute this order in the most satisfactory manner.

                              Yours faithfully,

                              HANKUK CO., LTD.
                              Dong-Woo Kim
                              Dong-Woo Kim, Export Manager

해설

※ 이 샘플은 전동식 스크루드라이버에 대한 수입상의 주문에 수출상이 대체품을 제시하는 예문이다.

1) solutions : 해결책
2) substitute : 대체품
3) bit torque : 비트를 돌리는 힘
4) the inconvenience you have been put to : 귀사가 겪은 불편
   (cf) put one to inconvenience : ~에게 불편을 끼치다
5) pneumatic : (압축) 공기에 의하여 작동되는

[샘플 38] 대체품 제안

20th September, 2020

London Importing Co., Ltd.
588 Regent Street, London, W. I
England

Dear Sirs,

    Your Order Sheet No. 57 has come to hand.[1] We regret to say that we are unable to execute your order for Muslin Curtains to the pattern enclosed.[2] These Muslin Curtains have gone entirely out of fashion[3] and are no longer manufactured. So it is now impossible to obtain them.

    Enclosed we send you samples of our new products which are very similar in appearance,[4] and nearly the same in quality. Therefore, we offer these goods subject to your reply reaching us by 30th September. The price of £1.75 C.I.F. London a piece, less usual discount,[5] is a recommendation.[6]

    We hope to hear from you soon.

Yours faithfully,

HANKUK CO., LTD.

Dong-Woo Kim
Dong-Woo Kim, Export Manager

> 해설

※ 이 샘플은 수출상이 수입상에게 주문한 커튼이 유행이 지나 이제 생산되지 않으므로 대체품을 제안하는 예문이다.
1) come to hand : 입수되다
2) to the pattern enclosed : 동봉된 견본
3) out of fashion : 유행이 지난
4) in appearance : 외견상
5) less usual discount : 통상의 가격 할인을 한
6) recommendation : 추천 가격

주문 수락 및 거절에 유용한 표현

- We are sorry to say that we *are unable to* fill your order, the lowest current price in this market being higher than your limit by about 10%.
  이곳 시장의 가장 낮은 현재 가격이 귀사의 한계 가격보다 약 10% 높으므로 귀사의 주문을 이행할 수 없음을 전하게 되어 유감입니다.

- *Owing to* the rush of orders for our canned sardine, we cannot promise you to make shipment by the date you specify.
  당사의 정어리 통조림에 대한 주문 쇄도로 인해 당사는 귀사가 지

정한 날짜까지 선적을 약속할 수가 없습니다.

- All these goods *are in stock* and we can guarantee shipment before 15th March.

 이들 모든 제품은 재고가 있으므로 당사는 3월 15일 이전에 선적을 보장할 수 있습니다.

- We *have requested(arranged with)* our bankers to open an irrevocable L/C by tele-transmission in your favor.

 당사는 당사의 거래 은행에 귀사를 수익자로 하여 전신으로 취소불능신용장을 개설하도록 요청하였습니다.

- We *are in urgent need of* the goods and ask you to ship them by November 30 at the latest.

 당사는 그 제품이 급하게 필요하므로 귀사가 늦어도 11월 30일까지 그 제품을 선적할 것을 요청합니다.

- We regret that we are unable to *book(accept)* your order at the price you are asking for.

 당사는 귀사가 요청하고 있는 가격으로는 귀사의 주문을 수락할 수 없어 유감입니다.

- Thank you very much for your order No. 30 of October 12. We are pleased to accept it and are *sending herewith(enclosing)* our Sales Note No. 120.

  10월 12일 자 귀사의 주문번호 30에 대하여 대단히 감사합니다. 당사는 그 주문을 수락하고 당사의 매도계약서 120번을 동봉합니다.

- As the goods *are in stock*, they will be shipped by the M/S "Arirang" leaving Pusan on the 15th October.

  그 제품은 재고가 있으므로 10월 15일에 부산을 출발하는 아리랑호 선박에 선적될 것입니다.

- The article you ordered *is* temporarily *out of* stock, but we can recommend No. 6 as a good substitute for No. 5. You will see in the enclosed sample that No. 6 is very close to No. 5 in quality, and we offer it at a specially reduced price of US$52.00

  귀사가 주문한 품목은 일시적으로 재고가 없습니다. 그러나 당사는 5번에 대한 좋은 대체품으로 6번을 추천할 수 있습니다. 귀사는 동봉된 샘플에서 6번이 품질 면에서 5번과 매우 유사하다는 것을 알게 될 것입니다. 그리고 당사는 6번을 특별히 인하된 가격인 미화 52달러로 오퍼합니다.

- We appreciate your order No. 50 for Fishing Tackle, but regret that we are unable to accept it at the old prices. *Owing to* the sudden rise in both material and wage, we had to revise(increase) all our prices.
  유감스럽게도 당사는 기존의 가격으로는 그 주문을 수락할 수 없습니다. 원재료와 임금 모두의 갑작스러운 상승으로 당사는 당사의 모든 가격을 인상시켜야 했습니다.

- As has been agreed upon, please open a Letter of Credit for two million yen in the Japanese currency, *upon receipt of* which we will execute the order with our best attention.
  합의된 바와 같이 일본 통화로 200만 엔에 대한 신용장을 개설하십시오. 그 신용장을 받자마자 당사는 최선을 다하여 주문을 이행하겠습니다.

- *We have received with thanks* your Order Sheet dated May 30 for one hundred(100) dozen (of) Assorted Toys.
  다양한 장난감 100다스에 대한 귀사의 5월 30일 자 주문서를 감사히 받았습니다.

- *We are doing everything possible* to effect the earliest shipment of your order in accordance with your instructions.
= In accordance with your instructions, we *are doing our best* to expedite the earliest shipment of your order.
  귀사의 지시에 따라 당사는 귀사의 주문품을 가장 빨리 선적할 수 있도록 최선을 다하고 있습니다.

- Your order No. 5 has already been executed.
  귀사의 주문번호 5는 이미 실행되었습니다.

- As(Since) we have this item in stock, we will send it to you *right away(at once)*.
  당사는 이들 제품의 재고를 가지고 있으므로 귀사에 그 제품을 즉시 발송할 수 있습니다.

- We *are compelled* to decline your order now because we have received so many orders from all over the world.
  당사는 세계 곳곳에서 너무 많은 주문을 받아 지금은 귀사의 주문을 거절하지 않을 수 없습니다.

- We thank you for your inquiry, but would ask you(wish you) to *contact* ABC Corporation, our sole agents for(in) your country.

귀사의 조회에 감사합니다만, 귀국에 있는 당사의 독점 대리점인 ABC상사와 접촉하시기 바랍니다.

- Since our prices are quoted for an minimum order of 500 units, we wish you to increase your order to this figure.

당사의 가격은 최소 주문량 500단위에 대해 제시한 것이므로, 귀사의 주문을 이 수치까지 늘려주시기 바랍니다.

- *Unfortunately*, the goods *are out of production* at present.
= It is unfortunate that the goods be out of production at present.

불행하게도 그 제품은 현재 생산되지 않고 있습니다.

- The work will be completed *in a month*.

그 작업은 한 달 지나서 완성될 것입니다.

- We have *a wide range of* blue jeans that will appeal to all ages, in particular, to teenagers.

당사는 모든 연령층, 특히 10대에게 인기 있는 다양한 청바지를 보유하고 있습니다.

- May we expect *a quantity discount* in addition to a 20% trade discount off your list prices?
  당사는 귀사의 가격에서 20% 거래 할인에 추가하여 수량 할인을 기대해도 되겠습니까?

4장

신용장·선적·보험에 관한 무역통신문

신용장에 관한 무역통신문

대금 결제 방법

수출 대금을 회수하는 방법에는 송금(Remittance), 추심(Collection), 신용장(Letter of Credit : L/C), 국제 팩토링(International Factoring) 등이 있다. 그리고 구체적인 결제 수단에는 송금 수표(Demand Draft : D/D), 우편환(Mail Transfer : M/T), 전신환(Telegraphic Transfer : T/T) 등이 있다.

대금 결제 방법의 종류

구분	종류

송금
(Remittance)
	• 사전 송금 방식 : 선불
	  -CWO(Cash With Order : 현금 출급 주문) : 주문 시 대금 지불
	• 사후 송금 방식 : 후불
	  -Open Account : 물품 및 운송 서류 인도 후 대금 결제하는 순수한 후불
	  -COD(Cash On Delivery : 화물 인도 대금 결제 방식) : 물품 인도와 동시에 대금 결제
	  -CAD(Cash Against Documents : 서류 상환 대금 결제 방식) : 운송 서류 인도와 동시에 대금 결제

추심
(Collection)
	• D/P(Documents against Payment : 선적서류 지급인도 조건) : 운송 서류와 환어음을 제시함과 동시에 대금 결제
	• D/A(Documents against Acceptance : 선적서류 인수인도 조건) : 외상 거래
	  -D/A(at 90 days after sight) : 일람 후 90일에 대금 결제
	  -D/A(at 90 days after the date of shipment) : 선적 후 90일에 대금 결제

신용장
(L/C : Letter of Credit)
	• Sight L/C(일람불신용장) : 운송서류 및 환어음 제시 즉시 대금 결제(은행보증)
	• Usance L/C(기한부신용장) : 외상 거래(은행 보증)
	  -Usance L/C(at 90 days after sight) : 일람 후 90일에 대금 결제
	  -Usance L/C(at 90 days after the date of shipment): 선적 후 90일에 대금 결제

국제 팩토링 (International Factoring)	• IFG(International Factors Group) 등 국제 팩토링 그룹에 가입되어 있는 Export Factor(수출국 팩토링 회사) 및 Import Factor(수입국 팩토링 회사)의 무역 금융 수혜 및 지급 보증으로 대금 결제가 이루어지는 최근의 결제 방법

[샘플 1] 신용장 개설 독촉

1st September, 2020

British Trading Co., Ltd.
110 Oxford Street, London, W. 1
England

Dear Sirs,

On 2nd August, we received your order for ten cases of Cotton Sewing Threads.

The goods will soon be ready for shipment and we are thinking of sending them by the m/s "Arirang" which is scheduled to sail[1] from Pusan towards 20th September.[2] However, your L/C to cover[3] this order has not reached us yet. Please arrange with your bank to open by cable a letter of credit for your order of 2nd August.

We trust that you will attend to[4] this matter without delay.

Yours faithfully,

ABC CO., LTD.

Nam-Sik Lee
Nam-Sik Lee, Export Manager

해설

※ 이 샘플은 수출상이 선적 준비가 되었으나 아직 신용장을 받지 못해 수입상에 신용장 개설 수배를 독촉하는 예문이다.

1) be scheduled to sail : 출항 예정인
2) toward 20th September : 9월 20일을 경과하지 않는 기한 내에서 9월 20일경

(cf) about (approximately) 20th September : 9월 15일부터 9월 25일까지 총 11일간 사이

3) to cover : ~에 관한, ~에 해당하는
4) attend to : 수배하다, ~에 관심을 두다

[샘플 2] 신용장 개설 독촉

10th May, 2020

XYZ Co., Ltd.
184 J1, Gajah Mada 3rd Floor
Jakarta, Indonesia

Dear Sirs,

　　Further to[1] our letters of 20th April and 4th May, we have to remind you that the credit to cover your Order No. 15 for Porcelain Ware has not yet reached us.

　　This contract was originally for May shipment and the goods were specially made to your order.[2] You will readily see the inconvenience[3] and actual losses we are suffering.

　　We might dispose of[4] the goods and have you make up for[5] the loss, but trusting your immediate attention, we wait for the early arrival of the L/C.

　　　　　　　　　　　　　　Yours faithfully,

　　　　　　　　　　　　　　ABC CO., LTD.

Nak-Sun Lee
Nak-Sun Lee, Export Manager

해설

※ 이 샘플은 수출상이 수입상을 위해 특별히 제조한 도자기 제품에 대해 아직 신용장을 받지 못해 독촉하는 예문이다.

1) further to : ~에 이어, ~에 더하여
2) specially made to your order : 귀사의 주문을 위하여 특별히 제작한
3) inconvenience : 불편, 부자유
4) dispose of ~ : ~을 처분하다
5) make up for ~ : ~을 보상하다

[샘플 3] 신용장 개설 통지 및 조속한 선적 요구

10th June, 2020

XYZ Co., Ltd.
110 Oxford Street, London, W. 1
England

Dear sirs,

    Your Sales Note No. 10 has been received. Having found it correct,[1] we enclose the duplicate duly signed by us.[2]

    We have arranged with[3] The Royal Bank of Canada for an Irrevocable Letter of Credit in your favour for US$1,719,00. The advising bank,[4] The First British Bank in your city, will send you the L/C shortly.

We require our order urgently, so please expedite shipment[5] as soon as possible.

Your attention will be appreciated.

Yours faithfully,

ABC CO., LTD.
Dong-Jin Park
Dong-Jin Park, Export Manager

해설

※이 샘플은 수출상이 보낸 매매계약서를 수입상이 확인·서명 후 동봉하고 신용장을 개설할 것을 지시하였으므로 가능한 한 조속히 선적하길 요구하는 예문이다.

1) Having found it correct : 그것에 하자가 없었으므로
2) the duplicate duly signed by us : 당사가 정식 서명한 부본
3) arrange with : 수배하다
4) advising bank : 통지은행
5) expedite shipment : 선적을 서두르다

[샘플 4] **신용장 접수 통지**

20th June, 2020

ABC Co., Ltd.
123 Samsung-dong, Gangnam-gu
Seoul 06170, Korea

Dear Sirs,

　Thank you for your prompt arrangement of the L/C.

　We have received today the L/C No. 45812 of The Royal Bank of Canada through The First British Bank, London.

　We have already started arranging shipment of your order No. 321.

　As soon as we finish shipping your order, we will let you know the name of the steamer and the estimated time of arrival.

　Thank you again for your attention.

　　　　　　　　　　　　Yours faithfully,

　　　　　　　　　　　　XYZ CO., LTD.

　　　　　　　　　　　　James Baker
　　　　　　　　　　　　James Baker, President

해설

※ 이 샘플은 앞 서한의 회답으로서 수출상이 신용장을 받았고 이미 선적 준비를 했으며 선적 완료 후 선적통지를 하겠다는 예문이다.

[샘플 5] 신용장 유효 기일 및 선적 기일 연장 요청

13th October, 2020

XYZ Co., Ltd.
456 Wall St., New York
N.Y. 1008, U.S.A.

Dear Sirs,

L/C No. 7890 for Order Nos. 10 & 11

We have received with thanks the letters of credit covering your orders No. 10 and 11.

Upon examination, however, we have found that the L/C No. 7890 for Order No. 10, which is to be shipped during this month, expires[1] on 15th October. On the other hand, the vessel "Earnest Venture" of Hyundai Shipping Lines, which the L/C specifies for the shipment, leaves Pusan on or around the 20th.

So we are asking you to extend the validity and the shipment time[2] of the L/C to the end of October and fax us to that effect by the 18th.

We trust that you will comply with[3] our request, since the shipment time agreed upon was "during October" and the goods are ready for shipment.

Yours faithfully,

ABC CO., LTD.

Jun-Ho Kim
Jun-Ho Kim, Director

해설

※ 이 샘플은 수출상이 신용장을 받았으나 선적 기일과 유효 기일이 너무 빨라서 수입상에 이를 연장해달라고 요청하는 예문이다.

1) expires : 유효기간이 만기되다
2) extend the validity and the shipment time : 신용장의 유효 기일 및 수출 상품의 선적 기일을 연장하다
3) comply with : 동의하다, 승낙하다

[샘플 6] 신용장 유효 기일 및 선적 기일 연장 요청

July 15, 2020

XYZ Co., Ltd.
456 Wall St., New York
N.Y. 1008, U.S.A.

Gentlemen :

    As we faxed[1] this morning, we have to ask you to extend[2] the shipment time of your order No. 100 for the following reasons :

    A few days ago, we received an advance sample[3] from the manufacturer and noticed that it was not quite[4] satisfactory in finish.[5]

    We instructed them to examine the whole lot[6] again and they say that they will deliver perfect goods by 25th July. This will make it impossible for us to ship the goods by S/S ARIRANG sailing on the 27th of July.

The next available vessel[7] is M/S DONGGUK scheduled to sail on 8th August.

We are sorry to trouble you, but shall be obliged if you will amend the L/C to extend the shipment time and validity[8] for two weeks respectively.

We believe that it is worth while to[9] wait for better goods and trust that you will comply with our request.

Yours faithfully,

HANKUK TRADING CO., LTD.
Jun-Ho Kim
Jun-Ho Kim, Director

해설

※이 샘플은 제조 지연에 따른 신용장의 선적 기일 및 유효 기일을 연장해달라고 요청하는 예문이다.

1) As we faxed : 당사가 팩스를 보낸 대로
2) extend : 연기하다, 연장하다
3) advance sample : 선발 견본
4) not quite : 아주 ~하지는 않은
5) in finish : 마무리
6) whole lot : 전 제품
7) available vessel : 이용 가능한 배
8) validity : 유효 기일
9) worth while to : ~할 가치가 있는

신용장의 내용과 형식

신용장(Letter of Credit : L/C)이란 수입자의 요청과 지시에 따라 수입자를 신용장 개설 의뢰인(Applicant Beneficiary)으로 하고 수출자를 수익자(Beneficiary)로 하여, 수입자의 거래 은행(L/C Issuing or Opening Bank)이 L/C에 명시된 조건과 일치하는 운송서류(Transport Documents)를 제시받으면 수출 대금인 신용장 금액을 수출자에게 틀림없이 지급하겠다는 확약서다.

신용장 거래의 메커니즘은 다음과 같다.

① 수출자는 수입자와 매매계약을 체결하고 Sales Note(또는 Offer Sheet)를 교환한다.

② 수입자는 수입 제한 승인 품목의 경우 Offer Sheet 등 수입 승인에 필요한 서류를 준비하여 관련 협회나 조합 등에서 I/L(Import License : 수입승인서)을 발급받는다.

③ I/L을 발급받은 수입자는 I/L 발급 후 거래 은행에 L/C 개설을 의뢰해야 한다.

④ 수입자로부터 L/C 개설 의뢰를 받은 L/C 개설 은행은 L/C를 발행하여 수출지 소재의 환거래 은행에 송부한다.

⑤ L/C를 접수한 통지은행은 지체 없이 수출자에게 L/C 도착을 통지하고, 이를 통보받은 수출자는 L/C를 수취한다.

⑥ L/C를 수취한 수출자는 수출 제한 승인 품목의 경우 L/C 등 수

출 승인에 필요한 서류를 준비하여 관련 협회나 조합 등에 가서 E/L(Export License : 수출승인서)을 신청하고 E/L을 발급받는다.

⑦~⑧ E/L을 발급받은 수출자는 수출 물품을 확보하여 수출 통관을 거친 후 운송회사에 수출 물품을 선적하고 B/L(Bill of Lading : 선하증권)을 교부받는다.

신용장 거래의 메커니즘

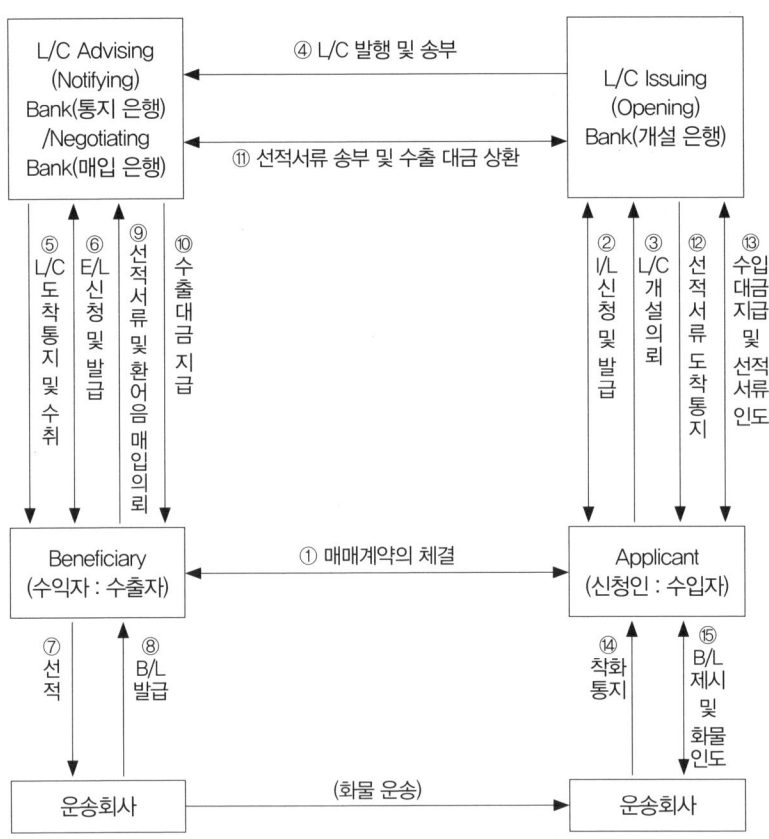

⑨ B/L을 교부받은 수출자는 보험증권(필요 시), 상업송장, 환어음 등 선적 서류를 준비하여 매입 은행에 환어음 매입을 의뢰한다.

⑩ 선적서류를 첨부한 환어음을 매입 의뢰받은 매입 은행은 서류를 검토하고 수출자에게 수출 대금을 지급한다.

⑪ 수출 대금을 지급한 매입 은행은 지급한 수출 대금을 결제받기 위해 L/C 개설 은행에 선적서류를 송부하고 환어음 대금을 상환받는다.

⑫ 선적서류를 받은 L/C 개설 은행은 수입자에게 선적서류 도착을 통지한다.

⑬ 선적서류 도착을 통지받은 수입자는 L/C 개설 은행에 수입 대금을 지급하고 선적서류를 인도받는다.

⑭ 운송회사는 화물이 도착하면 수입자에게 착화(화물 도착)를 통지한다.

⑮ 착화 통지를 받은 수입자는 수입통관 후 운송회사에 B/L을 제시하고 화물을 인도받음으로써 수출입 거래가 종결된다.

[샘플 7] 우편신용장(Mail L/C)

ORIGINAL   BANK OF OCEANIA LIMITED
                       P. O. Box 549 New Plymouth
                            New Zealand

☒ Advised by air mail
☒ Confirmation of our cable/telex of this date   Date : 28th January, 2020

IRREVOCABLE DOCUMENTARY CREDIT	Credit number : 8170708
Advising bank : The Shinhan Bank Limited Overseas Operation Center, Jung-gu Seoul 04534, Korea	Applicant : New Zealand Wire Industries Limited Private Bag, New Plymouth New Zealand
Beneficiary : Kalam Machine Co., Ltd. 19th floor, Korea Bldg. 456 Jongro 3-ga, Jongro-gu Seoul 03056, Korea	Amount : U.S.$125,400.00(SAY U.S. DOLLARS ONE HUNDRED AND TWENTY-FIVE THOUSAND FOUR HUNDRED ONLY)
	Expiry Date and Place : 31st July, 2020 in the country of the beneficiary for negotiation

Dear Sirs,
We hereby issue in your favour this documentary credit which is available by negotiation of your drafts at sight for 100% of invoice value drawn on Bank of Oceania Limited, 63 Wall Street, New York, NY 10005, U.S.A. bearing the clause "Drawn under Documentary Credit No. 8170708 of Bank of Oceania Limited. New Plymouth, New Zealand" and accompanied by the following documents(at least in duplicate unless otherwise specified) marked with :
☒ Signed commercial invoice
☒ Full set of clean "on board" ocean bills of lading dated not later than 20th July, 2020 made out to order and endorsed in blank, and marked "Freight Prepaid" and "Notify Applicant"
☒ Insurance policy or certificate for not less than 110% of the invoice value in the currency of drafts, endorsed in blank, with claims payable in New Zealand, covering ICC(A) 1/1/82
☐ Insurance to be covered by applicant
☒ Packing list
☒ Certified customs invoice
    Evidencing shipment of "Korea" brand Three Drawbenches as per Applicant's Order No. 5030 CIF

From Pusan port, Korea To Wellington port, New Zealand	Partial shipments and transhipment Prohibited
Special conditions : Fumigation certificate of packing materials Instructions to the negotiating bank : Drafts are to be forwarded to the drawee bank with reimbursement claim. All documents are to be despatched in two sets by consecutive airmails to the issuing branch.	

We undertake that drafts drawn and presented in conformity with the terms of this credit will be duly honoured.
The amount of each drawing must be endorsed on the reverse hereof by the negotiating bank.
                Yours faithfully,
                Bank of Gana Limited
                (signed)
                Authorized Signature
	Advising bank's notification :
	
	Our Advice No. 1456 on Feb. 4, 2020
	HANYANG BANK LIMITED
	(Signed)
	
	Place, date, name and signature of advising bank.

[샘플 8] 우편신용장(Mail L/C)

Name of Issuing Bank:	Irrevocable Documentary Credit	Number
CITI BANK 40 Liberty St., New York, N.Y. 1005, U.S.A.		SH-9838710

Place and Date of Issue: New York, November 10, 2020	Expiry Date and Place for Presentation of documents
Applicant: XYZ CO., LTD. 50 Liberty St., New York N.Y. 1005, U.S.A.	Expiry Date: January 31, 2020 Place for Presentation: At the counter of negotiating bank
	Beneficiary: ABC CO., LTD. 123 Samsung-Dong, Kangnam-Ku, Seoul, Korea
Advising Bank: Reference. No. HANIL BANK SEOUL, KOREA	Amount: U.S.$1,000,000.00(U.S. Dollars One Million only)

Partial shipments ☐ allowed ☒ not allowed	Credit available with Nominated Bank:
Transhipment ☒ allowed ☐ not allowed	☐ by payment at sight: ☐ by deferred payment at: ☐ by acceptance of drafts at: ☒ by negotiation
☐ Insurance covered by buyers	

Shipment as defined in UCP 500 Article 46	Against the documents detailed herein:
From: Busan Port, Korea For transportation to: New York Port, U.S.A. Not later than: January 21, 2020	☒ and Beneficiary's draft(s) at sight drawn on: issuing bank for full invoice value

Advice for the Beneficiary

1) Full 3/3 set of clean on board ocean Bills of Loading, to order of shipper, blank endorsed, marked "Freight prepaid" and notify XYZ CO., LTD.
2) Insurance Policy or Certificate for full invoice value plus 10%, with claims payble in New York in the same currency as the draft, covering Institute Cargo Clauses (All Risks) including War and SRCC risks.
3) Signed commercial Invoice in triplicate
4) Packing List in triplicate
5) Certificate of Origin in duplicate

Covering :
"50,000 pieces of blue jeans U.S.$20.00 per piece C.I.F. New York as per Contract No. 123"
Other conditions :
  All banking charges outside U.S.A. are for account of beneficiary.
Instructions for negotiating bank :
  Negotiating bank should forward the documents direct to issuing bank in two separate registered airmail.

Documents to be presented within [10] days after the date of shipment but within the validity of the Credit.

We hereby issue the Irrevocable Documentary Credit in your favour. It is subject to the Uniform Customs and Practice for Documentary Credits (1993 Revision, International Chamber of Commerce, Paris, France. Publication No. 500) and engages us in accordance with the terms thereof. The number and the date of the Credit and the name of our bank must be quoted on all drafts required. If the Credit is available by negotiation, each pressentation must be noted on the reverse side of the advice by the bank where the Credit is available.

The document consists of [1] signed page(s)   Name and signature of the Issuing Bank

[샘플 9] Telex L/C

RECEIPT NUMBER : 076260
DATE : 201113
TO : HANVIT BANK, SEOUL, KOREA
FM : CITI BANK
    40 LIBERTY ST., NEW YORK, N.Y.1005, U.S.A.
■ TESTED FOR USD 1,000,000.00

PLEASE ADVISE THIS CREDIT TO THE BENEFICIARY WITHOUT ADDING YOUR CONFIRMATION IMMEDIATELY ON RECEIPT OF THIS CREDIT.
WE OPEN IRREVOCABLE DOCUMENTARY CREDIT NO. 707
BENEFICIARY : ABC CO., LTD.
        123 SAMSUNG-DONG, KANGNAM-KU, SEOUL, KOREA
APPLICANT : XYZ CO., LTD.
        40 LIBERTY ST., NEW YORK, N.Y.1005, U.S.A.
AMOUNT : USD 1,000,000.00(U.S. DOLLARS ONE MILLION ONLY)
EXPIRY DATE AND PLACE : JULY 31, 2000 IN KOREA
TRADE TERM : CIF NEW YORK PORT,INCOTERMS 2020
AVAILABLE WITH ANY BANK BY NEGOTIATION OF BENEFICIARY'S DRAFT(S) AT SIGHT DRAWN ON ISSUING BANK FOR FULL INVOICE VALUE
DOCUMENTS REQUIRED :
1. SIGNED COMMERCIAL INVOICE IN TRIPLICATE
2. FULL 3/3 SET OF CLEAN ON BOARD OCEAN BILLS OF LADING MADE OUT TO ORDER OF SHIPPER AND BLANK ENDORSED, MARKED "FREIGHT PREPAID" AND NOTIFY THE APPLICANT
3. INSURANCE POLICY OR CERTIFICATE IN DUPLICATE, ENDORSED IN BLANK, FOR 110 PERCENT OF THE CIF INVOICE VALUE, WITH CLAIMS PAYABLE IN NEW YORK IN THE SAME CURRENCY AS THE DRAFT, COVERING INSTITUTE CARGO

CLAUSES(A) INCLUDING WAR AND STRIKES RISKS
4. PACKING LIST IN TRIPLICATE
5. CERTIFICATE OF ORIGIN IN DUPLICATE
COVERING : "50,000 PIECES OF BLUE JEANS USD 20.00 PER PIECE CIF NEW YORK PORT, INCOTERMS 2020 AS PER CONTRACT NO. 123"
SHIPMENT : FROM PUSAN PORT, KOREA FOR TRANSPORTATION TO NEW YORK PORT, U.S.A. NOT LATER THAN JANUARY 31, 2020
PARTIAL SHIPMENT : NOT ALLOWED
TRANSHIPMENT : ALLOWED
OTHER CONDITIONS :
- ALL BANKING CHARGES OUTSIDE U.S.A. ARE FOR ACCOUNT OF BENEFICIARY
- DOCUMENTS MUST BE PRESENTED WITHIN 10 DAYS AFTER THE DATE OF SHIPMENT, BUT NOT LATER THAN JANUARY 31, 2020 IN THE COUNTRY OF BENEFICIARY
- DRAFT(S) MUST QUOTE THE NUMBER, DATE AND NAME OF ISSUING BANK OF THIS CREDIT.

INSTRUCTIONS FOR NEGOTIATING BANK : NEGOTIATING BANK SHOULD FORWARD THE DOCUMENTS MUST BE ENDORSED ON THIS ADVICE BY NEGOTIATING BANK.
THIS CREDIT IS SUBJECT TO U.C.P. 600(2007 REVISION), AND THIS IS THE OPERATIVE INSTRUMENT AND NO MAIL CONFIRMATION FOLLOWS.
REGARDS,
CITI BANK, NEW YORK

[샘플 10] SWIFT L/C

* Advice Br. : 신한은행 신반포	* Advice Date : 2020. 05. 06
Advice of Issue of Documentary Credit	* Advice No : A-0688-905-01974 * Credit No : 9ASAL200199BU
* Beneficiary : TEL. 595-1616 ALLIED SIGNAL KOREA LTD. 44-1 BANPO-DONG, SEOCHO-GU, SEOUL	* Applicant : THE GIANT TAIWAN LTD. 91, SEC. 3, NANKING EAST ROAD, TAIPEI, TAIWAN, R.O.C.
* Amount : USD23,210.60 * Expiry Date : 2020. 08. 03	* Issuing Bank : SCSBTWTP SHANGHAI BANK, TAIPEI 2, MIN CHUAN EAST ROAD TAIPEI, TAIWAN

Gentlemen :

At the request of the issuing bank, and without any engagement or responsibility on our part, we are pleased to inform you that we have received the following AUTHENTICATED teletransmission dated 2020. 05. 04(7-0138-00)

: 700   Issue of Documentary Credit

: 27	Sequence of Total	: 1/1
: 40A	Form of Documentary Credit	: IRREVOCABLE
: 20	Documentary Credit Number	: 9ASAL200199BU
: 31C	Date of Issue	: 200504
: 31D	Date and Place of Expiry	: 200803KOREA
: 50	Applicant	: THE GIANT TAIWAN LTD. 91, SEC. 3, NANKING EAST ROAD, TAIPEI, TAIWAN, R.O.C.
: 59	Beneficiary	: ALLIED SIGNAL KOREA LTD. 44-1 BANPO-DONG SEOCHO-

	KU, SEOUL, KOREA
:32B Currency Code and Amount	: USD23,210.60
:41D Available With ... By ...	: WITH ANY BANK
	BY NEGOTIATION
:42C Drafts at ...	: SIGHT
:42D Drawee	: ISSUING BANK
:43P Partial Shipments	: PERMITTED
:43T Transshipment	: PROHIBITED

:44A Loading on Board/Dispatch/Taking in Charge at/from
                                                : JAPANESE PORT
:44B For transportation to ...   : TAIWANESE PORT
:44C Latest Date of Shipment   : 200803
:45A Description of Goods and/or Services
                                                : TURBOCHARGER X 60 PCS
                                                  FOB JAPANESE PORT
:46A Documents Required   :

    A. SIGNED COMMERCIAL INVOICE IN SEXTUPLICATE INDICATING THIS CREDIT NUMBER

    B. FULL SET OF ORIGINAL CLEAN ON BOARD OCEAN BILLS OF LADING MADE OUT TO ORDER OF ISSUING BANK SHOWING APPLICANT AS NOTIFY PARTY MARKED FREIGHT COLLECT AND THIS CREDIT NUMBER

    C. PACKING LIST IN SEXTUPLICATE

:47A Additional Conditions   :

ONE COMPLETE SET OF NONNEGOTIABLE DOCUMENTS TO BE SENT TO APPLICANT DIRECTLY AND BENEFICIARY'S CERTIFICATE TO THIS EFFECT IS REQUIRED

:71B Charges   :

ALL BANKING CHARGES OUTSIDE TAIWAN ARE FOR BENEFICIARY"S ACCOUNT

:48   Period for presentation   :

DOCUMENTS MUST BE PRESENTED WITHIN 10 DAYS AFTER

THE DATE OF SHIPMENT BUT WITHIN THE VALIDITY OF THIS CREDIT

: 49   Confirmation Instructions   : WITHOUT
: 78   Instruction to the Paying/Accepting/Negotiating Bank :
   1. A USD30.00 FEE PLUS ALL RELATIVE CABLE CHARGES WILL BE DEDUCTED FROM THE REIMBURSEMENT CLAIM FOR EACH PRESENTATION OF DISCREPANT DOCUMENTS UNDER THIS DOCUMENTARY CREDIT.
   2. UPON RECEIPT OF THE RELATIVE SHIPPING DOCUMENTS IN ORDER, WE SHALL REIMBURSE THE NEGOTIATING BANK ACCORDING TO THEIR INSTRUCTIONS.
   3. ALL DOCUMENTS TO BE SENT TO US IN ONE LOT.
      (ADD : 149, SEC. 2, MIN SHENG E. RD., TAIPEI, R.O.C.)
: 72   Sender to Receiver Information :
   NO MAIL CONFIRMATION WILL FOLLOW

Please note that we reserve the right to make such corrections to this advice as may be necessary upon receipt of the mail confirmation and assume no responsibility for any errors and/or omissions in the transmission and/or translation of the teletransmission, and for any forgery and/or alteration on the credit.

If the credit is available by negotiation, each presentation must be noted on the reverse of this advice by the bank where the credit is available.

THIS ADVICE IS SUBJECT TO THE UNIFORM CUSTOMS AND PRACTICE FOR DOCUMENTARY CREDITS(2007 REVISION, ICC PUBLICATION NO. 600).

Yours very truly,

_____
Authorized Signature

신용장 개설 및 독촉에 유용한 표현

- We now ask you to *arrange with* your bank to open the L/C for your Order No. 30 without delay.

  당사는 지금 귀사가 지체 없이 귀사의 주문번호 30에 대하여 귀사의 거래 은행에 신용장을 개설하도록 수배할 것을 요청합니다.

- We *have received* L/C No. 1567 issued by Bank of India but have to inform you that the name of the goods reads "Men's Blue Jeans" *instead of* "Women's Blue Jeans".

  당사는 인도 은행에 의해 발행된 신용장을 받았습니다만, 제품명이 '여성용 청바지' 대신에 '남성용 청바지'로 잘못 기재되어 있다는 것을 귀사에 통지해야만 합니다.

- Since our bankers do not overlook even the slightest discrepancy, we ask you to *request* your bank *to* amend the credit as soon as possible.

  당사의 거래 은행들은 사소한 하자도 간과하지 않으므로 당사는 귀사가 가능한 한 빨리 귀사의 거래 은행에 신용장을 변경할 것을 요청하기를 부탁합니다.

- We usually *do business* on an L/C at sight basis, but if you insist we may accept D/P terms.

  당사는 통상 일람불신용장을 기본으로 거래를 합니다. 그러나 귀사가 주장한다면 D/P 조건도 수락할 수 있습니다.

- We *request* you *to* issue an irrevocable L/C for sums not exceeding US$10,000.

  당사는 귀사에 미화 1만 달러를 초과하지 않는 금액에 대한 취소불능신용장을 개설할 것을 요청합니다.

- We have received a fax advice from our Hong Kong Bank *to the effect that* they have opened a letter of credit in your favour.

  당사는 당사의 거래 은행인 홍콩은행으로부터 귀사를 수익자로 하여 신용장을 개설하였다는 내용의 팩스 통지를 받았습니다.

- *Arrangements have been made with(We have arranged with)* our bankers for establishing(to establish) L/C to cover our order and we are enclosing a copy of the application for L/C for your reference.

  당사의 거래 은행에 당사의 주문을 커버하는 신용장을 개설하도록 조치하였습니다. 그리고 당사는 귀사가 참조하도록 신용장개설신청서 사본 한 부를 동봉합니다.

- We ask you to kindly make the following alterations (amendments) in the L/C.

  당사는 귀사가 신용장에 다음과 같은 변경을 하도록 요청합니다.

- As requested(At your request), we *have arranged with* our bank *to* amend the credit, so you will have no difficulty in negotiating your draft.

  귀사가 요청한 바와 같이 당사는 당사의 거래 은행에 그 신용장을 변경하도록 요청하였습니다. 그러므로 귀사는 귀사의 환어음을 네고(매입)하는 데 어려움이 없을 것입니다.

- We have opened *in your favor* an irrevocable L/C for sums not exceeding US$5,000.

  당사는 귀사를 수익자로 하여 미화 5,000달러를 초과하지 않는 금액에 대해 취소불능신용장을 개설하였습니다.

- Please extend the expiry date of L/C No. 40 till May 31.

  신용장 40번의 만기일을 5월 31일까지 연장해주십시오.

- We *shall be obliged if*(*We would appreciate it if*) you will extend (the validity of) the credit to September 30.
9월 30일까지 신용장의 유효 기일을 연장시켜주시면 감사하겠습니다.

- As requested, we have already *arranged with* our bankers to extend the expiry date of L/C No. 123 for two weeks up to(till) October 15, 2020.
귀사의 요청에 따라 당사는 이미 당사의 거래 은행에 신용장 123번의 만기일을 2020년 10월 15일까지 2주일간 연기하도록 조치하였습니다.

- *It* is customary *for* us *to* do business on an L/C at sight basis.
당사는 일람불신용장 베이스로 거래하는 것이 관례입니다.

- When you give us your order, we wish you would open an irrevocable L/C as usual.
당사에 주문을 할 때는 통상과 같이 취소불능신용장을 개설해주시기 바랍니다.

- *According to* your fax of (dated) April 18, you had *arranged with* the Rome Branch of the Hanvit Bank *to* open a letter of credit (in our favor) immediately. The credit, however, has not yet reached us.

4월 18일 자 귀사의 팩스에 의하면, 귀사는 한빛은행 로마지점에 (당사를 수익자로 하여) 즉시 신용장을 개설하도록 조치하였습니다. 그러나 신용장은 아직 당사에 도착하지 않았습니다.

- Our bank, Chicago Bank will open an Irrevocable and Confirmed Letter of Credit *covering (for)* our order.

  당사의 거래 은행인 시카고은행이 당사의 주문에 대한(주문을 커버하는) 취소불능확인신용장을 개설할 것입니다.

- In order to cover this business, we shall *instruct(request)* our bankers to open an Irrevocable Letter of Credit for the amount of this business *in your favor*.

  이 거래를 커버하기 위해 당사는 당사의 거래 은행에 귀사를 수익자로 하여 이 거래 금액에 대한 취소불능신용장을 개설하도록 지시하겠습니다.

- We do not business on a letter of credit for any order of less than US$ 5,000.00 because our bank charges are too high.

당사의 은행 거래 비용이 너무 높으므로 미화 5,000달러 미만의 주문에 대해서는 신용장 조건으로는 거래를 하지 않습니다.

- According to the Credit we received, the payment was to be made *at 60d/s(days after sight)*. But we wish it to be made *at sight*.

 당사가 받은 신용장에 따르면 대금 결제가 일람 후 60일로 되어 있습니다. 그러나 당사는 대금 결제가 일람불로 이루어지기를 원합니다.

- We wish you to pay *either* by TT(telegraphic transfer) in advance *or* by an Irrevocable Letter of Credit in our favour.

 당사는 귀사가 전신환으로 사전 결제하거나, 또는 당사를 수익자로 하여 취소불능신용장으로 결제하기를 바랍니다.

- We thank you very much for L/C and shipping instructions covering your *trial order*.

 귀사의 시험 주문에 대한 신용장과 선적 지시에 대해 대단히 감사합니다.

- We have learned that the L/C had been *issued(opened,*

established), but we have not received it yet.

신용장이 개설되었다고 들었습니다만, 당사는 아직 신용장을 받지 못했습니다.

- We *have instructed* our bankers *to* open a L/C in your favor for US$1000,000.00 covering our order No.123 of December 2, 2020.

당사는 2020년 12월 2일 자 당사 주문번호 123에 대한 미화 100만 달러에 대하여 귀사를 수익자로 하여 신용장을 개설하도록 당사의 거래은행에 지시하였습니다.

- We have been advised by our bankers of the credit No.123, but the unit price on it is stated incorrectly. Please amend it *in compliance with* the original contract.

당사는 당사의 거래은행으로부터 신용장 123번을 통지받았습니다. 그러나 신용장에 단가가 잘못 기재되어 있습니다. 그것을 당초 계약서와 일치하게 수정해주십시오.

- We have requested the Detroit Bank to open an irrevocable Letter of Credit in your favor yesterday and you may expect to receive the L/C in 10 days.

당사는 어제 디트로이트은행에 취소불능신용장을 개설하도록 요청하였으며, 귀사는 열흘 후에 그 신용장을 받을 것입니다.

신용장에서 유용한 표현

- The drafts are to be accompanied by *a complete set of* shipping documents.
  환어음은 선적서류 전통(全通)과 함께 수반(제출)되어야 합니다.

- All drafts drawn under this credit must be negotiated *on or before* November 30.
  본 신용장에 근거하여 발행된 모든 환어음은 11월 30일 이전에 매입되어야 합니다.

- We authorize you to *draw on* The Bank of Tokyo.
  당행은 귀사가 도쿄은행 앞으로 환어음을 발행할 권한을 부여합니다.

- Drafts are to be accompanied by shipping documents as stipulated in the letter of credit.

환어음은 신용장에 명시된 선적서류와 함께 수반(제출)되어야 합니다.

- All banking charges outside America *are for the account of* beneficiary(are for beneficiary's account).
  미국 밖에서 발생하는 모든 은행 비용은 수익자의 부담입니다.

- Documents *must(to)* be presented for negotiation within 10 days after the date of issuance of transport documents.
  서류는 운송 서류 발행일 후 10일 이내에 매입을 위해 제시되어야 합니다.

- This credit is *transferable* in Korea only.
  이 신용장은 한국에서만 양도 가능합니다.

- Negotiation under this credit *is restricted to* the advising bank only.
  본 신용장하의 네고(매입)는 통지 은행에 제한되어 있습니다.

- *Telegraphic transfer reimbursement* is prohibited.
  전신환 상환은 금지됩니다.

- Acceptance commission and discount charges *are for beneficiary's account.*

  인수 수수료와 할인 수수료는 수익자가 부담합니다.

- All documents must be counter signed by the Seoul office of our company.

  모든 서류는 당사 서울 사무소에 의해 연대 서명되어 있어야 합니다.

- *Documents presented later than 21 days after the date of shipment* are acceptable.

  선적일 후 21일이 지나 제시된 서류도 수리됩니다.

- *Stale Bills of Lading* are acceptable.

  시효경과선하증권도 수리됩니다.

- *Third party B/L* is acceptable

  제3자선적인선하증권도 수리됩니다.

- *The transport document indicating a party other than the beneficiary of the credit as the consignor of the goods* is acceptable.

신용장의 수익자 이외의 여타 당사자를 화물의 수하인으로 명시한 운송 서류도 수리됩니다.

- One complete set of non-negotiable documents must(to) be sent to applicant directly by DHL and beneficiary's certificate to this effect is accompanied(required) with the receipt required.
한 세트의 비유통 서류가 DHL로 개설 의뢰인에게 직접 송부되어야 하며, 수익자가 이것을 이행했다는 내용의 수익자 발행증명서가 해당 영수증과 함께 요구됩니다.

- Shipment *must(to)* be effected by Han Jin Shipping Co. only.
선적은 오로지 한진해운에 의해 이루어져야 합니다.

- Beneficiary's drafts drawn under this credit are negotiable on *a sight basis irrespective of the tenor of the draft*.
본 신용장하에 수익자가 발행한 환어음은 환어음의 기간에 관계없이 일람불 기본으로 네고(매입)됩니다.

- Shipment sample must be sent to applicant by air and the

relative receipt must be accompanied with the shipping documents.

선적품 샘플이 개설 의뢰인에게 항공으로 발송되어야 하며, 이를 이행하였다는 해당 영수증이 선적서류와 함께 제출되어야 합니다.

• Copy of telex or fax certified by beneficiary to the applicant before shipment date advising the name of carrying vessel, sailing date, No. of package, quantity to be shipped, draft amount and L/C No. must be attached to the drafts.

선적일 전에 운송 선박명, 선적 일자, 포장 수, 선적될 수량, 환어음 금액 및 신용장 번호를 통지한 수익자가 증명한 텔렉스 또는 팩스 사본이 환어음에 첨부되어야 합니다.

• All negotiable set of B/L *made* out to order must *be endorsed in blank* by the shipper.

지시인 앞으로 발행된 모든 유통 가능한 선하증권은 선적인(송하인)에 의해 백지 배서되어야 합니다.

• *A tolerance of 5% more or less* in amount and quantity is acceptable.

금액 및 수량에 있어서 5%의 과부족이 허용됩니다.

- A certificate from steamship company certifying that carrying vessel is *neither* Israeli owned *nor* registered and does not call at any Israeli ports and is not on the Israeli blacklist.
운송 선박이 이스라엘 소유도 아니며, 국적도 이스라엘이 아니고, 이스라엘 항구에 들르지 않으며, 이스라엘 블랙리스트(요사찰인 명부)에 있지 않다는 것을 증명하는 선박 회사가 발행하는 증명서

- This credit is available *with* Hanvit Bank *by* payment (at sight) (against the documents detailed herein).
본 신용장은 한빛은행에서 (명시된 서류를 제시하면) 즉시 (일람불로) 대금이 지급됩니다(지급신용장의 경우).

- This credit is available *with* Shinhan Bank *by* (deferred) payment at 90 days after the date of shipment (against the documents detailed herein).
본 신용장은 신한은행에서 (명시된 서류를 제시하면) 선적일 후 90일에 대금이 연지급됩니다(연지급신용장의 경우).

- This credit is available *with* Shinhan Bank *by* acceptance of beneficiary's drafts at 90 days after sight drawn on Shinhan Bank for full invoice value (against the documents detailed herein).

본 신용장은 수익자가 상업송장 금액 전액에 대하여 신한은행 앞으로 발행된 일람 후 90일에 대금이 결제되는 환어음을 (명시된 서류와 함께) 신한은행에 제시하면 환어음이 인수됩니다(인수신용장의 경우).

- This credit is available *with* any bank *by* negotiation of beneficiary's drafts at sight drawn on us for full invoice value (against the documents detailed herein).

본 신용장은 수익자가 상업송장 금액 전액에 대해 개설은행 앞으로 발행된 일람 즉시 대금이 결제되는 (일람불) 환어음을 (명시된 서류와 함께) 어떤 은행에나 제시하면 매입(네고)됩니다(일람불매입신용장의 경우).

- This credit is available *with* any bank *by* negotiation of beneficiary's drafts at 90 days after sight drawn on us for full invoice value (against the documents detailed herein).

본 신용장은 수익자가 상업송장 금액 전액에 대해 개설 은행 앞으로 발행된 일람 후 90일에 대금이 결제되는 (기한부) 환어음을 (명시된 서류와 함께) 어떤 은행에나 제시하면 매입(네고)됩니다(기한부매입신용장의 경우).

- We hereby issue an irrevocable documentary Letter of Credit in your favour available with any bank by negotiation of your drafts at 90 days after sight drawn on us.

당행은 귀사를 수익자로 하고 당행 앞으로 일람 후 90일에 대금이 결제되는 조건의 귀사 (발행) 환어음으로 어떤 은행에서든 매입(네고)이 가능한 취소불능화환신용장을 개설합니다.

- The Bill of Lading must indicate that the goods were boarded on the carrying vessel not later than December 31, 2020.

  선하증권은 화물이 2020년 12월 31일 이전에 운송 선박에 본선 적재되었다는 것을 표시하여야 합니다.

- Partial shipments is prohibited and transshipment are permitted.

  분할 선적은 금지되고, 환적은 허용됩니다.

- The amount of each draft drawn under this credit and the date of negotiation must be endorsed on the reverse of this credit by the negotiating bank.

  본 신용장에 근거하여 발행된 각 환어음 금액과 매입(네고) 일자가 매입(네고) 은행에 의해 본 신용장 뒷면에 배서되어 있어야 합니다.

선적에 관한 무역통신문

선적 절차

수출 통관 절차가 끝나면 드디어 선적하게 되는데, 선적 절차는 다음과 같다.

먼저 수출상은 출항예정표(Shipping Schedule)를 입수하여 최종 선적 기일 약 2주 전에 선박 회사에 선적요청서(Shipping Request)를 제출하여 선적 예약(Space Booking)을 한다.

그 후 세관으로부터 수출 물품의 통관을 완료하여 수출신고필증을 받으면 수출 통관된 물품을 선적항까지 운송한다. 수출 물품이 선적항에 도착하면 선박 회사에 수출신고필증을 제시하고, 선박 회사는 수출신고필증의 진위를 확인한 후, 수출 물품을 인수 또는 선적하고 드디어 선하증권(B/L)을 발급함으로써 선적 절차는 완료된다.

선적 절차

구분	내용
선적 예약	• Shipping Schedule 입수 후 선사에 S/R(Shipping Request : 선적요청서)을 제출하여 Space Booking(선적 예약)을 함.
내륙 운송	• 수출신고필 후 수출 통관된 물품을 선사가 지정한 장소까지 내륙 운송함.
화물 인도 · 선적 B/L 발행	• 재래식 화물 ① 선사에 물품 인도 : 수출신고필증 제시 ② 본선 적재 지시 : S/O(Shipping Order : 선적지시서) 발급 ③ 본선 적재 완료 : M/R(Mate's Receipt : 본선수취증) 발급 ④ B/L(Bill of Lading : 선하증권) 발행 : Shipped B/L(선적선하증권) • 컨테이너 화물 ① 선사에 물품 인도 : 수출신고필증 제시 ② 부두에서 물품 인수 : D/R(Dock Receipt : 부두인수증) 발급 ③ B/L 발행 : Received B/L(수취선하증권) ④ 본선 적재 ⑤ Received B/L에 On Board Notation(본선 적재 표시) : On Board B/L(본선적재선하증권)

주) 컨테이너 화물이라도 위의 재래식 화물과 마찬가지로 본선 적재 완료 후 Shipped B/L을 발행하는 경우가 있음.

[샘플 11] 선적 예약(Space Booking)

August 1, 2020

Hyundai Shipping Co., Ltd.
123 Samsung-dong, Gangnam-gu
Seoul 06170, Korea

Gentlemen :

    Will you be kind enough to reserve space of 8 CBM[1] on the m/s "Acacia" which is scheduled to sail from Pusan on August 20.

    The goods are four cases of our Porcelain Tea Set B, which will be warehoused by August 10 by our shipping agents, Multi Forwarding Co., Ltd.

    We are informed that there is a rising tendency in freight rate, and we are grateful to you for giving us your usual rate of US$50.00 per CBM.

    Your immediate confirmation would be greatly appreciated.

Yours faithfully,

HANKUK TRADING CO., LTD.
Si-Hak Oh
Si-Hak Oh, Export Manager

해설

※ 이 샘플은 수출상이 선사에 도자기 커피 세트를 선적 예약하는 예문이다.
  1) CBM : Cubic Meters의 약어(= m^3)

[샘플 12] 선적통지

August 20, 2020

Pacific Trading Co., Inc.
30 Water Street, New York
N.Y. 10003, U.S.A.

Gentlemen :

    We are pleased to advise you that your order for four hundred (400) dozen Porcelain Tea Set B was shipped on August 19 by the m/s "Arirang" which left here today.

    You will find enclosed a nonnegotiable copy[1] of B/L and copies of Marine Insurance Policy and our Invoice No. 499.

    Against this shipment we have drawn a draft on your bank[2] at 30 d/s for US$ 3,800 under L/C No. 10001, with documents attached,[3] and have negotiated it through[4] The Bank of Hanvit, Ltd., Seoul. We wish you would honor it upon presentation.[5]

    We trust that the goods will reach you in good order[6] and give you complete satisfaction.

                                 Yours very truly,

                                 HANKUK TRADING CO., LTD.

                               In-Ho Kim
                               In-Ho Kim, Export Manager

Incls. 1 Copy of B/L
      1 Copy of Marine Insurance Policy
      1 Copy of Invoice

해설

※ 이 샘플은 선적 후 선적 관련 서류를 동봉하여 선적통지를 하면서 네고(매입) 사실을 통보해주는 예문이다.

1) nonnegotiable copy : 양도 불능(유통 불능) 사본
2) have drawn a draft on your bank : 귀사 거래은행 앞으로 환어음을 발행하다
   (cf) Drawee : 환어음 지급인, Drawer : 환어음 발행인
3) with documents attached : 첨부된 선적서류와 함께
4) have negotiated it through : ~에 환어음을 네고(매입)하다
5) We wish you would honor it upon presentation : 환어음을 제시하자마자 귀사가 동 환어음을 결제하기를 바란다
6) in good order : 양호한 상태로(= in good condition)

[샘플 13] 선적통지

October 10, 2020

China Import Corporation
P. O. Box 95 Er-Li-Gou, Xi Jiao
Beijing, China

Dear Sirs,

<u>Shipment : Order No. 85EX-612</u>

    We are pleased to inform you that we shipped the following goods on October 10, by the m.s. "Neptune" of the East Asia Line as per enclosed copies of the relative shipping documents :

85EX-612
KOREA STEEL
SHANGHAI
BOX NOS. 1-70
MADE IN KOREA

70 bundles(92,257kgs) of
Seamless Carbon Steel Tubes
Covering your order
No. 85EX-612 of 21st June, 2020

To cover this shipment[1] we negotiated our draft through Hanvit Bank, Ltd., Seoul, Korea under the L/C No. A 36418 issued by Bank of China, Beijing and please honor[2] our draft upon presentation.[3]

We trust that the goods will reach you in good order and give you complete satisfaction so that you may favour us with further orders.

Yours faithfully,

KOREA STEEL CO., LTD.

Si-Hak Oh

Si-Hak Oh, President

Encls. 3 Invoices
     4 B/L copies
     4 Copies of Insurance Policy
     3 Packing Lists
     1 Letter of Attesting(Nationality of the Vessel)
     1 Certified Copy of Fax dispatched to you reporting the details of the shipment
     1 Mill Sheet(Inspection Certificate)

해설

※이 샘플은 선적 후 선적 관련 서류를 동봉하며 선적통지를 하는 예문이다.

1) To cover this shipment : 이 선적품에 대한 대금 회수를 위해
2) hono(u)r : 어음대금을 결제하다(= protect)
   (cf) 환어음의 종류에는 일람불환어음(sight bill of exchange)과 기한부환어음 (usance or time bill of exchange)이 있다.
3) presentation : 제시, 제출

[샘플 14] 선적, 포장, 하인 및 어음 발행 통지

Gentlemen :

Your Order No. 123 of May 15

We are pleased to inform you that the Transistor Radios have now been shipped to you as specified below[1] :

Packing : In 15 cases, 4 radios in a case.[2]
Marking & Numbering[3] : HTH in circle Los Angeles. Particulars[4] of weight and measurement[5] are given in the enclosed sheet.
Shipment : By s.s. "Arirang"of KSC Line, which sailed from Pusan on June 3, and is scheduled to arrive at Los Angeles on June 20.

A complete set[6] of Bills of Lading, together with Invoice and Insurance Certificate,[7] both in triplicate,[8] have been given to Hanvit Bank with sight draft[9] for US$ 2,000 under the terms of[10] the Letter of

Credit. We have received the sum[11] from the said bank.

We should appreciate your information on the arrival of the consignment.[12]

Very truly yours,

해설

※ 이 샘플은 선적통지를 하며 포장·하인·네고(환어음 매입) 사실도 함께 통보하는 예문이다.

1) as specified below : 하기에 명기한 대로
2) in a case : 1상자당
3) marking and numbering : 하인과 번호를 붙임
4) particulars : 명세
5) measurement : 치수
6) a complete set : 한 벌
7) Insurance Certificate : 보험증(명)서
8) in triplicate : 3통
9) sight draft : 일람출급어음
10) under the terms of : ~의 조건으로
11) sum : 총액
12) consignment : 인도품

[샘플 15] 선적지연통지

Dear Sirs,

<u>Your Order No. 501</u>

We greatly regret[1] to inform you that an accident in the machines of our maker's factory has made it impossible for us to ship the goods on your Order No. 501 by 30th September as arranged.[2]

Therefore, we are asking you to allow the postponement of shipment till the 8th of October. The goods will be sent out by a direct steamer[3] leaving our port on that day.

We trust that such a failure will not occur in future.

Yours faithfully,

해설

※이 샘플은 제조업체 공장의 기계 고장으로 선적 기일을 지키지 못하여 선적 기일을 연장 요청하는 예문이다.
1) regret : 유감으로 생각하다
2) as arranged : 협의된 바와 같이
3) direct steamer : 직항선(直航船)

[샘플 16] 선적 지연에 따른 분할 선적 허용 요청

10th December, 2020

Richard Hunt & Co. (Pty.) Ltd.
P. O. Box 7784
Johannesburg 2000
South Africa

Dear Sirs,

<u>Order Nos. 103 and 105</u>

We are sorry to inform you that it has become very difficult to complete shipment during January of your Order Nos. 103 and 105.

According to the manufacturers, all the recent orders including these two from you were booked on the basis of their expansion plan, a 20% increase in production by putting[1] a fully automated finishing line in operation[2] at the beginning of next year.

Contrary to their expectation, the new equipment arrived at their factory two weeks behind the schedule, and this is very likely to affect all the January shipments.

They say that the existing line[3] has been running at full capacity[4] as a stopgap[5] but some delay would be unavoidable. We ask you, therefore, to approve partial shipments, that is, one half of each indent in January and the other half in February.

Though the delay is beyond our control,[6] we are no less sorry for it and shall be obliged if you will kindly understand the situation and obtain your clients'[7] consent.

Yours faithfully,

KOREA TRADING CO., LTD.

Si-Hak Oh

Si-Hak Oh, Manager
Steel Department

해설

※ 이 샘플은 공장 확장 계획이 약 2주간 지연됨에 따라 선적 기일을 지키지 못하게 되어 2회 분할 선적을 허용해줄 것을 요청하는 예문이다.

1) putting : 가동하다
2) finishing line in operation : 최종 공정 설비
3) existing line : 기존 설비, 현 설비
4) running at full capacity : 전력을 다해 조업하다
5) as a stopgap : 임시변통으로, 미봉책으로
6) beyond our control : 당사가 통제할 수 없는, 즉 불가항력의
7) clients' : 고객들의(= customers')

[샘플 17] 선적지연통지

Dear Sirs,

<u>Your Order No. EPT-3178/D of August 16</u>

Further to your above-mentioned order, we informed you last Monday by telex that we had booked freight space on[1] the S.S. ATLAS.

We regret to say that owing to the longshoremen's strike[2] toward the end of this month we will not be able to effect shipment on the bove by the stipulated time.

Under the circumstances,[3] we will re-book[4] on the first available ship after the strike, which at present seems to be the S.S. QUEEN sailing from London around December 5.

We hope you will fully understand the situation.

Your faithfully,

해설

※ 이 샘플은 항만 노동자들의 파업으로 선적이 지연됨을 통지하는 예문이다.

1) book freight space on : 선박을 예약하다
2) longshoremen's strike : 항만 노동자들의 파업
3) Under the circumstances : 이러한 사정으로
4) re-book : 재예약하다

[샘플 18] 상업송장

HANKUK TRADING CO., LTD.
345 Dobong-dong, Dobong-gu, Seoul, Korea
TEL+82-2-551-1234 FAX+82-2-551-1235

August 20, 2020

COMMERCIAL INVOICE No. 499

INVOICE of Four(4) Cases (400dozen) of Porcelain Tea Set B

Description	Quantity	Unit Price	Amount
Porcelain Tea Set B	400 doz.	CIF New York US$ 9.50 per doz.	US$ 3,800.00

SOLD to   The Pacific Trading Co., Inc.
          30 Water Street, New York
          N.Y. 10003. U.S.A.
SHIPPED   per m/s "Arirang"
          On August 19, 2020
          From Pusan
          To New York, via Panama

⟨ PT ⟩
NEW YORK
via Panama
C/# 1/4
MADE IN KOREA

HANKUK TRADING CO., LTD.
Si-Hak Oh
Si-Hak Oh, Export Manager

[샘플 19] **상업송장**

HANKUK STEEL CO., LTD.
Central P. O. Box 123
Seoul 06170, Korea

October 11, 2020

COMMERCIAL INVOICE No. G-225

INVOICE of 92.006 M/T of Seamless Carbon Steel Tubes **shipped per** M/S "Neptune" **from** Busan **to** Shanghai **for account and risk of** China Import Corporation, P.O. Box 95 Er-Li-Gou, Xi Jiao, Beijing, China **by the undersigned against** Order No. 85EX-612 **dated** June 21, 2020

Marks & Nos.	Descriptions	Quantity	Unit Price	Amount
C.N.I.C 85EX-612 HANKUK STEEL SHANGHAI B/NOS. 1-70 MADE IN KOREA	Seamless Carbon Steel Tubes KS G 3445, STKM-11A Size(mm) 139.7×14 86 pcs. 152.4×10 123 pcs. Total : Length 6-12m but all nearly 11m	M/T 40.785 51.221 92.006	per M/T US$ 400 US$ 396	CIF Shanghai US$ 16,314.00 US$ 20,283.52 US$ 36,597.52

Manufacturers : Hankuk Steel Corporation, Seoul
Net Weight   : 92,006 kgs
Gross Weight : 92,257 kgs
Measurement   : 67.039 m³

Packing	: Strapped in 70 bundles weighing 1,000 to 1,500 kgs. each, with three metalic tags and oiled

Insured with The Pacific Fire & Marine Insurance Co., Ltd. Tokyo **for** US$ 40,257.27
L/C No. A36418 **issued by** Bank of China, Beijing
Draft drawn through Shinhan Bank, Ltd., Seoul

HANKUK STEEL CO., LTD.

Si-Hak Oh

Si-Hak Oh, President

[샘플 20] 상업송장

COMMERCIAL INVOICE

Seller	SAMSUNG TRADING CO., LTD. 123 Samsung-dong, Gangnam-gu Seoul 06170, Korea		Invoice No. and date 8905 BK 1007 May 20, 2020
Buyer	MONACH PRODUCTS CO., LTD. 520 Anthony St., Seattle Washington, U.S.A.		L/C No. and date 55352 APRIL 25, 2020
	Consignee To order of Citi Bank		Other references COUNTRY OF ORIGIN : REPUBLIC OF KOREA
	Notify MONACH PRODUCTS CO., LTD. 520 Anthony St., Seattle Washington, U.S.A.		
	Departure date : May 20, 2020 Vessel/Flight : PHEONIC From : PUSAN PORT, KOREA To : SEATTLE PORT, U.S.A.		Terms of delivery and payment FOB PUSAN PORT L/C AT SIGHT

Shipping marks	No. & kind of packages	Goods description	Quantity	Unit price	Amount
MON/T 0858	420 DP X 420D MATERIAL. AS PER MONARCH PRODUCTS ORDER NO. T. 858	NYLON OXFORD	60,000M 1,208.06KGS.	US$1.00/M	US$60,000.00

SAMSUNG TRADING CO., LTD.

Si-Hak Oh

Si-Hak Oh, President

[샘플 21] 포장명세서

PACKING LIST

Seller	**SAMSUNG TRADING CO., LTD.** 123 Samsung-dong, Gangnam-gu Seoul 06170, Korea	Invoice No. and date 8905 BK 1007 May 20, 2020	
Buyer	**MONACH PRODUCTS CO., LTD.** 520 Anthony St., Seattle Washington, U.S.A.	L/C No. and date 55352 APRIL 25, 2020	
Consignee To order of Citi Bank		Other references COUNTRY OF ORIGIN : REPUBLIC OF KOREA	
Notify MONACH PRODUCTS CO., LTD. 520 Anthony St., Seattle Washington, U.S.A.			
Departure date : May 20, 2020 Vessel/Flight : PHEONIC From : PUSAN PORT, KOREA To : SEATTLE PORT, U.S.A.			

Shipping marks	No. & kind of packages	Goods description	Quantity or Net weight	Gross weight	Measurement
MON/T 0858	420 DP X 420D MATERIAL. AS PER MONARCH PRODUCTS ORDER NO. T. 858	NYLON OXFORD	60,000M 1,208.06KGS.	1,250.00KGS.	9,000CBM

SAMSUNG TRADING CO., LTD.

Si-Hak Oh

Si-Hak Oh, President

선적에 관한 유용한 표현

- We *regret to inform* you that the sailing of S/S ARIRANG, by which your order No. 10 was to be shipped, has suddenly been cancelled.

  당사는 유감스럽게도 귀사의 주문번호 10이 선적될 아리랑호의 출항이 갑작스럽게 취소되었음을 알려드립니다.

- These goods were delayed in reaching us from the factory, and then *shut out* of M/S ARIRANG. They will now leave by M/S DORAGI due to sail on the 14th unless you let us know to the contrary.

  이들 제품이 공장에서 당사에 도착이 지연되어 아리랑호에 선적되지 못하였습니다. 그 화물은 이제 귀사가 당사에 반대 의사를 알리지 않는 한 14일에 출항할 예정인 도라지호로 떠나게 될 것입니다.

- The delay in shipment *is* entirely *due to* the delay on your part in *furnishing* us *with* the L/C and the shipping instructions.

  선적 지연은 귀사 측이 당사에 신용장과 선적통지를 지연한 것에 전적으로 기인한 것입니다.

- We are sorry that you have been put to a great deal of inconvenience by this delay, but it was a case of *force majeure* as you will see in the enclosed certificate of the Korean Chamber of Commerce and Industry.

  당사는 귀사가 이 지연으로 많은 불편을 겪은 것에 대하여 사죄합니다. 그러나 이 지연은 동봉한 대한상공회의소의 증명서에서 보듯이 불가항력의 경우입니다.

- We trust that the goods will reach you *in good condition* and prove to be a great satisfaction to you.

  당사는 그 화물이 양호한 상태로 도착하여 귀사에 큰 만족을 주리라 믿습니다.

- We wish you to ship our goods by the next vessel *bound for* London.

  당사는 귀사가 당사의 상품을 런던을 향해서 떠나기로 되어 있는 다음 선편에 선적하기를 바랍니다.

- We *are awaiting* your shipping instructions for this order.

  당사는 이 주문에 대한 귀사의 선적 지시를 기다립니다.

- *Please be advised(We inform you)* that your order has been shipped by the m/s "Mary".
  귀사의 주문품이 메리호에 선적되었음을 알려드립니다.

- *We are arranging* to ship your order by the m/s "Orient"
  당사는 귀사의 주문품을 오리엔트호에 선적하도록 수배하고 있습니다.

- *Owing to* the strike of longshoremen *at this end* we are unable to make shipment of your order by the stipulated date.
  이 지역 항만 노동자들의 파업으로 당사가 지정한 날짜까지 귀사의 주문품을 선적할 수 없습니다.

- *Be sure to inform us of* the exact date of shipment of our order as soon as it is determined.
  당사 주문품의 정확한 선적일이 결정되자마자 그 날짜를 당사에 틀림없이 통지해주십시오.

- *In reply to* your inquiry we are pleased to quote you US$50.00 per CBM.
  귀사의 조회에 답하여 당사는 귀사에 입방미터당 미화 50달러로 가격을 제시합니다.

- *According to* our contract with you, we have arranged to ship your order by the m/s "Orient", *sailing from* Pusan about October 10.
당사는 귀사와 계약한 바와 같이 귀사의 주문품을 10월 30일경 부산을 출발하는 오리엔트호로 선적할 것을 수배하였습니다.

- We enclose copies of shipping documents covering this order.
당사는 이 주문에 대한 선적서류 사본을 동봉합니다.

- We have sent you by airmail a sample of the article.
당사는 귀사에 그 제품의 샘플을 항공편으로 보냈습니다.

- We have arranged to reserve a space of 10 metric tons on a direct steamer *bound for* your port
당사는 귀사의 항구를 향해서 떠나기로 되어 있는 직항선에 10미터톤의 선복을 예약해놓았습니다.

- Fifty units of Computer on your order of February 10 have been shipped on the s/s "Santamo" *scheduled to leave* Pusan on March 20.

2월 10일 자 귀사의 주문품인 컴퓨터 50대가 3월 20일 부산을 출항하기로 되어 있는 산타모호에 선적되었습니다.

- We are sure that these goods will meet your requirements, and *look forward to* receiving prompt instructions from you.

당사는 이들 제품이 귀사의 요구 조건들을 충족시킬 것으로 확신하며, 귀사로부터 신속한 지시를 받기를 기대합니다.

- Our articles are packed in cases in such a manner that movement inside the cases is impossible.

당사의 제품은 상자 내에서 이동이 불가능하도록 포장되어 있습니다.

- We have to inform you that the goods shipped on board the "Sakura" on May 14 reached us two weeks later than schedule.

5월 14일 사쿠라호에 본선 적재된 화물이 스케줄보다 2주 늦게 당사에 도착하였음을 알려드립니다.

- Our stock is rapidly running low, so we wish you to make

shipment of our order as soon as possible.

당사의 재고가 급속히 감소하고 있어 당사는 귀사가 당사의 주문품을 가능한 한 빨리 선적해주시길 바랍니다.

- Shipment must *be effected* by November 30 *at the latest.*

늦어도 11월 30일까지 선적되어야 합니다.

- We are pleased to inform you that your order *is* now ready for shipment, and await your shipping instructions.

당사는 귀사의 주문품이 이제 선적될 준비가 되어 있음을 통보하며 귀사의 선적 지시를 기다립니다.

- As this article is to be displayed at retail shops around July 10, please ship it out by the end of *May at the latest.*

이 제품은 7월 10일경에 소매점에 전시될 예정이므로 늦어도 5월 말일까지 선적해주시기 바랍니다.

- Your order was cleared through our customs without any difficulty.

귀사의 주문은 아무 어려움 없이 우리 세관을 통관했습니다.

- We are thinking of *making shipment* of 150 units of the personal computer you ordered on August 30 by the "Arirang" leaving Pusan on October 25.

  당사는 귀사가 8월 30일 주문한 개인용 컴퓨터 150대를 10월 25일에 부산을 출발하는 아리랑호에 선적할 것을 고려하고 있습니다.

- All the goods *on* your order have been completed(finished) and are ready for shipment(dispatch).

  귀사가 주문한 모든 제품은 완료되어 선적할 준비가 되어 있습니다.

- *As to* your order, we are now arranging to make shipment by the "Queen" which *is scheduled to* leave Pusan toward(in, about) the middle of next month.

  귀사의 주문에 대해 이제 당사는 다음 달 중순(11~20일)에 부산을 출항 예정인 퀸호에 선적할 것을 수배하고 있습니다.

- We will take special care to see that the goods be packed as per your instructions.

  당사는 그 제품이 귀사의 지시에 따라 포장되도록 특별한 배려를 하겠습니다.

- The goods on your order(you ordered) will be shipped by the "Arirang" (which is) scheduled to leave our port on December 9.

  귀사가 주문한 제품은 12월 9일 당사의 항구를 출항할 예정인 아리랑호에 선적될 것입니다.

- We have reserved a space of 20 metric tons on a direct vessel for Hamburg.

  당사는 함부르크행 직항선에 20미터톤의 선복을 예약하였습니다.

- *Half (of) the order* can be shipped(sent out) at the end of July, and *the other half(the remainder, the balance)* at the end of August.

  주문품의 절반은 7월 하순(21~31일)에 선적될 수 있으며, 나머지 절반은 8월 하순(21~31일)에 선적될 수 있습니다.

- As the goods are breakable, we require them to be sent by air.

  그 제품은 파손되기 쉬우므로 당사는 그 제품을 항공편으로 보내도록 요구합니다.

- The shortage of *shipping space(ship's space)* has brought about a considerable rise in ocean freight rate.
  선복의 부족으로 해상 운임이 상당히 인상되었습니다.

- *Since(As) the goods(articles, items)* are fragile(easy to break), we wish you to send them by air.
  그 제품은 파손되기 쉬우므로 당사는 귀사가 그 제품을 항공편으로 보내기를 바랍니다.

- The goods were packed strictly *in accordance with* your instructions.
  그 상품은 귀사의 지시에 따라 엄격히 포장되었습니다.

- We will send you the goods you *desired(wished for)* by air freight upon their completion(as soon as they are completed).
  당사는 귀사가 원하는 제품을 완성되자마자 항공편으로 보내드리겠습니다.

- Please send us *one copy of* Bill of Lading as soon as you ship the goods stipulated.
  귀사가 당해 제품을 선적하자마자 선하증권 사본 한 부를 보내주십시오.

- We hope the goods will reach you in safety and *come up to your expectation*.

  당사는 그 제품이 귀사에 안전하게 도착하여 귀사의 기대에 일치하기를 바랍니다.

- The sewing machines are wrapped in stout water-proof material, and packed in a wooden case.

  재봉틀이 질긴 방수재로 감싸 있고 나무상자에 포장되어 있습니다.

- Overall measurements of each case must not exceed 80cm(Length)×50cm(Width)×40cm(Depth).

  각 상자는 80cm(길이)×50cm(폭)×40cm(깊이)를 초과해서는 안 됩니다.

- As requested, we have perfectly carried out *marking* and *numbering* on all cases.

  귀사가 요청한 바와 같이, 당사는 모든 상자에 마크 및 번호를 완벽히 부여하였습니다.

- The goods *are* already *on their way* and the documents were given to the Hanvit Bank.
그 화물은 이미 운송 중이며, 서류는 한빛은행에 보냈습니다.

운송 및 포장 관련 용어

운송 관련 용어

Conventional Ship : 재래선

Sigle-purpose Ship : 전용선

Pure Car Carrier : 자동차 전용선

Heavy Lifter : 중량물 전용선

Crude Oil Tanker : 유조선(원유 전용선)

Bulk Carrier : 산적화물(Bulk Cargo) 전용선

Multi-purpose Ship : 다목적선

LASH(Lighter Aboard Ship) : LASH선

Semi-container : 세미컨테이너선

Ro/Ro(Roll-on / Roll-off) : Ro/Ro선

Lo/Lo(Lift-on / Lift-off) : Lo/Lo선

포장 관련 용어

- '포장하다'의 영문 표기
  Make-up, Package, Packaging, Packing
  Inner Packing : 내부 포장
  Outer Packing : 외부 포장

- 포장의 형태
  Wooden Case : 나무상자
  Carton Box : 종이상자
  Bale : 포대
  Barrel, Cask, Keg : 통
  Crate : 바구니 모양의 격자 상자

화인 및 취급주의 표시

화인(Cargo Mark) 표시

○　Circle(원형)
□　Square(정방형)

△ Triangle(삼각형)

◇ Diamond(마름모형)

⬯ Oval(타원형)

☆ Star(별형)

▭ Rectangle(직사각형, 장방형)

✚ Cross(십자형)

⊖ Bisected Circle(원일자형)

⊕ Cross in Circle(원십자형)

⬖ Cross in Diamond(마름모십자형)

✢ Projecting Diamond(불쑥 내민 마름모형)

✡ Double Triangles(이중삼각형)

⧖ Hourglass(모래시계형)

⁂ Three Diamond(세마름모형)

♯ Intersecting Parallels(우물정자형)

♡ Heart(심장형)

∧ Angle(산형)

☾ Moon(초생달형)

✣ Circle in Projecting Diamond(불쑥 내민 마름모 원형)

◎ Double Circles(이중원형)

◬ Triangle in Circle(원삼각형)

⍉ T.s. Mixed(T.s. 겹친형, T.s. 중복형)

ⓢ Sin Pentagon(오각 S형)

화인 표시의 예

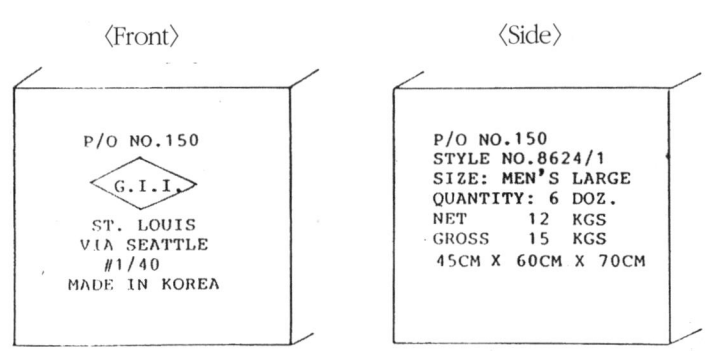

취급주의(Care Marks) 표시

ACID WITH CARE : 산(酸) 주의

DON'T STOW BELOW ANOTHER CARGO : 하적 금지

DON'T THROW : 던지기 엄금

DON'T TURN OVER : 전도(轉倒) 금지

DO NOT DROP : 낙하 금지

DO NOT STOW ON DECK : 갑판에 놓지 못함

FRAGILE : 부서지기 쉬운 물건(파손주의)

GLASS WITH CARE : 유리 주의

GUARD AGAINST DAMP : 습기 엄금

HANDLE WITH CARE : 취급 주의

INFLAMMABLE : 가연물

KEEP COOL : 냉소(冷所) 보관

KEEP DRY : 젖은 물건 주의

KEEP FLAT : 평평하게 놓음

KEEP UPRIGHT : 세로로 놓음

LIFT HERE : 이곳을 올림

LIQUID : 액체

NEVER LAY FLAT : 평적(平積) 금지

OPEN THIS END : 여기를 엶

PERISHABLE : 부패하기 쉬움

STOW AWAY FROM HEAT : 화기 엄금

THIS SIDE UP : 상하 바로 놓음

TOP : 이 방향이 위

USE NO HOOKS : 갈고리 사용 금지

해상 보험에 관한 무역통신문

해상 보험은 왜 부보할까?

B/L 약관상 운송인은 화물 운송 중 운송인의 취급 부주의로 인한 상업 과실(Commercial Loss)에 대해서만 화주에게 손해배상 책임을 지며, 운송인이 좌우할 수 없는 해상손해(Marine Loss)에 대해서는 면책된다고 규정하고 있다.

따라서 화주가 해상손해를 보상받기 위해서는 해상적하보험(Marine Cargo Insurance)을 부보하여야 한다.

[샘플 22] 해상적하보험 청약

August 2, 2020

Samsung Marine & Fire Insurance Co., Ltd.
123 Samsung-dong, Gangnam-gu
Seoul 01670, Korea

Gentlemen :

In confirmation of[1] our conversation by telephone this morning, we enclose an application[2] for Marine Cargo Insurance Contract[3] on four hundred (400) dozen of our Porcelain Tea Set B.

We hope that you will be good enough to make out the Insurance Policy and copies as mentioned in the Application and send them to us as soon as possible.

Yours truly,

HANKUK TRADING CO., LTD.

Sang-Won Lee
Sang-Won Lee, Export Manager

Inc. 1 Application for Marine Cargo Insurance

해설

※ 이 샘플은 보험회사에 해상적하보험을 청약하는 예문이다.

1) In confirmation of ~ : ~을 확인하기 위하여
2) application : 청약서
3) Marine Cargo Insurance Contract : 해상적하보험계약

[샘플 23] 해상적하보험 청약

Gentlemen :

This is to confirm our instructions via telephone yesterday. As per copy enclosed, we shall be pleased if you will effect insurance[1] for us subject to ICC(B)[2] on US$10,000 value of 100 cases canned provisions, to be shippd from Busan port on the S.S. ARIRANG sailing for Los Angeles port on or about[3] July 25.

Would you please send[4] us the insurance policy, together with the statement of premium due[5] soon.

Your prompt attention to this matter would be much appreciate :

Very truly yours,

해설

※ 이 샘플은 보험회사에 해상적하보험을 청약하는 예문이다.

1) effect insurance : 보험에 들다, 부보하다
2) ICC(B) : 협회적하약관(B)
3) on or about : ~경
4) Would you please send : 정중한 의뢰
5) the statement of premium due : 보험료명세서

[샘플 24] 보험료 문의

Gentlemen :

　　Please quote us your rate for Marine Cargo Insurance,[1] ICC(B) including war and strikes risks, on a shipment of 10 cases of cotton goods, valued at[2] US$30,000 by the s/s "Arirang" from Busan portto Hong Kong port.

　　The ship will sail from Busan port on 2nd September, and we hope to have your reply by return.[3]

　　　　　　　　　　　　　　　　Yours truly,

해설

※이 샘플은 보험회사에 면제품에 대한 해상적하보험료 요율을 문의하는 예문이다.
1) Please quote us your rate for Marine Insurance ~ : ~에 대한 조건의 해상보험료를 알려주십시오
2) value at : 가격에 대해
3) by return : 회신 편에

[샘플 25] 보험료 문의에 대한 회답

Gentlemen :

In response to your inquiry of 27th of this month, we wish to quote you the rate of Marine Cargo Insurance at 0.315 percent, ICC(B) including war risk, on the shipment referred to in[1] your letter.

This is exceptionally low rate, because many of the insurance companies will hesitate to take the risk at any premium whatever[2] dreading the heavy average[3] to which they are exposed on the South China Sea.

We hope that you will pass us your business.

Yours very truly,

해설

※ 이 샘플은 보험료 문의에 대한 회답 예문이다.

1) referred to in : ~에서 언급한
2) hesitate to take the risk at any premium whatever : 보험료가 많고 적고 간에 위험 인수를 주저한다
3) dreading the heavy average : 대해손(大海損)을 두려워하여

[샘플 26] 보험금의 지급

Gentlemen :

We have received your letter of May 26, regarding 600 bags damaged[1] Rice by s.s. "Arirang". We have pleasure in enclosing you a check for US$18,000 in settlement of[2] your claim.[3] We shall be glad to have your receipt[4] in due course.[5]

Yours very truly,

해설

※ 이 샘플은 보험금의 지급을 통지하며 영수증을 요청하는 예문이다.

1) damaged : 손상된
2) in settlement of : ~의 지급을 위하여
3) claim : 손해배상금
4) receipt : 영수증
5) in due course : 지체 없이, 정히

[샘플 27] 보험금 청구 서한

April 15, 2020

Samsung Marine & Fire Insurance Co., Ltd.
Samsung Insurance Bldg.,
123 Samsung-dong, Gangnam-gu
Seoul 101670, Korea

Attn. : Mr. Y. S. Jang / Marine Claim Section

Dear Sirs/Madam,

NOTIFICATION OF MISSINGING CARGO

MAWB	: 180-3682 2402
FLIGHT	: KE 631/27-3-20
NO. PACKAGE	: 1 SKD(15 CARTONS)-150 PCS
CONTENT	: SAMSUNG HARD DISK DRIVE,
MODEL	: SHD-3172A

We, Yoku Systems Pte Ltd, are cargo consignee[1] of MAWB 180-3682 2402 which was shipped by Samsung Corporation through Korean Airline KE631 and arrived at Changi Airport, Singapore on 27 March 2020 at 21:30 hours and this cargo's invoice(No. CI466940323041) value is US$ 63,300.00.

We received 1 SKD made up of[2] 15 cartons which is 150 pcs only. The value we received is US$31,650.00. The other balance of 1 SKD, 15 cartons(150PCS) was missing.[3]

On 29 March 2020, we were informed by our forwarder, Freight Express International Ltd. that this cargo was unlocated at Changi Airport. Immediately, we sent a fax message to the Cargo Tracing

Dept. of SATS(Singapore Airport Terminal Services Pte Ltd.) requesting a written advice on the unlocated cargo.

You are kindly requested to survey this case and to compensate our loss immediately.

For your easy reference, attached are some documents for your perusal.[4]
- Airway Bill No. 180 3682 2402
- Shipper's Invoice No. : CI466940323041
- SATS' reply fax dated 31 March 2020
- Marine Cargo Insurance policy No. OEA-948200218

Your prompt action in this matter is appreciated.

Yours truly,

Yoku Systems Pte Ltd.

Robert H. Brown
Robert H. Brown, Assistant Manager

해설

※ 이 샘플은 수입상이 보험회사에 행방불명된 화물에 대한 보험금을 청구하는 예문이다.
1) cargo consignee : 화물수하인
2) made up of : ~으로 구성된
3) be missing : 행방불명되다
4) perusal : 숙독, 정독, 통독

[샘플 28] 신용장의 보험 조건이 상이하지만 수락한다는 통보

Gentlemen :

We have received with thanks Shinhan Bank's Letter of Credit No. 23568 covering your Order No. 160, and are glad to note that everything stipulated therein[1] is quite all right except that your buyer specified that insurance is to be against ICC(A). You will doubtless recall that there is an understanding between you and us that we quote CIF prices on the basis of ICC(B), with additional clauses[2] for the buyer's account. This means that ICC(A), War and Strikes Risks are to be borne by the buyer.[3]

In this instance, we will absorb the difference[4] between ICC(B) and ICC(A), but from now on please do not fail to insert a notation[5] on your purchase note that any additional coverage other than ICC(B) shall be for the account of the buyer.

Very truly yours,

해설

※ 이 샘플은 신용장상 보험 조건이 당초 제시한 ICC(B)가 아니라 ICC(A) 및 War/Strikes Risks로 되어 있어, 이번에는 수출상이 신용장 조건대로 해주지만 다음부터는 ICC(B)로 해야 한다고 통보하는 예문이다.

1) everything stipulated therein : ~신용장에 명시된 모든 조건
2) additional clauses : 추가 적하약관
3) be borne by the buyer : 매수인에 의해 지급되다
4) absorb the difference : 차이를 부담하다
5) insert a notation : 단서를 삽입하다

해상보험에 관한 유용한 표현

- Please *insure* the silk goods, *on* ICC(C), *for* the amount of US$3,000.

  그 실크 제품을 협회적하약관(C) 조건으로 미화 3,000달러에 대하여 부보하십시오.

- Please *quote* us your rate *for* Marine cargo insurance with ICC(WA) *on* a shipment of two cases Rayon Goods.

  인조견사 제품 두 상자의 선적에 대해 협회적하약관(분손담보) 조건으로 해상적하보험에 대한 귀사의 요율을 당사에 제시해주십시오.

- *In compliance with* your instructions, we *have effected insurance with* the Samsung Marine Insurance Co., Ltd., for US$2,500 on 10 cases Sunglasses, to be shipped by the m/s "Arirang", against ICC(A).

  귀사의 지시에 따라 아리랑호에 선적될 예정인 선글라스 10상자에 대한 미화 2,000달러를 협회적하약관(A) 조건으로 삼성해상보험회사에 부보하였습니다.

- The vessel *encountered heavy weather* and *in consequence* one case was damaged by sea-water. We enclose the Survey Report and the Policy against All Risks. Kindly adjust the claim.

  그 배는 악천후를 만나서 한 상자가 해수로 손상되었습니다. 당사는 손해검정보고서와 전위험(담보 조건의) 보험증권을 동봉합니다. 클레임을 정산해주시기 바랍니다.

- We *have made Marine Cargo Insurance Contract* with the Samsung Marine Insurance Co., Ltd. as you instructed.

  당사는 귀사가 지시한 대로 삼성해상보험회사에 해상적하보험계약을 체결하였습니다

- This shipment is covered(insured) *for* 110% of the invoice amount(the invoice amount plus 10%) *against* All Risks.

  이 선적품은 전위험담보 조건으로 송장 금액의 100%에 대해 부보되었습니다.

- Please *effect insurance* on the above goods to be shipped (sent) by the "Arirang" *against* all risks.

  아리랑호에 선적 예정인 상기 (연급) 제품에 대해 전위험담보 조건

으로 보험을 부보하십시오.

- We enclose the marine cargo insurance policy for US$510,000 on wheat, by the "Arirang" from Pusan to London.
  당사는 부산에서 런던으로 가는 아리랑호에 의해 운송되는 밀 미화 51만 달러에 대한 해상적하보험을 동봉합니다.

- Please *insure against* ICC(A) *for* US$500,000 *on* the shipment by S.S. "Arirang".
  아리랑호 선적품 미화 50만 달러에 대해 협회적하약관(A)로 부보해주십시오.

- Please effect insurance on the cargo for US$10 million by s.s. "Arirang", from Pusan to Singapore.
  부산에서 싱가포르로 가는 아리랑호로 운송되는 1,000만 달러의 화물에 대해 부보해주십시오.

- Please insure the goods by s.s. "Arirang" from Incheon to Sydney, for US$20 million.
  인천에서 시드니로 가는 아리랑호에 의해 운송되는 화물에 대해 2,000만 달러로 부보해주십시오.

- Please insure against ICC(A) for US$100,000, value of one thousand sewing machines, shipped at San Francisco to Incheon.

샌프란시스코 선적 인천행의 재봉 기계 1,000대의 10만 달러에 대해 협회적하약관(A) 조건으로 부보해주십시오.

보험 관련 용어

Abandonment : 위부

All Risks(A/R) : 전위험담보

Average(Partial Loss) : 분손

Average Deposit : 해손공탁금

Average Statement : 해손정산서

Barratry : 선원의 불법행위(비행)

Cover Note : 보험승낙서

Free of(from) Particular Average(F.P.A.) : 단독해손부담보

General Average(G.A.) : 공동해손

Insurable Value : 보험가액

Insurance Broker : 보험중개인

Insurance Company(Underwriter) : 보험회사

Insurance Policy : 보험증권

Insurance Premium : 보험료

Insurance Premium Rate : 보험료율

Insured Amount(Sum) : 보험금액

Insurer : 보험업자

Jettison : 투하

Leakage : 누손

Marine Cargo Insurance : 해상보험

Particular Average(P.A.) : 단독해손

Pilferage : 발하(좀도둑)

Subject Matter Insured : (피)보험목적(물)

The Insured(Assured) : 피보험자

Total Loss(T.L.) : 전손

Total Loss Only(T.L.O.) : 전손만 담보

With Average(W.A.) : 분손담보

5장

대금 결제·클레임·
기타 무역 관련 통신문

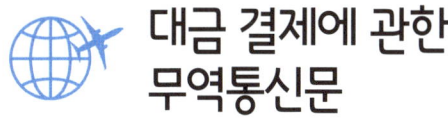
대금 결제에 관한 무역통신문

대금 회수 방법

마라톤 경기에서 결승점이 가장 중요하듯이, 무역에서도 대금 결제가 가장 중요하다. 따라서 대금 결제와 관련하여 환어음, 상업송장, 포장명세서 등의 서류를 작성할 줄 알아야 한다.

그리고 대금 결제가 제때 이루어지지 않아 대금 회수 서한을 보낼 때는 거래 및 상대 회사의 중요도에 따라 정중한 서한과 함께 청구서를 보낸다.

우편 일수를 감안하여 그때까지도 회신이나 대금 지불이 없을 때에는 재차 'Overdue, please remit' 또는 'Please remit and oblige' 또는 'Long overdue, please remit by return' 등으로 상대편의 주의를 환기시킨다.

이와 같은 서한에도 반응이 없을 때는 최종 수단으로 'The matter

will be now handed over to a solicitor, or to a Best Collection Agency'라는 서한을 제시하거나, 법적 조치를 취하지 않을 수 없다고 통고한다.

[샘플 1] 환어음

```
NO. _____      BILL OF EXCHANGE      Date: _____ Seoul, Korea
FOR   USD6,121.17
AT    XXXXXXXXXXXXXXXXXXXX  SIGHT OF THIS ORIGINAL BILL OF EXCHANGE(DUPLICATE UNPAID)
PAY TO THE ORDER OF          Shinhan Bank
THE SUM OF  SAY US DOLLARS SIX THOUSAND ONE HUNDRED TWENTY ONE AND CENTS
            SEVENTEEN ONLY.
VALUE RECEIVED AND CHARGE THE SAME TO ACCOUNT OF  BUCKLE PTY LTD
            ANZ BANKING GROUP LTD 10/20 MARTIN PLACE, SYDNEY NSW 2000,
DRAWN UNDER AUSTRALIA
L/C NO.  85374/2092                      DATED   OCT 29, 1999  CO., LTD.
TO  AUSTRALIA AND NEW ZEALAND BANKING GROUP LIMITED 10/20 MARTIN PLACE,
    SYDNEY NSW 2000 AUSTRALIA
                                             S  CHUNG  PRESIDENT
(27-0225) (20.8 × 9.3) (85.3.20) 1/2
```

해설

※ 환어음이 선적서류와 함께 발행되면 화환어음, 선적서류가 수반되지 않으면 무화환어음이라고 한다. 그리고 환어음을 일람 즉시 지급하는 것은 일람출급환어음, 발행되어 일정 기간이 지난 후 지급하는 것을 기한부환어음이라고 한다. 환어음은 보통 2통이 발행되고 그중 하나가 결제되면 나머지는 자동적으로 효력을 상실한다.

[샘플 2] 환어음

> **BILL OF EXCHANGE**[1]
>
> No. 450[2]   Seoul, Korea[3], August 20, 2020[4]
> For U.S.$ 3,800.00[5]
> At 30 days after **sight**[6] **of this FIRST of Exchange(SECOND being unpaid)**[7] **pay to** Shinhan Bank **or order**[8] **the sum of**
> Say U.S. Dollars Three Thousand Eight Hundred only.[9]
> **Value received**[10] **and charge the same to account of** PACIFIC TRADING, INC.[11]
> **Drawn under** L/C No. 1001[12] dated August 5, 2020[13]
> issued by The Bank of America, New York, U.S.A.[14]
> **TO : THE BANK OF AMERICA**[15]   HANKUK TRADING CO., LTD.[16]
> 345 Wall St., New York   *Kil-Dong Hong*
> NY 10005, U.S.A.   Kil-Dong Hong, President

해설

※ 이 샘플은 환어음 예문으로서 전 세계적으로 널리 사용되는 표준 양식이다.

1) 환어음 표시 : 모든 환어음은 환어음(Bill of Exchange 또는 Draft)이라는 표시가 되어 있어야 한다.
2) 환어음 번호 : 환어음 번호는 환어음을 발행하는 수출상이 부여, 기재한다. 환어음 번호는 환어음의 효력을 발생시키는 필수 기재 사항은 아니다. 그러므로 실무적으로는 환어음 번호를 생략하는 것이 일반적이다.
3) 환어음 발행지 : 환어음은 분쟁 발생 시 행위지의 법률에 따르므로 반드시 환어음 발행지를 기재하여야만 분쟁을 해결하기 위해 준거법을 규명할 수 있다.
4) 환어음 발행 일자 : 연월일을 전부 풀어서 기재하는 것이 원칙이므로, 줄여서 약식으로 쓰는 것은 피해야 한다.
5) 결제 통화 및 환어음 금액 : 환어음에서 가장 중요한 내용으로, 환어음 금액, 즉 대금 청구 금액(숫자 금액)을 나타낸다.
6) 환어음 지불(결제) 기일 : 환어음의 결제 기일을 나타내는 것으로, 환어음 제시(일

람) 즉시 결제되어야 하는 일람불환어음(At Sight B/E)의 경우는 'At Sight'로 기재되며, 환어음 제시(일람) 후 일정 기일이 지나서 결제되는 기한부환어음(Usance B/E)의 경우는 'At 30 days after sight'로 기재된다.

7) 환어음 발행 부수 : 환어음은 통상 원본 2부가 발행되며 2부 중 어느 1부로 대금이 결제되면 다른 1부는 무효가 된다. 즉, 어느 1부로 대금을 결제받으려면 다른 1부가 대금이 결제되지 않았을 때 대금이 결제된다.

8) 환어음 수취인(환어음 수령인) : 환어음 대금을 결제(지급)받아야 할 환어음 대금 수취인으로서 수출상이 거래 은행에 네고(환어음 매입)를 하였을 경우는 매입 은행(기명식) 또는 매입 은행의 지시인(지시식)이 되며, 수출상이 네고(환어음 매입)를 하지 않고 추심 후 환어음 대금을 결제받을 경우는 수출상 자신(기명식) 또는 수출상이 지시하는 사람(지시식)이 된다.

9) 환어음 금액 : 환어음 금액을 문자 금액으로 재차 확인하는 문언이다.

10) 대가 문언(代價文言) : 환어음 발행인이 매입 은행으로부터 동 환어음 금액을 수령하였다는 대가 문언으로, 환어음이 최초 대금 수령의 영수증으로부터 유래했기 때문이다. 오늘날은 이러한 문구가 환어음의 필수 기재 사항은 아니나 지금도 관례적으로 사용하고 있다. 물론 환어음을 매입하지 않고 추심 후 대금을 결제받을 경우는 이 대가 문언을 사용해서는 안 되지만 환어음 대금 수령인이 수출상 자신이므로 대가 문언을 그대로 두어도 상관은 없다.

11) 환어음 지급인에게 지시 문언 : 수출상(환어음 발행인)이 매입 은행으로부터 환어음 대금을 받았으므로 환어음 지급인인 개설 은행은 환어음 수령인인 매입 은행에 동 금액을 지불하고 수입상으로부터 동 금액을 받아내라는 지시 문언이다. 이는 당연한 사실이므로 오늘날 사족에 불과하지만, 관행상 기재할 뿐이며 필수 기재 사항은 아니다. 물론 신용장 거래가 아닌 추심거래(D/P 및 D/A)의 경우는 환어음 지급인이 수입상 자신이므로 환어음 지급인인 수입상 자신이 매입 은행에 동 금액을 지불하고 수입상인 자신으로부터 동 금액을 받아내라는 지시 문언은 의미가 없으므로 이 문언을 아예 생략하거나 아니면 수입상란에 공란을 두는데, 일반적으로 공란을 두는 경우가 많다.

12) 신용장 번호, 13) 신용장 발행 일자, 14) 신용장 발행 은행명 : 본 환어음을 발행하는 근거를 제공한 신용장 번호, 발행 일자 및 발행 은행명을 기재한다. 즉, Drawn

under ~는 This bill of exchange is drawn under ~(본 환어음은 ~에 근거하여 발행되었음)을 줄인 표현이다.
15) 환어음 지급인 : 신용장 거래의 경우는 대부분 개설 은행이 되지만, 때로는 제3의 상환은행이 될 수도 있다. 그러나 추심거래(D/P 및 D/A)의 경우는 항상 수입상이 된다. 어느 경우든 상호 및 주소까지 정확히 기재하여야 한다.
16) 환어음 발행인 : 환어음 발행인은 수출상으로, 신용장 거래의 경우는 신용장상의 수익자(Beneficiary)란에 기재된 수출상 상호 및 주소와 완벽히 일치하여야 한다. 한편 기타 거래의 경우는 매매계약서상에 기재된 수출상 상호 및 주소와 완벽히 일치하여야 한다.

환어음 매입(네고) 시 배서 예

- Shinhan Bank(기명식) : 환어음 뒷면에 아무런 배서 없이 백지 상태로 신한은행이 환어음 지급인에게 제시하면 대금이 결제된다.
- the Order of Shinhan Bank(지시식) : 환어음 뒷면에 반드시 신한은행의 배서가 있어야만 동 환어음을 환어음 지급인에게 제시하여 대금이 결제된다. 이 경우 환어음 뒷면에 배서하는 방법은 "Pay to Seoul Bank", "Pay to the Order of Seoul Bank", "Pay to Seoul Bank or Order" 등이 있다.
- Shinhan Bank or Order(기명식과 지시식의 선택식) : 아무런 배서 없이 백지상태로 신한은행이 동 환어음을 환어음 지급인에게 제시하면 대금을 결제받을 수 있으며, 또한 환어음 뒷면에 신한은행이 배서한 동 환어음을 환어음 지급인에게 제시하여도 대금이 결제된다.

[샘플 3] 송금수표(Demand Draft)

THE BANK OF SEOUL, LTD.

K-AD 014741[1]   Seoul, 14th December, 2020[2]

For Stg. £180[3]
Pay against this cheque[4]
to the order of Henry Herman[5]
the sum of Sterling Pounds One Hundred and Eighty only[6]

To : WEST CITY BANK OF   THE BANK OF SEOUL, LTD.[8]
     ENGLAND LONDON[7]   *Chul-Soo Kim*
                                  Chul-Soo Kim, Manager

해설

※ 이 샘플은 서울은행이 발행하는 송금수표로, 지급 은행은 런던에 있는 웨스트시티잉글랜드은행이다.

1) 송금수표 번호
2) 발행지 및 발행 일자
3) 송금수표의 결제 통화 및 금액(숫자 금액)
4) 지불 문언(본 수표를 제시하면 아래 금액을 ~에게 지불하시오)
5) 송금수표 수취인
6) 송금수표 금액 확인 문언(문자 금액)
7) 지불(지급) 은행명
8) 발행(송금) 은행명

[샘플 4] 대금 결제 독촉

Dear Sirs,

May we remind you that our January statement[1] amounting to £51[2] is overdue?[3]

We should be grateful to receive your cheque at your early convenience.[4]

Yours faithfully,

해설

※ 이 샘플은 결제 기간의 경과를 상기시키며 조속한 결제를 요구하는 예문으로, 중요한 고객에게 보내는 첫 번째 독촉문이다.

1) statement : 계산서
2) £51 : 51파운드
3) be overdue : 미불 상태다, 기간이 경과하다
4) at your early convenience : 귀하가 편리한 대로 조속히

[샘플 5] 대금 결제 독촉

Dear Sirs,

We have submitted[1] our January statement twice and regret that the amount of £34 is still outstanding. We would appreciate an early settlement.[2]

Yours faithfully,

해설

※ 이 샘플은 대금 결제를 재차 독촉하는 정중한 표현의 예문이다.
1) submit : (계산서 따위를) 제출하다(= render)
2) early settlement : 조속한 결제

[샘플 6] 대금 결제 독촉

Dear Sirs,

Your account shows[1] an overdue balance[2] of £24 which was payable on 20 February.

Please send us your cheque by return mail.

Yours faithfully,

해설

※ 이 샘플은 대금 결제를 독촉하는, 상당한 유감을 표현하는 예문이다.
1) account shows : ~계정에 ~이 나타나 있다(남아 있다)
2) overdue balance : 미불 잔액

[샘플 7] 대금 결제 독촉

Dear Sirs,

　　We regret that we had no reply to our letter of 15th March. We are at a loss[1] to understand your attitude and wonder if[2] there are any reasons for your silence.[3] If our service has been in any way unsatisfactory or if we have unknowingly made a mistake, we should be obliged if you would inform us in order that we may make the necessary adjustment.[4]

　　We shall appreciate an early reply.

　　　　　　　　　　　　　　　Yours faithfully,

해설

※ 이 샘플은 침묵으로 일관하는 상대방에게 대금 결제를 독촉하는 비교적 정중한 표현의 예문이다.
1) be at a loss : 당황하다
2) wonder if : ~가 궁금하다, ~인지를 잘 모르겠다
3) reasons for your silence : 회답이 없는 이유
4) make the necessary adjustment : 필요한 조치를 취하다

[샘플 8] 대금 결제 독촉

Dear Sirs,

Though we have reminded you in our letter of 5th. March of the overdue balance[1] of your account, we have so far[2] not received your check.

We are unable to keep this balance open[3] any longer[4] and must request payment of the amount of £24.45 by the 30th of March at the latest.

Yours faithfully,

해설

※ 이 샘플은 대금 결제를 독촉하는, 불만스러운 감정을 표현하는 예문이다.

1) of the overdue balance : 미불 잔액에 대하여
2) so far : 지금까지
3) keep this balance open : 이 잔액을 미해결 상태로 두다
4) not ~ any longer : 더 이상 ~않다(= no longer)

[샘플 9] 대금 결제 독촉

Dear Sirs,

We have submitted our statement for your January account three times and have asked you for settlement of the overdue amount of £ 50.20 in our letters of 15th and 29th April. We are surprised that we have not even had a reply to our letters.

No items of the account is in dispute[1] and we must now insist on an immediate settlement.

Please note that we shall have to hand this matter[2] to our solicitors[3] if your check is not received[4] by the 20th May.

We need not tell you how much we should regret to take such a step after the long and friendly connection with your firm and we hope that you will help us to avoid it by giving this matter your immediate attention.

Yours faithfully,

해설

※ 이 샘플은 대금 결제를 재삼 독촉하면서 이제 변호사에게 넘겨 법적 절차를 취하겠다는 표현의 예문이다.

1) No items of the account is in dispute : 거래 품목 중 어떤 것도 분쟁 중에 있는 것은 없다
2) hand this matter : 본건을 넘기다
3) solicitor : 사무 변호사(법정에는 서지 않는 하급 변호사)
4) be not received : 도착하지 않으면(접수되지 않으면)

[샘플 10] 대금 결제 독촉

Dear Sirs,

Neither our repeated statements nor our letters of 15th March and 2nd April have met with any response on your part[1] and we must reluctantly conclude that you are not facing your responsibilities in a correct manner.[2]

We have to inform you accordingly that we shall place the matter in other hands[3] unless we receive payment of the balance of £34 within 5 days.

We are very regretful to have to write to you in this way but your attitude does not leave us any choice.[4] We still hope that you will settle this account without further delay and thus save yourself the inconvenience and considerable costs of a legal action.

Yours faithfully,

해설

※ 이 샘플은 대금 결제를 최종적으로 독촉하는 예문으로, 법적 절차를 취하겠다는 단호한 표현이다.

1) meet with response on your part : 귀사의 회답을 얻다
2) in a correct manner : 온당한 자세(태도)로
3) place the matter in other hands : 타인(변호사)에게 이 문제를 넘기다
4) your attitude does not leave us any choice : 귀사의 태도로 보아 어쩔 수가 없다, 다른 도리(방법)가 없다

[샘플 11] 대금 결제 청구

4th December, 2020

Hankuk Trading Co., Ltd.
123 Samsung-dong, Gangam-gu
Seoul 01670, Korea

Dear Sirs,

As we wrote to you previously, your account for Stg.[1] £180 to cover our agent commission has been outstanding[2] for some time.

For this account we are enclosing our Debit Note[3] No. 10

We hope you will kindly settle it as soon as possible.

Yours faithfully,

PACIFIC TRADING CO., INC.
Robert H. Brown
Robert H. Brown, Export Manager

Enc. 1 Debit Note

해설

※ 이 샘플은 한국회사의 대리점인 퍼시픽회사가 한국회사에 미지급된 대리점수수료에 대한 대금청구서를 동봉하며 대금을 청구하는 예문이다.

1) Stg. : sterling의 약어. 영화(英貨)
2) outstanding : 미결제된, 미지급된
3) Debit Note : 대금청구서, 대금명세표

[샘플 12] 대금청구서

DEBIT NOTE

No. 10　　　　　　　　　　　　　　London, 4th December, 2020

Debited to[1] Hankuk Trading Co., Ltd.

Description	Amount
Agent Commission[2]	Stg. £180
////////////////////	///////////
Total	Stg. £180

EAST RIVER TRADING CO., LTD.
Henry Herman
Henry Herman, Export Manager

해설

※ 이 샘플은 이스트리버회사가 한국회사에 대리점 수수료를 청구하는 대금청구서 예문이다.

1) Debited to ~ : ~앞으로 대금을 청구하다, 채무자 ~앞
　(cf) Debt : 채무, 빚, 부채
2) Agent Commission : 대리점 수수료

[샘플 13] 위탁판매매출계산서 송부 통보

10th January, 2020

ABC CO., LTD.
123 Samsung-dong, Gangnam-gu
Seoul 01670, Korea

Dear Sirs,

Your consignment[1] of 50(fifty) Photocopiers Model No. 102R has been successfully disposed of and we are sending herewith the Account Sales.

For the net proceeds,[2] please draw on us at sight as usual and we shall be glad to honour your draft.

Your goods are so popular in this market that we await further consignments, which will always receive our best attention.

Yours faithfully,

XYZ CO., LTD.

Robert H. Brown
Robert H. Brown, Sales Manager

Encl. Account Sales

해설

※ 이 샘플은 위탁판매매출계산서를 송부하며 추가 위탁을 부탁하는 예문이다.
1) consignment : 위탁판매, 위탁판매품
2) proceeds : 매출금, 대금

[샘플 14] 위탁판매매출계산서

ACCOUNT SALES

No. 122   Wellington, 10th January, 2020

Account Sales of 50(fifty) Photocopiers Model No. 102R ex M/S GODWIT sold by XYZ Co., Ltd. by order and for account of[1] ABC Co. Ltd., Seoul, Korea.

△ MB WELLINGTON Nos. 1-50	50(fifth) at US$240,000 Charges[2] Commission[3] 5% Net Proceeds[4]	Model No. 102R Photocopiers US$ 12,000,000 (-)US$ 300,000 (-) US$ 600,000 US$ 11,100,000

                                    XYZ CO., LTD.
                                    W. M. Groves
                                    W. M. Groves, Sales Manager

해설

※ 이 샘플은 ABC회사의 의뢰와 부담으로 XYZ회사에 의해 판매된 복사기 위탁판매 출계산서 예문이다.

1) by order and for account of : ~의 의뢰와 부담으로
2) Charges : 비용
3) Commission : 수수료
4) Net Proceeds : 순(매출)대금

[샘플 15] 대리점 수수료 독촉

20th February, 2020

Messrs. Kim & Co., Ltd.
123 Samsung-dong, Gangnam-gu
Seoul 01670, Korea

Dear Sirs,

　　Further to our letter of 15th January, we wish to call your attention to the unusual delay in your remittance[1] of our commission for the last quarter of 2020 amounting to Stg. £2,532.

　　We have heard more than once that you are expecting your treasurer's approval to the remittance very soon, and we should think it is about time your cheque reached us.

　　Since we work entirely on commission, we ask you to understand our difficulty and expedite the remittance.

　　If you have already attended to this matter, please forget about this letter, but if not, when may we expect your cheque?

　　　　　　　　　　　Yours faithfully,

　　　　　　　　　　　PACIFIC TRADING CO., INC.

　　　　　　　　　　　Robert H. Brown
　　　　　　　　　　　Robert H. Brown, Director

해설

※ 이 샘플은 대리섬 수수료를 독촉하는 예문이다.
  1) remittance : 송금 (cf) to remit : 송금하다

[샘플 16] 대금지불통지

14th December, 2020

East River Trading Co., Ltd.
65 High Holborn, London, W. C. 1
England

Dear Sirs,

    We have received your letter of 4th December enclosing your Debit Note No. 10. We are very sorry not to have paid your commission earlier by an oversight.[1]

    In payment of the account we enclose a cheque for Stg. £180 covering your commission up to 31st October, 2020.

    We shall be obliged if you will send us a receipt[2] by return of post.

Yours faithfully,

HANKUK TRADING CO., LTD.
Si-Hak Oh
Si-Hak Oh, Sales Manager

Enc. 1 Cheque

해설

※이 샘플은 수수료에 대한 수표를 동봉하면서 영수증을 요청하는 예문이다.

  1) by an oversignt : 실수로, 잘못해서
  2) receipt : 영수증, 인수증

[샘플 17] 대금수령통지

21st December, 2020

Hankuk Trading Co., Ltd.
123 Samsung-dong, Gangnam-gu
Seoul 01670, Korea

Dear Sirs,

    We have received with many thanks your cheque[1] for Stg. £180 covering our Debit Note No.10, for which our receipt is enclosed.[2]

                       Yours faithfully,

                         EAST RIVER TRADING CO., LTD.
                         Henry Herman
                         Henry Herman, Export Manager

Enc. 1 Receipt

해설

※ 이 샘플은 대금 수령을 통지하는 예문이다.
  1) cheque : 수표(영국)
     (cf) check : 수표(미국)
  2) enclose : 동봉하다

[샘플 18] 대금수령통지

26th February, 2020

Kim & Co., Ltd.
6th floor, Central Bldg.
123 Samsung-dong, Gangnam-gu
Seoul 01670, Korea

Dear Sirs,

 Your letter of 19th February crossed[1] ours of the 20th. Our bank has advised us of our account being credited[2] with £2,532, which we believe to be our commission for the last quarter of 2020. Enclosed is our receipt for it.

 We appreciate your effort in expediting the remittance and wait for your further commands.

Yours faithfully,

PACIFIC TRADING CO., INC.
Robert H. Brown
Robert H. Brown, Director

Encl. 1 Receipt

해설

※이 샘플은 대금 수령을 통지하는 예문이다.
 1) crossed : 서로 엇갈리다
 2) being credited : 입금되다, 대기(貸記)되다

[샘플 19] 대금수령영수증

RECEIPT

For Stg. £180   21st December, 2020

  Received of[1] Hankuk Trading Co., Ltd., Seoul, the Sum of Sterling One Hundred and Eighty Pounds only in settlement of[2] our account up to[3] 31st October, 2020.

          EAST RIVER TRADING CO., LTD.
          Henry Herman
          Henry Herman, Export Manager

해설

※ 이 샘플은 한국회사로부터 2020년 10월 31일까지의 정산금 180파운드를 받았다는 대금수령영수증 예문이다.

1) Received of~ : ~로부터 받다(수령하다)
2) in settlement of : 정산으로
3) up to : ~까지

[샘플 20] **대금수령영수증**

RECEIPT

26th February, 2020

Kim & Co., Ltd.
123 Samsung-dong, Gangnam-gu
Seoul 01670, Korea

For Stg. £2,532.00
Received from Messrs. Kim & Co., Ltd. Seoul, Korea the sum of Two Thousand Five Hundred and Thirty-Two Pounds Only in settlement of Commission Account for the last quarter of 2020.

PACIFIC TRADING CO., INC.
Robert H. Brown
Robert H. Brown, Director

해설

※ 이 샘플은 2020년 4/4분기에 대한 수수료 정산금 2,532파운드를 받았다는 대금수령영수증 예문이다.

대금 결제에 관한 유용한 표현

- For the balance(outstanding) of Stg. £5,250 in your favor, you may *draw* on us at sight as usual.
  귀사가 받아야 할 5,250파운드의 잔액(미지급금)에 대해, 귀사는 당사 앞으로 여느 때처럼 일람불로 환어음을 발행하시면 됩니다.

- Your bank check we received for US$12,000 *has been credited* to your account, which is now completely clear.
  미화 12,000달러에 대해 당사가 받은 귀사의 은행수표는 귀사 계정에서 인출되어 이제 완전히 정산되었습니다.

- We enclose the statement of your account showing a *balance of* US$12,500.
  당사는 미지급금(잔액) 미화 12,500달러에 대해 귀사 계정의(귀사가 지급하여야 할) 계산서를 동봉합니다.

- Please note that the *usance* of our drafts is 30 days after sight.
  당사가 발행한 환어음의 기간은 일람 후 30일임을 주지하시기 바랍니다.

- We ask for your *protection* of our draft on presentation.
  귀사는 당사의 어음을 즉시 결제해줄 것을 요청합니다.

- As your draft was *dishonored*, please negotiate for the matter with the drawees and let them protect it at once.

귀사의 환어음은 부도되었으므로, 이 문제에 대해 환어음 지급인과 협의하여 즉시 환어음을 결제하도록 하십시오.

- This is to *call your attention* to the fact that your account of US$ 25,000 is still unpaid.
 이것은 귀사의 계정 미화 25,000달러가 여전히 미지급되었다는 사실에 대해 귀사의 주의를 상기시키는 것입니다.

- This is to remind you that your remittance of our commission for the first quarter of this year is now more than a month *over due*.
 이것은 금년 1/4분기 당사 수수료에 대한 귀사의 송금이 한 달 이상이나 미지급되었다(만기가 지났다)는 것을 상기시키는 것입니다.

- We *have drawn on* you the draft(bill of exchange) at 60 days after sight under L/C No. 125.
 당사는 신용장 125번에 근거하여 귀사 앞으로 일람 후 60일 결제 조건으로 환어음을 발행하였습니다.

- We ask you to *protect the above draft* on presentation, which was drawn under L/C No. 301.

당사는 귀사에 상기 환어음을 제시하자마자 결제해주실 것을 요청하며, 동 환어음은 신용장 301번에 근거하여 발행되었습니다.

- *Enclosed* you will find our check for US$2,000.00 in payment for the samples you sent us by airmail on December 3.
동봉된 바와 같이 귀사가 12월 3일 항공편으로 당사에 보낸 샘플에 대한 대금 결제로 미화 2,000달러짜리 당사 수표를 보내드립니다.

- We are enclosing a statement of our account with you showing a balance of US$3,617.00 in our favor, and ask for your early settlement.
당사가 받아야 할 미지급액(잔액) 미화 3,617달러에 대한 당사의 계산서를 귀사에 동봉하오니 귀사의 조기 결제를 바랍니다.

- We thank you very much for your letter of January 10 enclosing a check for US$1,350 as our commission for November/December.
11~12월에 대한 당사의 수수료로 미화 1,350달러짜리 수표를 동봉한 귀사의 1월 10일 자 편지에 대해 대단히 감사합니다.

- Should you have any reason for not paying the above sum, you might let us know instead of keeping silent. We could yet come to some mutually satisfactory arrangement. Please fax to us as soon as you receive this fax.

  귀사가 상기 금액을 지급하지 않는 이유가 있다면, 침묵만 지키는 대신 당사에 알려줄 수 있을 것입니다. 그러나 당사는 아직 만족스러운 합의에 이르지 못하였습니다. 이 팩스를 받으면 바로 즉시 답변을 보내주시기 바랍니다.

- A sight draft was drawn on you *for* the invoice amount.

  일람불환어음이 송장 금액에 대해 귀사 앞으로 발행되었습니다.

- You will please take the trouble of sending us a check for US$584.00 covering our commission for the last quarter.

  지난 분기 당사의 수수료에 대한 미화 584달러짜리 수표를 당사에 보내주십시오.

- Please oblige us by instructing your bankers to tele-transmit remittance within a week.

  귀사의 거래 은행에 1주일 이내에 전신 송금하도록 지시해주면 감사하겠습니다.

- The enclosed Statement of Account covers *the balance* payable to us.

  동봉된 계산서는 귀사가 당사에 지불해야 할 미지급금(잔액)을 나타냅니다.

- After *allowing for* our expenses, there remains a balance of US$100 in your favor.

  귀사에 지불할 잔액이 당사의 비용을 공제하고 미화 100달러 남아 있습니다.

- Unless the account is settled by the end of October, we shall *be compelled to take legal steps* for its collection.

  그 금액이 10월 말까지 결제되지 않으면 당사는 동 대금의 회수를 위해 법적 절차를 취하지 않을 수 없습니다.

- We wish to *call your attention* to the enclosed account, which is now nearly three months overdue.

  귀사의 결제 기간이 3개월 가까이 경과하였는바, 귀사는 동봉된 계산서에 관심을 가지기 바랍니다.

- We have duly received your check for US$255.00 to settle

your account *up to* December 31.
당사는 12월 31일까지 귀사의 채무를 정산(결제)하는 미화 255달러짜리 귀사의 수표를 정히 잘 받았습니다.

- *In answer to* your letter of September 14 regarding our outstanding account, we are enclosing a check for US$ 3,000.
당사의 미지급 채무에 대한 9월 14일 자 귀사의 편지에 답하여, 당사는 미화 3,000달러짜리 수표를 동봉합니다.

- The shipping documents will *be handed to* you by the Hanvit Bank against settlement of the account shown.
선적서류는 표시된 채무의 결제 조건으로 한빛은행에 의해 귀사에 전달될 것입니다.

- In payment for 10 units of cassette tape-recorders, we will today send you a check for US$1,500 by airmail.
카세트 녹음기 10대에 대한 대금 결제로, 당사는 오늘 귀사에 항공편으로 미화 1,500달러짜리 수표를 보내겠습니다.

- Today we *have drawn (a draft) on* you at sight for (the amount of) US$1,000.

금일 당사는 미화 1,000달러에 대한 일람불로 귀사에 환어음을 발행하였습니다.

- Neither of your bills is correct.
= Both (of) your bills are incorrect.
= Your bills are both incorrect.
  귀사의 대금청구서(계산서)는 모두 옳지 않습니다.

클레임 제기에 관한 무역통신문

클레임 제기

무역은 일반적으로 먼 거리를 두고 떨어져 있는 당사자 사이에 이루어지고 있어, 계약의 성립부터 인도가 끝날 때까지 시일이나 장소의 간격이 있으므로, 물품은 품질이나 가격상의 변화가 일어나고 거래는 계약 이행상의 불능, 지연, 과오 등을 초래할 위험이 있다.

따라서 실제로 무역을 하면 거래의 성립이나 수행 과정에서 당사자 사이에 각종 분쟁이 일어나기 쉽다. 그 결과 손해를 입은 쪽에서 상대방에 배상을 요구하면 클레임(Claim)이 된다.

[샘플 21] 클레임 제기

January 19, 2020

Hankuk Co., Ltd.
123 Samsung-dong, Gangnam-gu
Seoul 01670, Korea

Gentlmen :

    Nylon Hose on our Order No. 5 has reached us, but we are regretful to say that its quality is inferior to the sample on which we passed you the order.

    You will find enclosed a culling sample from the goods we received. You will admit that your shipments do not come up to the sample.[1]

    Please look into the matter and let us know what you can do about it.

Yours truly,

JOHN WILLIAMS CO., INC.

John H. Williams
John H. Williams, Import Manager

해설

※ 이 샘플은 나일론 스타킹의 품질 불량에 대해 클레임을 제기하는 예문이다.

1) come up to the sample : 샘플(견본)과 일치하다

[샘플 22] **클레임 제기**

November 4, 2020

Shin Yue Metal Co., Ltd.
10th Fl. No. 205
Nanking East Road, Sec. 2
Taipei, Taiwan, R. O. C

Attention : Mr. S. L. Cheng
　　　　　 Managing Director

Gentlemen :

Order No. 105 Black Iron Sheets[1]
ex[2] M/S KAOHSIUNG

　　This is to confirm my phone call this morning about the unsatisfactory manner in which you executed the order mentioned above.

　　Upon unpacking[3] this shipment, we have found that (1) the size is wrong, the length of each sheet being short by about 10mm and (2) most sheets are rusty and corroded.

　　Moreover, you will recall that we had to extend the validity of the relative credit because of the delay in shipment.

　　You will readily agree that any one of these irregularities[4] can be a good reason for canceling this order unconditionally or reshipping[5] the goods at your expense. But our customers say that they would oblige us by accepting[6] these defective goods[7] at a reduction of 20% on the invoice amount.

　　We consider it quite[8] a reasonable proposition and ask you to help us out of this awkward situation[9] by placing the same amount to our credit.[10]

We wait for your immediate reply.

Yours faithfully,

KOREA HARDWARE CO., LTD.
Si-Hak Oh
Si-Hak Oh, Manager
Import Department

해설

※ 이 샘플은 열연박철판의 규격 상이 및 녹 부식에 대한 클레임을 제기하며 해결책으로 20%의 감액을 요구하는 예문이다.

1) Black Iron Sheets : 열연박철판(熱延薄鐵板)
2) ex : from의 뜻을 가진 라틴어로서 전치사의 역할을 한다
3) unpacking : 포장을 풀다
4) irregularities : (계약) 위반
5) reshipping : 반송하다(reship = backship)
6) oblige us by ~ing : ~하는 호의를 당사에 베풀다
7) defective goods : 불량품
8) quite : 완전히, 아주(부사)
9) awkward situation : 곤란한(어려운) 입장
10) placing the same amount to our credit : 당사로부터 받을 금액, 즉 당사가 지불해야 할 금액에서 동 금액을 공제하다

[샘플 23] 클레임 제기

10th July, 2020

Hankuk Trading Co., Ltd.
123 Samsung-dong, Gangnam-gu
Seoul 01670, Korea

Attn. : Mr. Si-Hak Oh, Export Manager

Dear Sirs,

    We have just received 15 cases Porcelain Ware you shipped by M/S ARIRANG on our Order No. 15 of 20th March, but regret to have to inform you that the cases Nos. 3, 4 and 6 are broken and their contens badly damaged evidently through faulty packing.[1] Some photos are enclosed as evidence.

    We ask you therefore either to send us a credit note[2] for the amount of these cases together with the duty[3] paid on them, US$1,500, or to pass the duty to our credit and send us a replacement[4] at your expense.[5]

    Your immediate attention to this matter would be appreciated.

                       Yours faithfully,

                       CENTRAL TRADING COMPANY
                       Robert H. Brown
                       Robert H. Brown, Director

Encls. Photographs

> 해설

※ 이 샘플은 포장 불량으로 인한 도자기 파손에 대해 클레임을 제기하며, 해결책으로 파손품에 대한 관세 1,500달러를 포함하여 손해 금액을 보상하거나, 아니면 관세 1,500달러를 보상하고 파손품을 대체해줄 것을 요구하는 예문이다.

1) evidently through faulty packing : 명백히 포장 잘못으로
2) credit note : 대기표(貸記票), 지불통지서
   (cf) debit note : 차기표(借記票), 받을 통지서
3) the duty : 수입관세(= import duty)
   (cf) the duty paid on them, US$1,500 : 손상된 상품에 대해 지급된 관세
4) replacement : 대체품
5) at your expense : 귀사의 비용으로

[샘플 24] 클레임 제기

May 5, 2020

Hankuk Computer Co., Ltd.
123 Samsung-dong, Gangnam-gu
Seoul 01670, Korea

Gentlemen :

    We have received your shipment[1] covering our order No. 615 for 100 uinits of computer, but have found that several of the cases are in a badly damaged condition.[2] Among the goods, eight units are broken and the mechanisms[3] are exposed beyond repair.[4] It seems that some accident[5] was made on account of the wrong packing.[6]

    As you see in our survey report[7] stating[8] eight units of computers⁹⁾ are badly damaged on account of the inferior packing,¹⁰⁾ they are quite unsaleable.¹¹⁾ Therefore we would ask you to ship the good replacement¹²⁾ for the broken goods¹³⁾ as soon as possible.

It is the first time¹⁴⁾ in all these years of business¹⁵⁾ that we have to lodge our claim¹⁶⁾ with you. We trust that you will pay your immediate attention¹⁷⁾ to this matter.

Yours faithfully,

CENTRAL TRADING COMPANY
Robert H. Brown
Robert H. Brown, Director

해설

※ 이 샘플은 포장 불량으로 파손된 컴퓨터의 대체품을 요구하는 예문이다.

1) your shipment : 귀사의 선적품

2) in a badly damaged condition : 심하게 파손된 상태로

3) mechanism : 기구, 기능

4) exposed beyond repair : 수리할 수 없는 상태다

5) some accident : 어떤 사고

6) on account of the wrong packing : 불량 포장 때문에

7) survey report : 손해검정(감정)보고서

8) stating : 기술하다

9) eight units of computers : 컴퓨터 8대

10) the inferior packing : 조악한 포장

11) quite unsaleable : 완전히 판매할 수 없는

12) good replacement : 훌륭한 대체품

13) the broken goods : 파손된 상품

14) the first time : 처음의 것
15) in all these years of business : 거래를 하는 수년 동안
16) lodge our claim : 클레임을 제기하다
17) pay your immediate attention : 귀사가 조속한 배려를 하다

클레임 제기에 유용한 표현

- You told us that our order No. 50 *was* almost *ready for* shipment and that your shipping advice would follow "in due course." More than a fortnight has passed since then, yet we have not heard from you anything about the shipment.
귀사는 당사의 주문번호 50이 선적 준비가 거의 되어 있으며 귀사의 선적통지가 '정히' 수반될 것이라고 말했습니다. 그러나 그로부터 2주 이상이나 경과하였으며 귀사로부터 그 선적건에 대하여 어떤 소식도 듣지 못했습니다.

- On unpacking the 10 cases of Printed Poplin ex M/S ARIRANG, we have found that the goods are much *inferior* in quality to your counter sample and slightly different in shade also.
당사는 아리랑호로 보내진 염색된 포플린 10상자를 풀자마자, 그 제품이 귀사가 제공한 샘플에 비하여 품질이 훨씬 떨어지며 색상

도 다소 상이하다는 것을 발견하였습니다.

- We cannot possibly deliver the merchandise in this condition to our customers, but might accept the lot *at a reduction of 20%* on the contract price.
  당사는 이 조건으로 당사의 고객에게 이 상품을 인도할 수 없습니다. 그러나 계약 가격에서 20%를 감한 가격으로는 그 상품을 인수할 용의가 있습니다.

- Please compare the *cuttings(cullings)* enclosed and you will readily admit the reasonableness of our claim.
  동봉된 발췌물을 비교해보시면 당사 클레임의 타당성을 기꺼이 인정할 것입니다.

- To prove the shortage, we *are enclosing* a Certificate of a Sworn Measurer.
  당사는 수량 부족을 입증하기 위해 공인검정인의 증명서를 동봉합니다.

- The goods sent by the m/s "Arirang" reached here, but they are *far from* being satisfactory.

아리랑호로 보내진 화물이 이곳에 도착하였습니다. 그러나 그 화물은 매우 만족스럽지 못합니다.

- *We regret that* two cases of your shipment arrived in a damaged condition.
  귀사의 선적품 중 두 상자가 손상된 상태로 도착하여 당사는 유감입니다.

- We ordered Model MR-50 camera, but today we have received Model QR-55, and the quantity is 5 pieces *short*.
  당사는 모델 MR-50 카메라를 주문했습니다. 그러나 오늘 당사는 모델 QR-55를 받았으며 더욱이 수량이 5개 부족합니다.

- *To our surprise*, most of the goods arrived badly damaged.
  놀랍게도 화물의 대부분이 심하게 손상되어 도착했습니다.

- The machine we bought from you *has broken down* again and again.
  당사가 귀사로부터 구매한 기계가 자주 고장이 납니다.

- *When we checked(checking)* your invoice, we (have) found the following discrepancy(discrepancies).

당사가 귀사의 송장을 점검해본 결과, 당사는 다음과 같은 하자(불일치)를 발견했습니다.

- We have found that the goods received are different from the sample(s).
= The goods received were found(proved) to be different from the sample(s).

  귀사는 수령한 제품이 샘플과 상이하다는 것을 알았습니다.

- The performance is *far from being satisfactory(a long way off satisfaction)*.

  성과가 매우 만족스럽지 못합니다.

- It is *regrettable(regretful)* that you did not ship our order earlier.

  귀사가 당사의 주문품을 조속히 선적하지 않아 유감스럽습니다.

- You *ought to* have shipped our order earlier.

  귀사는 당사의 주문품을 조속히 선적해야 했습니다.

- We *see to it that* the goods might not be damaged in transit.

= We take care that the goods might not be damaged in transit.
당사는 그 제품이 운송 중에 손상되지 않았을 것으로 판단됩니다.

- Apparently they did not notice the defect.
= They appeared not to notice the defect.
외견상 하자가 나타나지 않았습니다

- The finish is not good and the gilt *comes off* partly.
마무리가 좋지 않아 금박이 부분적으로 떨어져 나갔습니다.

- You have delivered the goods below the standard we expected from the samples
귀사는 당사가 샘플로부터 기대한 수준 아래의 제품을 인도하였습니다.

- The screw-heads should be below the outer surface, but they *stand out* above it.
나사못 머리가 바깥 표면 아래에 있어야 하는데 그보다 위에 있습니다.

- We *are possibly unable to* supply our customers with the

products received from you.

귀사로부터 받은 물품을 당사의 고객에게 공급할 수 없습니다.

- We *are checking up* the missing goods with our packers.

  당사는 당사의 포장업자와 행방불명된 화물을 체크하고 있습니다.

- You will remember that the goods would be shipped by November 15.

  귀사는 그 화물이 11월 15일까지 선적되어야 한다는 것을 기억할 것입니다.

- If the goods have not yet been shipped, we must ask you to send them by air.

  만일 그 화물이 아직도 선적되지 않았다면 당사는 귀사에 그 화물을 항공편으로 보내도록 요청해야 합니다.

- We *pointed out* before placing an order that prompt delivery is essential.

  당사는 주문하기 전에 신속한 인도가 필수적이라는 것을 지적했습니다.

- This terrible delay has caused us a great loss of business.
  이 엄청난 지연이 당사에 커다란 거래 손실을 야기시켰습니다.

- It is essential that the delivery should *be punctual*, otherwise our summer sale cannot *be carried out*.
  인도가 제때에 이루어져야 하는 것이 필수적입니다. 그렇지 않으면 당사의 여름 판매는 이루어질 수 없습니다.

- The delivery time was clearly mentioned in our letter and you duly acknowledged it.
  인도 기일은 분명히 당사의 편지에 언급되었으며, 귀사도 그것을 정히 인정했습니다.

- Your letter must *have crossed with* ours informing you of the shipment of your order.
  귀사의 편지가 주문품의 선적을 통지하는 당사의 편지와 서로 엇갈린 것이 틀림없습니다.

- The stuffing inside the case was so loose *that* some cups and plates have been broken.
  상자 내부 적입이 너무 느슨해서 일부 컵과 접시가 파손되었습니다.

클레임 해결에 관한 무역통신문

클레임의 해결 방법

무역 클레임을 해결하는 방법에는 당사자 간 화합에 의한 원만한 해결, 즉 화해(Compromise, Amicable Settlement), 조정(Conciliation), 중재(Arbitration), 소송(Litigation, Lawsuit) 등이 있다. 그리고 잘못을 인정할 경우만 'sorry'나 'regret'라는 표현을 쓰고, 잘못을 인정하지 못할 경우는 이러한 표현을 쓰지 않는다.

[샘플 25] 클레임 해결

January 27, 2020

Messrs. John Williams Co., Inc.
310 Market Street, San Francisco, CA
U.S.A.

Gentlemen :

We regret to learn from your letter of January 19 that you received inferior goods against your Order No. 5.

Tracing our records,[1] we find that our shipping clerk shipped the goods of Item No. 3 Nylon Hoses[2] instead of those of Item No. 1 for which your order was given.

We are very sorry for this carelessness on our part. In order to adjust the matter, we would like either to send you the right goods as soon as possible or to give you a special allowance[3] of 20% for the invoice amount.

Please accept our apologies[4] for the inconvenience we have caused you and let us know which of the above two adjustments[5] is preferable to you.

Yours very truly,

HANKUK CO., LTD.
Si-Hak Oh
Si-Hak Oh, President

> **해설**

※ 이 샘플은 수출상이 선적 담당 직원의 과실로 물품을 잘못 선적하였음을 인정하고, 정상 물품을 보내거나 20%의 할인 중 선택하라는 내용의 클레임 해결 예문이다.

1) Tracing our records : 당사의 기록을 조사한 결과
2) Nylon Hoses : 나일론 스타킹(긴 양말)
3) allowance : 할인
4) Please accept our apologies : 당사의 잘못(사죄)을 받아주십시오
5) adjustments : 조정

[샘플 26] 클레임 해결

November 6, 2020

Thomas Hardware Co., Ltd.
123 Wall St., New York
N.Y. 10005, U.S.A.

Attn. : Tom H. Baker, Import Manager

Gentlemen :

    We are writing this to confirm the conversation I had with you over the telephone in reply to your phone call and fax on November 4 concerning the Black Iron Sheets on your Order No. 105.

    It is true that the shipment was delayed, but it was beyond our control since some of our machines had gone out of order because of a local heavy rain[1] which flooded the factory. We then asked for your understanding and you were good enough to extend the credit.

As to the size and corrosion, you will recall the fact that Mr. Brown, a representative[2] of your Seoul office, inspected our rolling operations[3] and approved of the products. We ourselves conducted a rigorous inspection[4] and found the sheets perfectly conforming to the standards,[5] as you will see in our mill sheets.[6]

Realizing, however, that you are in an awkward position,[7] we will meet you halfway[8] by making a 10% reduction.

We consider it advisable for your customers to accept this liberal settlement.

Yours faithfully,

KOREA METAL CO., LTD.
Si-Hak Oh
Si-Hak Oh, Managing Director

Encl. Mill Sheets

해설

※ 이 샘플은 열연박철판의 선적 지연은 불가항력인 홍수에 의한 것이며 규격 및 부식은 선적된 수입상의 서울사무소 직원이 검사하였으므로 면책임을 상기시키고, 난처한 입장을 고려하여 반분해서 10%의 감액을 허용한다는 예문이다.

1) local heavy rain : 국지적 호우
2) representative : 사원, 대표자
3) rolling operations : 압연작업
4) rigorous inspection : 엄격한 검사
5) conforming to the standards : 규격과 일치하는
6) mill sheets : (공장에서 발행하는) 검사증명서

7) be in an awkward position : 난처한 입장에 있다

8) meet you halfway : 양분 양보하다, 타협하다

[샘플 27] 클레임 해결

February 15, 2020

Ridgewood Food Inc.
Carson, California 90745
U.S.A.

Dear Sirs,

<u>Canned Tuna</u>

    Thank you for your letter of 4 February 2020 regarding complaints[1] about broken glass[2] in canned tuna shipped to you under our invoice No. QE42315.

    The canner[3] is now investigating[4] the matter, and we will inform you of the results as soon as they are available.

    In order to clarify the matter[5] and to help the canner to prevent the recurrence of the problem,[6] we should appreciate it if you would send us samples of the glass that has been found in the canned mackerel, if possible.

    We assure you that the canner regards this matter as seriously as you do and is taking every step[7] to see that it does not happen again.

Yours faithfully,

HANKUK CO., LTD.

Si-Hak Oh
Si-Hak Oh, Managing Director

해설

※ 이 샘플은 참치 통조림의 유리 조각에 대한 원인 규명 및 재발 방지를 약속하는 예문이다.

1) complaints : 불평, 불만
2) broken glass : 깨어진 유리
3) canner : 통조림 제조업자
4) investigating : 조사 중
5) clarify the matter : 본건을 해명하다
6) prevent the recurrence of the problem : 문제의 재발을 예방하다
7) taking every step : 모든 수단을 강구하다

[샘플 28] 클레임 거절

20th July, 2020

P. T. Central Trading Company
184 Jl. Gajah Mada 3rd Floor
Jakarta, Indonesia

Dear Sirs,

 Your letter of 10th July on the 15 cases Porcelain Ware of your order No. 15 has received our most careful attention.

 We are, however, unable to account for[1] the breakage, since we paid the best possible attention to the packing of all the 15 cases and the shipping company received the whole lot in perfect condition as is evident from the clean B/L[2] we obtained.

 Moreover, the goods have been covered against the risk of breakage. We advise you, therefore, that you file your claim with[3] the insurance company.

 We understand the inconvenience you have been put to, and shall be glad to do anything in our power to assist you in pushing[4] your claim.

Yours faithfully,

HANKUK CO., LTD.

Chul-Soo Lee
Chul-Soo Lee, Export Manager

해설

※이 샘플은 도자기 파손에 대한 클레임에 대해 수출상은 무하자 선하증권을 교부받았으므로 책임이 없으며 보험회사에 클레임을 청구하라는 예문이다.

1) account for : 설명하다, 책임을 지다
2) clean B/L : 무하자(무고장, 무사고)선하증권
   (cf) foul B/L의 경우 L/I(Letter of Indemnity)를 선사에 제출하고 clean B/L을 발급받을 수도 있다
3) file your claim with ~ : ~에 클레임을 제기하다(file = lodge = advance = enter)
4) pushing : (목적·요구)를 추구하다

클레임 해결에 관한 유용한 표현

- We admit that the wrong goods have been shipped through an error of our shipping clerk. We *were* temporarily *understaffed* and had to hire new men, but all this is no excuse. We only wish you to understand that this is really an exception.

당사 선적 담당 직원의 실수로 잘못된 화물이 선적되었다는 것을 인정합니다. 당사는 일시적으로 인원이 부족하여 새로 사람을 고용했어야 했습니다. 그러나 이 모든 것에는 변명의 여지가 없습니다. 당사는 단지 이것이 정말로 예외라는 것을 귀사가 이해해주시길 바랍니다.

- From the Clean B/L you will see that the goods were shipped in good condition. We suggest, therefore, that you *lodge your claim with* the shipping company.

  무하자선하증권을 보면 그 화물이 양호한 상태로 선적되었음을 알게 될 것입니다. 그러므로 당사는 귀사가 운송 회사에 클레임을 제기할 것을 제안합니다.

- Though we find no difference between the shipping sample and the duplicate sample in our hands, we will *meet you halfway* by offering a discount of 5% *in view of* our long pleasant relations.

  선적 샘플과 당사가 가지고 있는 부분 샘플과의 차이를 발견하지 못했지만, 당사는 귀사와 오래되고 원만한 관계를 고려하여 5%의 할인을 제안함으로써 귀사의 손해를 반분(반을 부담)하겠습니다.

- We apologize for the inconvenience this business has caused you and assure you of our best attention to your future orders.

  이번 거래가 귀사에 야기한 불편에 대하여 사죄하며, 귀사의 추후 주문에 대해서는 당사가 최선의 배려를 할 것을 약속합니다.

- We *are prepared to* give you *a 10% allowance* to compensate you for the defects in the goods shipped.
  당사는 귀사에 선적 물품의 하자를 보상하기 위해 10%를 할인할 준비가 되어 있습니다.

- We will ship by the next vessel one case to replace the damaged goods.
  당사는 손상된 화물을 대체하기 위해 다음 선박편으로 한 상자를 선적하겠습니다.

- We *assure you of* our full attention not to repeat such a mistake.
  당사는 그러한 실수가 재발되지 않도록 최선을 다할 것을 귀사에 약속합니다.

- The loss must be *made up for* by all means.
  그 손해는 모든 수단을 다하여 보상되어야 합니다.

- We are of the opinion that rough handling in transit was the cause of the damage.
  당사는 운송 중 부주의한 취급이 손상의 원인이라고 봅니다.

- This amount will be large enough to *make up for* the loss you have suffered.
이 금액은 귀사가 당한 손실을 보상하기에 충분할 것입니다.

- At the time of packing, the above-mentioned goods were in a perfect condition.
포장할 때는 상기 언급 물품이 완벽한 상태였습니다.

- By some mistake the goods have been wrongly delivered.
약간의 실수로 화물이 잘못 배달되었습니다.

- We are very sorry for our mistake in the number, which *resulted in* your receiving the wrong goods.
당사가 번호를 잘못 매김으로 인해 귀사가 잘못된 물품을 받게 되어 죄송합니다.

- The defect may be *due to* a fault in a machine, and we are now checking up all the machines.
하자는 기계의 하자에 기인된 것입니다. 따라서 당사는 지금 모든 기계를 점검하고 있습니다.

- We should appreciate returning the goods to us, as the expense for returning them will, of course, be borne by us.
당사에 그 물품을 반송해주시면 감사하겠습니다. 물론 반송 비용은 당사가 부담할 것입니다.

- We are very sorry to learn that the goods sent to you were not of the quality you expected.
귀사에 보낸 화물이 귀사가 기대한 품질이 아니어서 대단히 죄송합니다.

- As soon as we received your letter, we asked the packers to *looks into* the matter.
당사는 귀사의 편지를 받자마자 포장업자에게 그것을 조사하도록 요청했습니다.

- We are very sorry for this delay, which you will understand was due to circumstances *beyond our control*.
당사는 이 지연에 대하여 사과드립니다. 그러나 이 지연이 당사가 통제할 수 없는 상황 때문이었다는 것을 이해하실 겁니다.

기타 무역 관련 통신문

해외 출장 전 면담 요청 통신문

[샘플 29] 면담 요청

> Our Export Manager, Mr. Chul-Soo Kim, will soon visit your country. He intends to stay[1] in your city from September 10 to 17. He earnestly wishes to meet your Import Manager. Will you please let us know if one of those days will be convenient[2] for your Manager. We should like to have your reply by return of mail.

해설

※ 이 샘플은 수출부장인 김철수 씨가 수입국에 9월 10일에서 17일까지 머무를 예정이며, 동 기간 중 수입부장을 만나고 싶은데 어떤 날짜가 편리한지 알려달라는 예문이다.

1) intend to stay : 머무를 예정이다
2) convenient : 형편이 좋은, 편리한

[샘플 30] 면담 요청에 대한 회신

Thank you for your letter informing us of Mr. Kim's visit to our city. Our Import Manager, Mr. Robert H. Brown, will be pleased to meet him on September 15. We hope Mr. Kim will confirm the appointment[1] by telephone on his arrival[2] in this city.

해설

※ 이 샘플은 수입부장인 브라운 씨가 9월 15일에 수출부장을 만날 수 있음을 통보하는 예문이다.

1) appointment : 약속
   (cf) meet a person by appointment : 미리 약속하고 만나다
2) on his arrival : 도착하자마자

소개장

[샘플 31] 소개장

Dear Mr. Harris,

It gives us pleasure to introduce to you Mr. Kil-Dong Hong, Managing Director of Hankuk Trading Co., Ltd., who is one of our business friends of many years.

Mr. Hong is going to visit your country at the beginning of August for the purpose of surveying the recent market conditions[1] in your country.

We should greatly appreciate it[2] if you would give him any assistance he may require. We will consider your assistance as a personal favor[3] to us.

Yours faithfully,

해설

※ 이 샘플은 한국회사의 홍길동 상무를 소개하며 협조를 부탁하는 예문이다.

1) for the purpose of surveying the recent market conditions : 최근 시장 조건(시황) 조사의 목적으로
2) it : 가목적어로 if 이하가 진목적어
3) personal favor : 개인적인 호의

해외 출장 시 만난 사람들에 대한 감사의 통신문

[샘플 32] 출장 시 환대에 대한 감사문

Dear Mr. Wilson,

    I wish to thank you warmly for the cordial hospitality you extended to me[1] during my stay in your place. The opportunity to meet you and your staff[2] is what I had long been wishing for, and I hope I can receive a visit here from you some day.[3] I thank you again for your hospitality.

                                            Sincerely yours,

해설

※ 이 샘플은 방문 시 베풀어준 호의에 감사하며 추후 이곳에 방문하면 보답하겠다는 예문이다.

1) cordial hospitality you extended to me : 당신이 본인에게 베푼 후한 대접
2) staff : 사원, 직원
3) some day : (미래의) 언젠가

경축 및 조의에 대한 통신문

[샘플 33] 경축문

We are very pleased to hear that you have recently been appointed to the Board.[1] We should like to congratulate[2] you and wish you every success.

해설

※ 이 샘플은 중역 임명을 축하하는 예문이다.
  1) be appointed to the Board : 중역(重役)으로 임명되다
  2) congratulate : 축하하다

[샘플 34] 조의문

We were deeply grieved[1] to hear of the sudden death of Mr. Arthur Klein of your firm. His passing[2] must mean a great loss to your firm. We, who knew him, are very grateful to[3] him for his many years' cooperation with us.

My staff join[4] me in conveying our sincere sympathy[5] to the members of his family.

해설

※ 이 샘플은 거래 회사 직원의 갑작스러운 사망 소식을 듣고 애도의 뜻을 전달하는 예

문이다.

1) grieve : 슬프게 하다

   (cf) be grieved to hear : ~을 듣고 슬퍼하다

2) passing : 죽음(= death)

3) be very grateful to ~ : ~에 은혜를 입고 있다

4) join : 함께하다

5) in conveying our sincere sympathy : 당사의 진실한 조의(문상)를 전달함에 있어서

사무소 이전 통지문

[샘플 35] 사무소 이전 통지문

HANKUK TRADING CO., LTD.
We take pleasure in announcing that,
effective April 1, 2020,
our Seoul Office will be located at
789 Samsung-dong, Kangnam-ku, Seoul 135-090, Korea
Telephone : +82-2-551-5611   Fax : +82-2-551-5615

해설

※ 이 샘플은 사무실 이전과 아울러 주소 및 연락처를 알리는 예문이다.

광고문

[샘플 36] 광고문

NEW speed record :
From zero to 1 million in 31months.

The Matiz's speed is not just a matter of a snappy engine. Think of the speed with which it has won the favour of 1 million car lovers in such a short time. The Matiz was the first car in Europe to sell a million in only 31 months.

Can this be due to its compact, modern styling, its manoeuverability? Indeed, it can.

Can this be due to its very lively, but very economical engine? Indeed, it can.

Can this be due to its big, roomy, comfortable interior? Indeed, it can.

Can this be due to its vast luggage space behind the tailgate that can be enlarged from 350 litres to 1,100 litres? Indeed, it can.

And indeed, the Matiz got that far in the popularity stakes just because it is fun driving a car with all these good features.

Matiz, the compact Daewoo. Lots of power. Lots of room. Lots of fun. From zero to 1 million in 31months.

Daewoo quality. Made in Korea.

해설

※ 이 샘플은 31개월 만에 100만 대의 초고속 판매를 기록한 마티즈자동차에 대한 광고 예문이다.

구직에 관한 통신문

[샘플 37] 구직문

February 15, 2020

Hankuk Trading Co., Inc.
345 Samsung-dong, Gangnam-gu
Seoul 01670, Korea

Gentlemen :

 From the Employment Section[1] of our university, I have learned that you are looking for a young man having some knowledge of International Trade and Business English. I wish to apply for the position since I have learned International Trade, Business English, Bookkeeping and Typewriting at university, and believe I can fill your requirement. As to the details of my personal history, I have enclosed a brief statement.[2]

 I am allowed to mention[3] Mr. Si-Hak Oh, professor of our university, as reference.[4]

 I hope you will give me the pleasure of a personal interview at your convenience.

Respectfully yours,

Chul-Soo Kim

Inc. 1 Personal History
P.S. I enclose an addressed and stamped envelope[5] for your reply.

해설

※이 샘플은 대학 취업과로부터 구인 정보를 듣고 이력서를 동봉하며 구직을 신청하는 예문이다.

1) the Employment Section : 취업과, 취직계
2) statement : 보고서
3) mention : 진술하다, 언급하다
4) as reference : 조회처로서
   (cf) refer : 조회하다
5) addressed and stamped envelope : 주소가 기재되고 우표가 붙은 반신용 봉투

[샘플 38] 구직문

6th March, 2020

Dear Sirs,

I should like to apply for[1] the position of export department clerk that you advertised in the "Daily Journal" of 5th March, 2020.

I am twenty-nine years of age[2] and have had more than two years' experience as clerk[3] of a trading company, as you will see from the enclosed history of mine.

My reason for seeking a change[4] is that such a large firm as yours will certainly give me a better opportunity for developing my ability.

Mr. Si-Hak Oh, President of Hankuk Trading Co., Ltd., will gladly reply to any inquiries about my character and ability.

I shall be glad to come to your office for an interview at any time you may specify.

Yours very sincerely,

Kil-Dong Hong

Enc. 1 Personal History

해설

※ 이 샘플은 구인광고를 보고 이력서를 동봉하며 구직을 신청하는 예문이다.

1) apply for : ~에 지원하다
2) of age : 나이가 얼마인(= old)
3) clerk : 직원
4) change : 전직(轉職)

이력서

[샘플 39] 이력서

Personal History[1)]

6th March, 2020

Name in Full　　　　: Jin-Ho Kim
Date of Birth　　　　: 12th August, 2020
Permanent Address　: 301 Samsung-dong, Gangnam-gu
　　　　　　　　　　 Seoul 01670, Korea
Present Address　　 : 123 Samsung-dong, Gangnam-gu
　　　　　　　　　　 Seoul 01670, Korea

Education :
　　March 1996 - February 2002　Lira Primary School
　　March 2002 - February 2005　Hangang Middle School
　　March 2005 - February 2008　Hangang High School
　　March 2008 - February 2012　Hankuk University
　　　　　　　　　　　　　　　　　(Majored in International Trade)

Military Affairs :
　　March 2012 - June 2014　　Intelligence Officer as first lieutenant

Employment :
Since July 2014 I have been with ABC Trading Co., Ltd.,
　　　　　　　104 Sangdo-dong, Dongjak-gu, Seoul, Korea, as an
　　　　　　　assistant manager.

Qualifications :
　I passed the A Class Examination in Business English in 2012.

I passed the Examination in International Trader in 2012.

Remarks :
　Typing speed 45 words per minute.

I certify that the above statement is true to the best of my knowledge and belief.[2]

Jin-Ho Kim

해설

※ 이 샘플은 전형적인 이력서 예문이다.
1) Personal History : 이력서(= resume)
2) I ~ belief : 이 문구는 한국식 표현으로, 생략하여도 무방하다.

기타 무역에 관한 유용한 표현

- When you pause "Cool-Drink" refreshes you best! People in constant activity refresh with ice-cold "Cool-Drink"! Any time, anywhere, "Cool-Drink" gives you a sparkling life, a refreshing new feeling. Enjoy delicious "Cool-Drink" …… for the Pause that Refreshes.
  휴식을 취할 때에는 "쿨드링크"가 여러분들을 최상의 상태로 재충전해줍니다. 끊임없이 활동적인 사람들은 얼음처럼 시원한 "쿨드링크"로 재충전합니다. 언제, 어디서든 '쿨드링크'는 여러분들에게 활기찬 삶, 상쾌한 기분을 줍니다. 상쾌한 휴식을 위해 맛있는 '쿨드링크'를 즐기세요. (광고문)

- I have a good knowledge of international trade and thoroughly experienced in all types of export and import.
본인은 국제무역에 관한 전문 지식을 가지고 있으며, 모든 형태의 수출입을 경험하였습니다.

- In March 2020 the company *went bankrupt* and my position was terminated.
2020년 3월 그 회사는 파산했으며, 본인의 직위는 종료되었습니다(본인은 그 회사를 그만두게 되었습니다).

- I trust that these qualifications will meet your requirements and am glad to present myself for an interview at any time you may specify.
본인은 이들 자격이 귀사의 요구 조건을 충족시킬 것으로 믿으며, 귀사가 정하는 어느 때든 기꺼이 면접에 응하겠습니다.

- I expect to *graduate from* Hankuk University in March next year.
본인은 내년 3월 한국대학을 졸업할 예정입니다.

- I *am good at* international trade and English correspondence.
본인은 국제무역 및 영어 회화에 능통합니다.

- I enclose *a letter of recommendation* by the professor of our university and my photograph.
본인 대학교 교수의 추천서와 본인 사진을 동봉합니다.

- Since I graduated from Hankuk University in March last year, I have helped my father in his business.
본인은 지난 3월 한국대학을 졸업한 이후 사업을 하시는 부친을 돕고 있습니다.

- I *passed* the Ⅱ Class Examination in Business English last year.
본인은 지난해 무역 영어 Ⅱ급 자격을 획득했습니다.

6장

Incoterms 2020 해설

Incoterms의 개념

Incoterms란 International Commercial Terms의 약칭으로, 정식 명칭은 '무역 조건의 해석에 관한 국제 규칙(International Rules for the Interpretation of Trade Terms)'이다.

국제상업회의소(ICC)가 중심이 되어 제정된 Incoterms는 외국과의 무역에 가장 일반적으로 사용되는 무역 거래 조건의 해석에 관해 일련의 국제 규칙을 제공하는 데 그 목적이 있다.

Incoterms는 1936년 제정된 이래 1967년, 1976년, 1980년, 1990년, 2000년, 2010년, 2020년에 각각 개정 또는 보완되어 현재 11가지의 거래 조건을 사용하고 있으며, 매매 가격의 산출에 있어서 세계적으로 가장 널리 채택되어 사용되고 있다.

Incoterms 2020 특징

2020년 1월 1일 시행되는 Incoterms 2020의 특징은 다음과 같다.

DAT를 DPU로 명칭을 변경히고 DAP와 배열 순서를 바꿈

Incoterms 2010의 DAT 조건은 사용 지침(Guidance Note)에서 'Terminal'이라는 용어를 광범위하게 정의하여 터미널은 물론 지붕의 유무를 불문하고 모든 장소를 포함하도록 정의되었다.

Incoterms 2010에서 DAT와 DAP의 유일한 차이점은, DAT 조건은 매도인이 물품을 도착 운송수단으로부터 양하 후 매수인에게 인도해야 하고, DAP 조건은 매도인이 물품을 도착 운송수단으로부터 양하하지 않고 도착 운송수단에 적재된 상태에서 매수인에게 인도하는 것이었다.

Incoterms 2010 개정 당시 매도인의 위험부담 순서로 배열한다면,

당초에 도착 운송수단에 적재된 채 인도되는 DAP가 앞에 배열되고 도착 운송수단에서 양하 후 인도되는 DAT가 나중에 배열되어야 했다.

따라서 Incoterms 2020에서는 DAT(Delivered At Terminal)를 DPU(Delivered at Place Unloaded)로 명칭을 변경하고, 매도인의 위험부담 범위 순서에 따라, 매도인이 도착 운송수단에 적재된 채 인도되는 DAP를 앞에 배열하고, 매도인이 도착 운송수단에서 양하 후 인도되는 DPU를 그다음에 배열하게 되었다.

CIF 조건의 최소 부보 의무는 기존의 ICC(C)와 동일하고 CIP 조건의 부보 의무는 ICC(A)로 확대

Incoterms 2010에서는 CIF 및 CIP 조건 모두 최소 부보 의무는 ICC(C)였다.

그러나 Incoterms 2020에서 CIF 조건의 최소 부보 의무는 기존의 ICC(C)와 동일하고, CIP 조건의 부보 의무는 ICC(A)로 확대되었다.

개정 당초에는 CIF 및 CIP 조건 모두 ICC(A)로 확대하려 했으나, 1차 상품의 경우 ICC(C)로 부보하는 경우가 많아 이를 감안하여 CIF 조건의 최소 부보 의무는 기존의 ICC(C)와 동일하게 하고, CIP 조건의 부보 의무는 ICC(A)로 확대했다.

그러나 Incoterms 2020에서 이번에 개정된 CIP 조건의 담보 범위의 확대는 그다지 중요하지 않다. CIF 조건에서도 계약 당사자 간에 담보 범위가 넓은 ICC(A)로 하고 거래 가격을 높게 계약할 수 있으며, CIP 조건에서도 계약 당사자 간에 담보 범위가 좁은 ICC(C)로 하고 거래 가격을 낮게 계약할 수 있기 때문이다.

FCA 조건에서 해상운송의 경우, 당사자 간 합의 시 본선적재표기(on-board notation) 선하증권(B/L)도 사용 가능

선사는 운송 계약상 통상 물품이 실제로 선적된 후에 당초 발행된 수취선하증권(Received B/L)에 본선적재표기(On-Board Notation)를 하여 본선적재선하증권(On-Board B/L)의 효력을 가지도록 하는 것이 일반적이다.

물론 계약 당사자 간에 물품이 FCA 조건으로 매매되고 해상으로 운송될 경우, 매도인이나 매수인(또는 신용장 거래 시 신용장 개설 은행)이 처음부터 본선적재선하증권(On-Board B/L) 또는 선적선하증권(Shipped B/L)을 요구할 수 있다.

특히 신용장 거래 시에 본선적재선하증권(On-Ooard B/L) 또는 선적선하증권(Shipped B/L)을 요구하는 것이 국제 상관례다.

이러한 관례를 감안하여 Incoterms 2020의 FCA 조건 A6/B6 조항에서, 매도인과 매수인이 합의한 경우 매수인은 선사에 매도인에게 본선적재선하증권을 발행하게끔 지시할 수 있도록 새로 규정하였다.

그러나 매도인은 선적에 대해 어떠한 의무도 없음을 강조하였다.

FCA, DAP, DPU 및 DDP 조건에서 매도인 또는 매수인 자신의 운송수단에 의한 운송도 가능함을 명시

Incoterms 2010에서는 물품이 매도인으로부터 매수인에게 운송되는 경우에 제3자 운송인에게 아웃소싱하여 물품을 운송하는 것으로 가정했다. 즉, Incoterms 2010에서는 매도인이나 매수인 자신의 운송수단에 의한 운송이 가능한지 여부를 명시적으로 규정하지 않았다.

그러나 Incoterms 2020에서는 매수인이나 매도인이 운송을 제3자 운송인에게 아웃소싱할 수도 있고, 매도인이나 매수인 자신의 운송수단에 의한 운송할 수도 있음을 명시적으로 규정하였다.

즉, Incoterms 2020의 FCA 조건에서 매수인은 자신의 물품을 수취하기 위해 자신의 운송수단을 사용할 수 있으며, DAP 및 DPU 조건에서 매도인은 운송을 제3자 운송인에게 아웃소싱하지 않고 자신의 운송수단을 사용할 수 있다.

Incoterms 2020의 11개 조건 내의 조항 배열 순서를 변경

물품의 인도 및 인수, 위험 이전, 운송 및 보험 등 중요도에 따라 배열 순서를 변경하였다.

Incoterms 2010 각 조건 내의 조항 배열	Incoterms 2020 각 조건 내의 조항 배열
A1. General Obligation 일반의무(개정 후와 동일)	A1. General Obligation 일반의무(개정 전과 동일)
A2. Licences, authorizations, security clearances and otherformalities 허가, 인가, 보안통관 및 기타 절차(개정 후 A7)	A2. Delivery /Taking delivery 인도/인수(개정 전 A4)
A3. Contracts of carriage and insurance 운송계약과 보험계약(개정 후 A4와 A5 분리)	A3. Transfer of risks 위험이전(개정 전 A5)
A4. Delivery/Taking delivery 인도/인수(개정 후 A2)	A4. Carriage 운송(개정 전 A3)
A5. Transfer of risks 위험이전(개정 후 A3)	A5. Insurance 보험(개정 전 A3)
A6. Allocation of costs 비용 분담(개정 후 A9)	A6. Delivery/transport document 인도/운송 서류(개정 전 A8)
A7. Notices to the buyer/the seller 매수인/매도인에 대한 통지(개정 후 A10)	A7. Export/Import Clearance 수출/수입 통관(개정 전 A2)
A8. Delivery document/Proof of delivery 인도서류/인도의 증명(개정 후 A6)	A8. Checking/packing/marking 검사/포장/확인(개정 전 A9)
A9. Checking – packing – marking 검사 – 포장 – 확인(개정 후 A8)	A9. Allocation of costs 비용분담(개정 전 A6)
A10. Assistance with information and related costs 정보에 관한 협조 및 관련 비용(개정 후 A4, A7, A9)	A10. Notices 통지(개정 전 A7)

무역 조건 내의 여러 조항에 비용 부담에 대한 내용이 있지만 A9/B9(Allocation of costs : 비용 분담)**에 매도인과 매수인이 부담해야 하는 비용을 일목요연하게 나열**

Incoterms 2010에서는 매도인과 매수인이 부담할 비용 부담에 대한 내용이 여러 조항에 있으므로, A6. Allocation of costs(비용 분담) 조항에 매도인과 매수인이 부담할 비용 부담에 대한 내용을 포괄적으로 규정하였다.

그러나 Incoterms 2020에서는 매도인과 매수인이 부담할 비용 부담에 대한 내용이 앞의 여러 조항에 명시되어 있지만, 다시 한번 A9. Allocation of costs(비용 분담) 조항에 매도인과 매수인이 부담해야 하는 비용을 운임, 보험료, 통관 비용, 보안 비용 등 구체적으로 일목요연하게 나열하여 명시하였다.

이렇게 개정된 이유는 매도인과 매수인이 각자 부담해야 할 비용을 최종적으로 한눈에 쉽게 알 수 있도록 하기 위해서다.

Incoterms 2020의 A4(Carriage : 운송)**와 A7**(Export/Import Clearance : 수출 통관)**에 보안 관련 의무를 강화하고 보안 관련 비용도 A9/B9**(Allocation of costs : 비용 분담)**에 명시 규정**

Incoterms 2010에서는 보안 관련 요건이 A2/B2(Licenses, authorizations,

security clearances and other formalities : 허가, 인가, 보안 통관 및 기타 절차)와 A10/B10(Assistance with information and related costs : 정보에 관한 협조 및 관련 비용)에 강력하지 않고 미미하게 규정되어 있었다.

그러나 Incoterms 2020에서는 테러 등을 고려하여 보안 관련 의무를 강화하여 A4(Carriage : 운송)와 A7(Export/Import Clearance : 수출 통관)에 강화된 보안 관련 의무를 명시하고, 보안 관련 비용도 A9/B9(Allocation of costs : 비용 분담)에 명확히 규정하였다.

11개 무역 조건의 서두에, Incoterms 2010의 '안내 지침(Guidance Note)'을, Incoterms 2020에서는 '사용자를 위한 안내 지침(Explanatory Notes for Users)'으로 변경하면서 설명문의 내용이 확대

Incoterms 2010에서는 11개 무역 조건별 '안내 지침(Guidance Note)'의 내용이 위험 이전 위주로 1페이지 내외였다.

그러나 Incoterms 2020에서는 11개 무역 조건의 서두가 '사용자를 위한 안내 지침(Explanatory Notes for Users)'으로 변경되면서 위험 이전은 물론 비용 부담과 수출입 절차 등의 설명이 추가됨으로써 내용이 3페이지 내외로 확대되었다.

Incoterms 2020
무역 조건별 해설

RULES FOR ANY MODE OR MODES OF TRANSPORT
(단일 또는 복수의 운송 방식에 사용 가능한 규칙)

1. EXW : Ex Works(공장 인도 조건)
2. FCA : Free Carrier(운송인 인도 조건)
3. CPT : Carriage Paid To(운송비 지급 인도 조건)
4. CIP : Carriage and Insurance Paid to(운송비·보험료 지급 인도 조건)
5. DAP : Delivered at Place(도착 장소 인도 조건)
6. DPU : Delivered at Place Unloaded(도착지 양하 인도 조건)
7. DDP : Delivered Duty Paid(관세 지급 인도 조건)

RULES FOR SEA AND INLAND WATERWAY TRANSPORT
(해상운송과 내수로 운송에 사용 가능한 규칙)

8. FAS : Free Alongside Ship(선측 인도 조건)

9. FOB : Free on Board(본선 인도 조건)

10. CFR : Cost and Freight(운임 포함 인도 조건)

11. CIF : Cost, Insurance and Frieght(운임·보험료 포함 인도 조건)

1. EXW(Ex Works) : 공장 인도 조건

- 위험 이전 : 매도인의 작업장 구내에서 매수인이 임의 처분할 수 있도록 물품을 인도 시
- 비용 부담 : 매도인은 '위험 이전'까지의 제비용 부담
- 통관 : 수출 통관 및 수입 통관 모두 매수인

2. FCA(Free Carrier) : 운송인 인도 조건

- 위험 이전 : 매도인이 매수인이 지정한 운송인에게 수출 통관된 물품을 인도 시(매도인 영업 구내에서 인도 시는 적재 인도, 영업 구내가 아닌 경

우 적재된 채 인도)
- 비용 부담 : 매도인은 '위험 이전'까지의 제비용 부담(선적선하증권 및 자가 운송 가능)
- 통관 : 수출 통관은 매도인 / 수입 통관은 매수인

3. CPT(Carriage Paid To) : 운송비 지급 인도 조건

- 위험 이전 : 물품이 약정된 일자 또는 기간 내에 지정 목적지까지 운송할 운송인의 보관하에, 또는 후속 운송인이 있을 경우 최초의 운송인에게 물품 인도 시
- 비용 부담 : 매도인은 FCA 조건 + 지정된 목적지까지의 물품 운송비 부담
- 통관 : 수출 통관은 매도인 / 수입 통관은 매수인

4. CIP(Carriage And Insurance Paid To) : 운송비 보험료 지급 인도 조건

- 위험 이전 : 물품이 약정된 일자 또는 기간 내에 지정 목적지까지 운송할 운송인의 보관하에, 또는 후속 운송인이 있을 경우 최초의 운송인에게 물품 인도 시

- 비용 부담 : 매도인은 CPT 조건 + 지정된 목적지까지의 적하보험료 부담(ICC(A))
- 통관 : 수출 통관은 매도인 / 수입 통관은 매수인

5. DAP(Delivered At Place) : 도착 장소 인도 조건

- 위험 이전 : 지정 목적지에서 도착 운송수단에 실린 채 양하 준비된 상태로 매수인의 처분하에 놓인 때
- 비용 부담 : 매도인은 '위험 이전'까지의 제비용 부담(자가 운송 가능)
- 통관 : 수출 통관은 매도인 / 수입 통관은 매수인

6. DPU(Delivered at Place Unloaded) : 도착지 양하 인도 조건

- 위험 이전 : 도착 운송수단으로부터 양하된 상태로 지정 목적항이나 지정 목적지의 지정 터미널에서 매수인의 처분하에 놓인 때
- 비용 부담 : 매도인은 '위험 이전'까지의 제비용 부담(자가 운송 가능)
- 통관 : 수출 통관은 매도인 / 수입 통관은 매수인

7. DDP(Delivered Duty Paid) : 관세 지급 인도 조건

- 위험 이전 : 약정된 일자 또는 기간 내에 매도인이 지정된 수입국 내의 목적 지점에서 도착 운송수단에 적재된 채로 매수인의 임의처분하에 인도한 때
- 비용 부담 : 매도인은 '위험 이전'까지의 제비용 부담(자가 운송 허용) + 관세
- 통관 : 수출 통관 및 수입 통관 모두 매도인

8. FAS(Free Alongside Ship) : 선측 인도 조건

- 위험 이전 : 물품이 지정 선적항의 부두에 또는 부선으로 본선의 선측에 인도했을 때, 또는 그렇게 인도된 물품을 조달한 때
- 비용 부담 : 매도인은 '위험 이전'까지의 제비용 부담
- 통관 : 수출 통관은 매도인 / 수입 통관은 매수인

9. FOB(Free On Board) : 본선 인도 조건

- 위험 이전 : 물품이 지정 선적항에서 본선에 적재했을 때(on board),

또는 그렇게 인도된 물품을 조달한 때
- 비용 부담 : 매도인은 '위험 이전'까지의 제비용 부담
- 통관 : 수출 통관은 매도인 / 수입 통관은 매수인

10. CFR(Cost And Freight) : 운임 포함 인도 조건

- 위험 이전 : 물품이 지정 선적항에서 본선에 적재했을 때(on board), 또는 그렇게 인도된 물품을 조달한 때
- 비용 부담 : 매도인은 FOB 조건 + 목적항까지의 운임 부담
- 통관 : 수출 통관은 매도인 / 수입 통관은 매수인

11. CIF(Cost Insurance and Freight) : 운임보험료 포함 인도 조건

- 위험 이전 : 물품이 지정 선적항에서 본선에 적재했을 때(on board), 또는 그렇게 인도된 물품을 조달한 때
- 비용 부담 : 매도인은 CFR 조건 + 목적항까지 보험료 부담(부보 : ICC(C))
- 통관 : 수출 통관은 매도인 / 수입 통관은 매수인

부록
자주 쓰는 무역 용어

[A]

Acceptance (오퍼 수락)

Accepting Bank (인수 은행)

Acknowledging (주문 승락)

Actual Total Loss (현실 전손)

Ad Valorem Duties (종가세)

Additional Clause (부보위험담보 조건)

Advising Bank (통지 은행)

Airway Bills (항공 화물 운송장)

All Risks ; A/R (전위험담보 조건)

Applicant for the credit (신용장 개설 의뢰인)

Arbitration Clause (중재 조항)

Automatic Approval Item ; A/A Item (자동 승인 품목)

Restricted Item (제한 승인 품목)

[B]

Back to Back Credit (구상무역신용장 또는 동시개설신용장)

Escrow Credit (기탁신용장)

Bareboat Charter (나용선 계약)

Beneficiary (수익자, 수혜자)

Bill of Exchange or Draft (환어음)

Bill of Lading (선하증권)

Blank Endorsement ; Endorsed in blank (백지 배서)

Bona Fide Holder (정당한 혹은 선의의 소지자)

Bonded Area (보세 구역)

Bonded Transportation (보세 운송)

Bulk Cargo (산적화물)

Buyer's Market (매입 주 시장)

[C]

Cable Credit (신용장 전신 개설)

Carnet Temporary Admission (ATA 카르네 제도)

Cargo Insurance (적하보험)

Cash Against Documents ; CAD (서류 상환불)

Cash on Delivery ; COD (대금 교환불)

Certificate of Orign ; C/O (원산지증명서)

Charter (용선)

Charterer (용선자)

Charterage (용선료)

Charter Party B/L (용선계약선하증권)

Claim (무역상의 분쟁)

Clean B/L (무결함선하증권)

Clean L/C (무화환 또는 무담보신용장)

Commercial Invoice (상업송장)

Confirmed L/C (확인신용장)

Confirming Bank (확인 은행)

Consignee (수하인)

Constructive Total Loss (추정 전손)

Correspondent Bank (환거래 은행)

Depositary Correspondent Bank (예치환거래 은행)

Non-depositaryCorrespondentBank (무예치환거래 은행)

Cover Note (보험인수장)

Credit Inquiry (신용조회)

Combined Transport Documents ; CTD (복합운송증권)

Conditional Offer (확인조건부 오퍼)

Container Freight Station ; CFS (소량 화물 집합소)

Container yard ; C.Y (야적장)

Counter Offer (반대 오퍼)

Customary Quick Dispatch ; C.Q.D (관습적 조속 하역)

[D]

Dead Freight (부적 또는 공적 운임)

Deferred Payment (연불)

Delivery Order ; D/O (화물인도지시서)

Debit Note (차변표)

Demand Draft ; D/D (송금환)

Demurrage (채선료)

Dispatch Money (조출료)

Dirty or foul B/L (결함선하증권)

Dock Receipt ; D/R (부두수취증)

Document against Acceptance ; D/A (인수인도 조건)

Document against Payment ; D/P (지급인도 조건)

Documentary L/C (화환신용장)

[E]

Electronic Data Interchange ; EDI (전자식 자료 교환)

Estimated time of Departure ; ETD (출항 예정일)

Estimated time of Arrival ; ETA (도착 예정일)

Exchange Commission (환가료)

Exclusive Contract (독점계약서)

Expected Profit ; Imaginary Profit (희망 이익)

Expiry Date ; E/D (신용장 유효 기일)

Export Declaration (수출 신고)

Export Inspection (수출 검사)

Export License ; E/L (수출 승인)

Export Packing (수출 포장)

Export Permit (수출 면장)

[F]

FIATA FBL ; Int'l Federation of Freight Forwarders Association FBL ; (국제운송주선인협회연맹) 발행 선하증권

Firm Offer (확정 오퍼)

Fixture Note (선복확약서 또는 성약각서)

Forwarder's Cargo Receipt ; FCR (운송 주선인의 화물수령증)

Freight (운임) 미국 (육상 + 해상 운임), 영국 (해상 : freight, 육상 : carrige)

Freight Collect (운임 후불)

Freight Prepaid (운임 선불)

Full Container Load ; FCL (만적 화물)

[G]

Gross Weight (총중량), Net Weight (순중량)

General L/C (보통 신용장), Special or Restricted L/C (특정신용장)

Generalized System of Preferences C/O ; G.S.P. C/O (특혜관세원산지 증명서)

[H]

H.S ; The harmonized Commodity description and coding system

Harmonized System (국제통일상품분류번호)

[I]

Import License ; I/L (수입 승인)

Incoterms (International Rules for the Interpretation of Trade Terms) (무역 조건 해석에 관한 국제 규칙)

Infringement Clause (권리 침해 조항)

Inland Storage Extension ; ISE (내륙 보관 확장 담보 조건)

Inland Transit Extension ; ITE (내륙 운송 확장 담보 조건)

Inquiry (조회)

Institute Cargo Clause ; I.C.C (협회 적하 약관)

Insurable Interest (피보험 이익)

Insurance Premium (보험료)

Insurance Terms (보험 조건)

Irrevocable L/C (취소불가능신용장), Revocable L/C (취소가능신용장)

Issuing Bank or Opening Bank or Establishing Bank (신용장 개설 은행)

[L]

Laydays ; Laytimes (정박 기간)

Less than Container Load ; LCL (혼재 화물)

Letter of Credit (신용장)

Letter of Guarantee ; L/G (수입화물선취보증장)

Liner (정기선)

Local Credit (내국신용장)

Lump-sum Charter (선복 용선 계약)

[M]

Mail Credit (신용장 우편 개설)

Mail Transfer ; M/T (우편환)

Manifest ; M/F (적하 목록)

Marine Insurance Act ; MIA (영국해상보험법)

Mate's Receipt ; M/R (본선수취증)

Minimum Freight (최저 운임)

[N]

Negotiating Bank (매입 은행)

Non-Tariff Barrier ; NTB (비관세 장벽)

[O]

Ocean or Marine B/L(해양선하증권)과 Local B/L(국내선하증권)

Offer Agent (무역 대리업자)

Offer subject to Prior Sale (선착순 판매 조건 오퍼)

Official Invoice (공용송장)

Open Account or Account Current or Running Account (장부 결제, 상호 계산, 청산 계정)

[P]

Packing List (포장명세서)

Partial Loss of Average (분손 또는 해손)

Paying Bank (지급 은행)

Payment in Advanced or Cash with Order (선불, 주문불)

Progressive Payment or Installment payment (누진불 또는 분할 지급)

[Q]

Quality Terms (품질 조건)

Quantity Terms (수량 조건)

[R]

Received B/L (수취선하증권)

Red Clause L/C or Packing L/C (전대신용장)

Revenue Ton or Freight Ton (운임 톤)

Revolving L/C (회전신용장)

[S]

Sailing Schedule (배선표)

Seaworthiness (내항성, 감항성)

Settling Bank (결제 은행)

Shipment Terms (선적 조건)

Shipped or On Board B/L (선적선하증권)

Shipper or Consignor (선적인 또는 송화인)

Shipping Advise, Notice of Shipment (선적통지서)

Shipping marks (화인)

Shipping Conference or Freight Conference (해운동맹 또는 운임동맹)

Shipping Order ; S/O (선적지시서)

Shipping Request ; S/R (선복요청서)

Short Form B/L (양식선하증권)

Sight L/C (일람출급신용장)과 Usance L/C (기한부신용장)

Special Instructions or Conditions (신용장상의 특수 지시 사항)

Specific Duties (종량세)

Stand-by Credit (보증신용장)

Stale B/L (기간경과선하증권)

Stowage (선내 하역비)

Straight B/L (기명식선하증권)과 Order B/L (지시식선하증권)

[T]

Telegraphic Transfer ; T/T (전신환)

Tenor (환어음의 결제 기한)

Tenor of Draft (환어음의 결제 조건)

Time Charter (정기 혹은 기간 용선 계약)

Total Loss (전손)

Transaction as principal to principal (본인 대 본인의 거래)

Transferable L/C (양도 가능 신용장)

Transportation Siberian Railroad ; TSR (시베리아 횡단철도 운송)

Through B/L (통과 선하 증권)

Trust Receipt ; T/R (대여 인도)

[U]

U.C.P ; Uniform Customs and Practice for Documentary Credit (외환신용장에 관한 통일 규칙 및 관례)

[V]

Voluntary Export Restraint ; VER (수출 자유 규제)

Voyage Charter ; Trip Charter (항해 혹은 항로 용선 계약)

[W]

Waiver (국적선 불취항 증명서)

War/Strike, Riots and Civil Commotions ; W/SRCC (협회 전쟁 및 협회 동맹파업·소요·폭동·담보 조건)

Wharfage (부두 사용료)

중앙경제평론사 Joongang Economy Publishing Co.
중앙생활사 | 중앙에듀북스 Joongang Life Publishing Co./Joongang Edubooks Publishing Co.

중앙경제평론사는 오늘보다 나은 내일을 창조한다는 신념 아래 설립된 경제·경영서 전문 출판사로서
성공을 꿈꾸는 직장인, 경영인에게 전문지식과 자기계발의 지혜를 주는 책을 발간하고 있습니다.

샘플로 쉽게 배우는 **무역 실무영어 첫걸음**

초판 1쇄 발행 | 2021년 6월 22일
초판 2쇄 발행 | 2024년 10월 15일

지은이 | 오시학(SiHak Oh)
펴낸이 | 최점옥(JeomOg Choi)
펴낸곳 | 중앙경제평론사(Joongang Economy Publishing Co.)

대　　표 | 김용주
책임편집 | 한　홍
본문디자인 | 박근영

출력 | 삼신문화　종이 | 한솔PNS　인쇄 | 삼신문화　제본 | 은정제책사

잘못된 책은 구입한 서점에서 교환해드립니다.
가격은 표지 뒷면에 있습니다.

ISBN 978-89-6054-272-3(03320)

등록 | 1991년 4월 10일 제2-1153호
주소 | ㈜ 04590 서울시 중구 다산로20길 5(신당4동 340-128) 중앙빌딩
전화 | (02)2253-4463(代)　팩스 | (02)2253-7988
홈페이지 | www.japub.co.kr　블로그 | http://blog.naver.com/japub
네이버 스마트스토어 | https://smartstore.naver.com/jaub　이메일 | japub@naver.com

♣ 중앙경제평론사는 중앙생활사·중앙에듀북스와 자매회사입니다.

Copyright ⓒ 2021 by 오시학
이 책은 중앙경제평론사가 저작권자와의 계약에 따라 발행한 것이므로 본사의 서면 허락 없이는
어떠한 형태나 수단으로도 이 책의 내용을 이용하지 못합니다.
※ 이 책은 《실전 무역영어 길라잡이》를 독자들의 요구에 맞춰 새롭게 출간하였습니다.

도서주문 www.japub.co.kr
전화주문 : (02) 2253-4463

https://smartstore.naver.com/jaub
네이버 스마트스토어

중앙경제평론사/중앙생활사/중앙에듀북스에서는 여러분의 소중한 원고를 기다리고 있습니다. 원고 투고는 이메일을
이용해주세요. 최선을 다해 독자들에게 사랑받는 양서로 만들어드리겠습니다. 이메일 | japub@naver.com